Board + CUET

CL MASTER SERIES

CBSE STUDY GUIDE

12th CLASS

with special focus on CUET examination

PSYCHOLOGY

Includes

CUET Solved Paper 2022 &
CBSE Solved Papers 2022 (Term I and II)

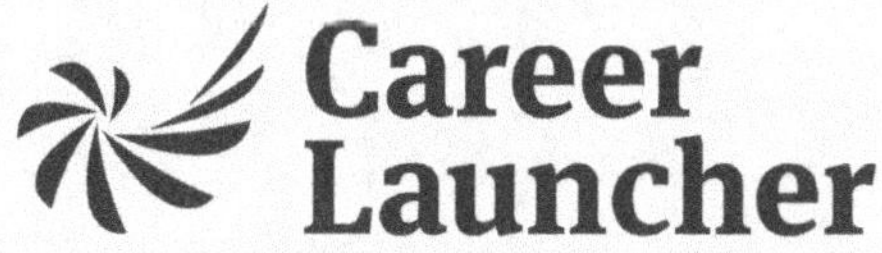

Career
Launcher

Title   : **CL Master Series :** CBSE Class XII - Psychology (Study Guide)

Language   : English

Editor's Name : Pravin Choubey

Copyright ©   : 2022 CLIP

Typeset & Published by :

Career Launcher Infrastructure (P) Ltd.

A-45, Mohan Cooperative Industrial Area, Near Mohan Estate Metro Station, New Delhi - 110044

Marketed by :

G.K. Publications (P) Ltd.

Plot No. 9A, Sector-27A, Mathura Road, Faridabad, Haryana-121003

ISBN   : **978-93-95101-46-2**

Printer's Details

For product information :

Visit *www.gkpublications.com* or email to *gkp@gkpublications.com*

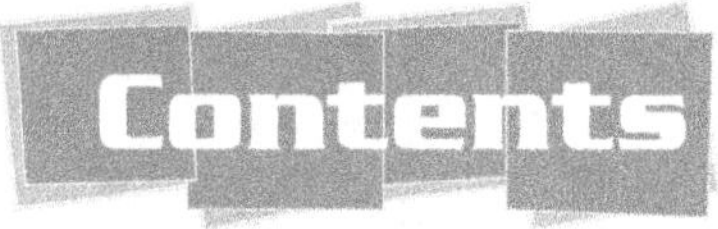

Contents

CHAPTER 1

Variations in Psychological Attributes

Summary

Individual Differences in Human Functioning

Variability is a fact of nature, and individuals are no exception to this. The list of variations can be endless. Different traits can exist in varying degrees in an individual.

Situationism, which states that situations and circumstances in which one is placed influence one's behaviour. The situationist perspective views human behaviour relatively more as a result of influence of external factors.

Assessment of Psychological Attributes

Assessment refers to the measurement of psychological attributes of individuals and their evaluation, often using multiple methods in terms of certain standards of comparison.

Our assessment may be informal or formal. Formal assessment is objective, standardised, and organised. On the other hand, informal assessment varies from case to case and from one assessor to another and, therefore, is open to subjective interpretations.

Psychological assessment uses systematic testing procedures to evaluate abilities, behaviours, and personal qualities of individuals.

Some Domains of Psychological Attributes

Intelligence is the global capacity to understand the world, think rationally, and use available resources effectively when faced with challenges.

Aptitude refers to an individual's underlying potential for acquiring skills.

Interest is an individual's preference for engaging in one or more specific activities relative to others.

Personality refers to relatively enduring characteristics of a person that make her or him distinct from others.

Values are enduring beliefs about an ideal mode of behaviour.

Multiple Choice Questions [1 Mark]

Q.1. Which of the following is the first step in understanding a psychological attribute?

(a) Assessment

(b) Intelligence

(c) Situtationism

(d) Aptitude

Ans. (a)

Q.2. Psychologists are trained in making ____________ assessment of psychological attributes.

(a) Formal

(b) Informal

(c) Personal

(d) External

Ans. (a)

Q.3. Which of the following evaluate by using systematic testing procedures?

(a) Evaluate abilities　(b) Behaviours,

(c) Personal qualities　(d) All the above

Ans. (d)

Very Short Answer Type　　　[1 Mark]

Q.1. Define Variability.

Ans. Variability is a fact of nature, and individuals are no exception to this. They vary in terms of physical characteristics, such as height, weight, strength, hair colour, and so on.

Q.2. Give an example of situationism?

Ans. A person, who is generally aggressive, may behave in a submissive manner in the presence of her/his top boss.

Q.3. What is the first step in understanding a psychological attribute ?

Ans. Assessment is the first step in understanding a psychological attribute. Assessment refers to the measurement of psychological attributes of individuals and their evaluation, often using multiple methods in terms of certain standards of comparison.

Q.4. When the behaviour is influenced more by situational factors it is called as __________.

Ans. Situationism

Short Answer Type - I　　　[2 Marks]

Q.1. What is individual difference?

Ans. For psychologists, individual differences refer to distinctiveness and variations among people's characteristics and behaviour patterns.

Short Answer Type - II　　　[3 Marks]

Q.1. Is situationism depends on external factor? Explain.

Ans. Behaviours are influenced more by situational factors. This latter view is known as situationism, which states that situations and circumstances in which one is placed influence one's behaviour.

Intelligence

- Intelligence as the power of perceiving, learning, understanding, and knowing.

- Aptitude refers to an individual's underlying potential for acquiring skills.

- Interest is an individual's preference for engaging in one or more specific activities relative to others.

- Personality refers to relatively enduring characteristics of a person that make her or him distinct from others.

- Values are enduring beliefs about an ideal mode of behaviour.

TOPIC 2

Summary

Assessment Methods

Psychological Test is an objective and standardised measure of an individual's mental and/or behavioural characteristics.

Interview involves seeking information from a person on a one-to-one basis.

Case Study is an in-depth study of the individual in terms of her/his psychological attributes, psychological history in the context of her/his psychosocial and physical environment.

Observation involves employing systematic, organised, and objective procedures to record behavioural phenomena occurring naturally in real time.

Self-Report is a method in which a person provides factual information about herself/himself and/or opinions, beliefs, etc. that s/he holds. Such information may be obtained by using an interview schedule or a questionnaire, a psychological test, or a personal diary.

Intelligence

The Oxford Dictionary explains intelligence as the power of perceiving, learning, understanding, and knowing.

Theories of Intelligence

Alfred Binet was the first psychologist who tried to formalise the concept of intelligence in terms of mental operations. He, therefore, conceptualised intelligence as consisting of one similar set of abilities which can be used for solving any or every problem in an individual's environment.

The psychometric approach considers intelligence as an aggregate of abilities. It expresses the individual's performance in terms of a single index of cognitive abilities.

In 1927, Charles Spearman proposed a two-factor theory of intelligence employing a statistical method called factor analysis. He showed that intelligence consisted of a general factor (g-factor) and some specific factors (s-factors).

J.P. Guilford proposed the structureof-intellect model which classifies intellectual traits among three dimensions: operations, contents, and products. Operations are what the respondent does. These include cognition, memory recording, memory retention, divergent production, convergent production, and evaluation.

Multiple Choice Questions [1 Mark]

Q.1. Generally, students having low intelligence are not likely to do so well in school-related examinations, but their success in life is not associated only with their intelligence test scores is signify which of the following:

(a) Aptitude

(b) Intelligence

(c) Value

(d) Personality

Ans. (b)

Q.2. Which one of the following helps us to explain an individual's behaviour and predict how she/he will behave in future?

(a) Personality   (b) Intelligence

(c) Value   (d) Interest

Ans. (a)

Q.3. Structure of intellect model was given by ____________.

(a) Arthur Jensen

(b) Charles Spearman

(c) J.P. Guilford

(d) Alfred Binet

Ans. (c)

Q.4. Level I and Level II belong to which type of model of Inteliigence?

(a) Hierarchical model of intelligence

(b) structureof-intellect model

(c) two-factor theory

(d) None of the above

Ans. (a)

Q.5. Which of the following attributes help to decide what subjects or courses student can pursue comfortably and with pleasure.

(a) Personality

(b) Interest

(c) Value

(d) Attitude

Ans. (b)

6. Certain phenomena such as mother child interactions can be easily studied through__________.

(a) Case study   (b) Self-report

(c) Observation   (d) Psychological test

Ans. (c)

Very Short Answer Type [1 Mark]

Q.1. Define psychometric approach.

Ans. The psychometric approach considers intelligence as an aggregate of abilities. It expresses the individual's performance in terms of a single index of cognitive abilities.

Q.2. Who had given Theory of Multiple Intelligences?

Ans. Howard Gardner proposed the theory of multiple intelligences. According to him, intelligence is not a single entity; rather distinct types of intelligences exist.

Q.3. Who was the first psychologist tried to formalise the concept of intelligence?

Ans. Alfred Binet was the first psychologist who tried to formalise the concept of intelligence in terms of mental operations.

Short Answer Type - I　　[2 Marks]

Q.1. Mention any two Psychological assessment methods.

Ans. i. Observation involves employing systematic, organised, and objective procedures to record behavioural phenomena occurring naturally in real time.

　ii. Self-Report is a method in which a person provides factual information about herself/himself and/or opinions, beliefs, etc. that s/he holds.

Q.2. What was two – factor theory?

Ans. In 1927, Charles Spearman proposed a two-factor theory of intelligence employing a statistical method called factor analysis. He showed that intelligence consisted of a general factor (g-factor) and some specific factors (s-factors).

　i. The g-factor includes mental operations which are primary and common to all performances.

　ii. Many specific abilities. These are contained in what he called the s-factor.

Short Answer Type - II　　[3 Marks]

Q.1. Write a short notes on Triarchic Theory of Intelligence.

Ans. Robert Sternberg (1985) proposed the triarchic theory of intelligence. According to this theory, there are three basic types of intelligence: Componential, Experiential, and Contextual.

　i. Componential Intelligence : Componential or analytical intelligence is the analysis of information to solve problems.

　ii. Experiential Intelligence: Experiential or creative intelligence is involved in using past experiences creatively to solve novel problems.

　iii. Contextual Intelligence : Contextual or practical intelligence involves the ability to deal with environmental demands encountered on a daily basis.

Q.2. Mention any 3 types of intelligence as studied by Howard Gardner.

Ans. Howard Gardner proposed the theory of multiple intelligences. According to him, intelligence is not a single entity; rather distinct types of intelligences exist

　i. Linguistic (an ability to produce and use language) : It is the capacity to use language fluently and flexibly to express one's thinking and understand others.

　ii. Interpersonal (an ability to understand to subtle aspects of others' behaviours) : This is the ability to understand the motives, feelings and behaviours of other people so as to bond into a comfortable relationship with others.

　iii. Logical-Mathematical (an ability to think logically and critically, and solve problems) : Persons high on this type of intelligence can think logically and critically.

TOPIC 3

Summary

Planning, Attention-arousal, and Simultaneous-successive (PASS) Model of Intelligence

This model has been developed by J.P. Das, Jack Naglieri, and Kirby (1994). According to this model, intellectual activity involves the interdependent functioning of three neurological systems, called the functional units of brain. These units are responsible for arousal/attention, coding or processing, and planning respectively. These PASS processes operate on a knowledge base developed either formally (by reading, writing, and experimenting) or informally from the environment. These processes are interactive and dynamic in nature; yet each has its own distinctive functions.

Individual Differences in Intelligence

In 1912, William Stern, a German psychologist, devised the concept of Intelligence Quotient (IQ). IQ refers to mental age divided by chronological age, and multiplied by 100.

Types of Intelligence Tests

Individual or Group Tests : An individual intelligence test is one which can be administered to one person at a time. A group intelligence test can be administered to several persons simultaneously.

Verbal, Non-Verbal, or Performance Tests

Verbal tests can be administered only to literate people. Raven's Progressive Matrices (RPM) Test is an example of a non-verbal test. In this test, the subject examines an incomplete pattern and chooses a figure from the alternatives that will complete the pattern

Culture-Fair or Culture-Biased Tests

Psychologists have tried to develop tests that are culture-fair or culturally appropriate, i.e. one that does not discriminate against individuals belonging to different cultures.

Intelligence Testing in India

S.M. Mohsin made a pioneering attempt in constructing an intelligence test in Hindi (NCERT) has documented Indian tests.

Culture and Intelligence: The cultural environment provides a context for intelligence to develop. A person's intelligence is likely to be tuned by these cultural parameters. Many theorists have regarded intelligence as attributes specific to the person without regard to their cultural background.

Q.1. The concept of "Two factor theory of Intelligence" proposed by

(a) Charles Spearman (b) J.P Guilford

(c) Alfred Binet   (d) Arthur Jensen

Ans. (a)

Q.2. _________________ ability to understand of one's own feelings, motives, and desires.

(a) Interpersonal   (b) Intrapersonal

(c) Naturalistic   (d) Spatial

Ans. (b)

Q.3. Triarchic Theory of Intelligence was proposed by?

(a) Jack Naglieri   (b) Kirby

(c) Robert Sternberg (d) Alfred Binet

Ans. (c)

Q.1. What is Cognitive Assessment System (CAS)?

Ans. It consists of verbal as well as non-verbal tasks that measure basic cognitive functions presumed to be independent of schooling.

Q.2. Who had given the Planning, Attention-arousal, and Simultaneous-successive (PASS) Model?

Ans. This model has been developed by J.P. Das, Jack Naglieri, and Kirby (1994).

Q.1. Differentiate between Intellectual Deficiency and Intellectual Giftedness.

Ans. Because the standard deviation of an IQ test is about 15, this means that about 2% of people score above an IQ of 130, often considered the threshold for giftedness, and about the same percentage score below an IQ of 70, often being considered the threshold for an intellectual disability.

Long Answer Type [5 Marks]

Q.1. How do psychologists characterize and define intelligence?

Ans. Psychological motion of intelligence is quite different from the common sensed motion of intelligence.

Generally people saw intelligence as mental alertness, ready art, quickness in learning and ability to understand relationships.

Oxford dictionary explained intelligence as the power of perceiving, learning understanding and knowing.

Accordingly Alfred Binet also used these attributes and defined intelligence as ability to judge well, understand well and reason well.Later Wechsler gave a comprehensive definition in terms of its functionality, i.e., its value for adaptation to environment. He defined intelligence as "the global and aggregate capacity of an individual to think rationally, act purposefully and to deal effectively with his/her environment."

Present day psychologists such as Gardner and Sternberg emphasized that "Intelligent individual not only adapts to the environment, but actively modifies or shapes it."

Sternberg views intelligence as "the ability to adapt, to shape and select environment to accomplish ones goals and those of ones society and culture."

TOPIC 4

Summary

Emotional Intelligence

Emotional intelligence is a set of skills that underlie accurate appraisal, expression, and regulation of emotions. It is the feeling side of intelligence.

Emotional Quotient (EQ) is used to express emotional intelligence in the same way as IQ is used to express intelligence.

Special Abilities

Aptitude refers to special abilities in a particular field of activity. It is a combination of characteristics that indicates an individual's capacity to acquire some specific knowledge or skill after training.

Interest is a preference for a particular activity; aptitude is the potentiality to perform that activity.

Creativity

Einstein's theory of relativity is an example of the highest level of creativity which implies bringing out altogether new ideas, facts, theory, or a product. Another level of creativity is working on what has already been established earlier by way of modifications, by putting things in new perspectives or to new use

Creativity and Intelligence

Researchers have found that the relationship between creativity and intelligence is positive. All creative acts require some minimum ability to acquire knowledge and capacity to comprehend, retain, and retrieve.

Creativity tests came into existence to assess variations in terms of the potential for creativity in contrast to intelligence.

Multiple Choice Questions [1 Mark]

Q.1. _______________ approach considers intelligence as an aggregate of abilities.

(a) Psychmetric

(b) Emotional Intelligence

(c) Values

(d) Aptitude

Ans. (a)

Q.2. _____________ refers to an individual's underlying potential for acquiring skills.

(a) Intelligence

(b) Aptitude

(c) Interest

(d) Personality

Ans. (b)

Q.3. Name the psychologist who proposed the concept of Intelligence Quotient.

    (a) Alfred Binet

    (b) Theodore Simon

    (c) William Stern

    (d) Jack Naglieri

Ans. (c)

Q.4. .__________ refers to the abilities involved in forming, using, and transforming mental images.

    (a) Spatial

    (b) Musical

    (c) Naturalistic

    (d) Intrapersonal

Ans. (a)

Q.5. Who among the following is not associated with PASS model?

    (a) J.P. Das

    (b) Jack Naglieri

    (c) Kirby

    (d) Theodore Simon

Ans. (d)

Q.6. The knowledge of______________ can help us to predict an individual's future performance.

    (a) Emotional Intelligence

    (b) Interest

    (c) Creativity

    (d) Aptitude

Ans. (d)

Q.7. Identify the formula for calculating intelligence quotient.

    (a) $IQ = MA/CA \times 100$

    (b) $IQ = CA/MA \times 100$

    (c) $IQ = MA + CA \times 100$

    (d) $IQ = MA \times CA \times 100$

Ans. (a)

Very Short Answer Type   [2 Marks]

Q.1. Which of the two lQ or EQ, do you think would be more related to success in life and Why?

Ans. **(i)** IQ is a good predictor of potential.

    (ii) EQ is a good predictor of success.

- Researchers had proved that—EQ helps in dealing with students who are stressed and face challenges of the outside world.

- It improves the academic performance.

- It is very useful in preparing students to face the challenges of life outside the classroom.

- They are less anti-social and more co-operative.

Long Answer Type   [5 Marks]

Q.1. How can you differentiate between verbal and performance tests of intelligence?

(CBSE 2008, 2014)

Ans. Types of Intelligence Tests:

Individual or group tests based on contact:

Individual Test:

(i) Administered to one individual at a time.

(ii) Requires the administrator to establish a rapport with the subject and be sensitive to his/her feelings, mood and expressions during the testing sessions which provides understanding of other aspects of subjects personality.

(iii) Allows people to answer orally or in written form or manipulate the objects as per the tester's instructions.

- Example: Stanford Binet intelligence scale, WAIS, WISSC, Alexander Pass along test.

Group Test:

(i) Administered to several individuals at a time simultaneously.

(ii) Do not allow an opportunity to be familiar with the subjects' feelings.

(iii) Seek answers in a Multiple-choice format.

(iv) It is relatively economical and less time consuming.

(v) Example: Group Test of Intelligence by Prayag Mehta, Group Test on Intelligence by S. Jalota.

Verbal, Non-verbal and Performance Tests based on Mode of Administration: Verbal Tests:

(i) Requires subject to give verbal responses either orally or in written form.

(ii) Can be administered to literates only. ,

(iii) Example: CIE, Verbal Group Test, Stanford Binet Intelligence Scale.

Non-verbal Test:

- Has pictures or illustrations as test items.

- Example: Ravens progressive matrices. In this test the subject examines an incomplete pattern and chooses a figure from the alternatives that will complete the pattern.

- Reduces culture biases.

- Example: SRPM, CIE Non-verbal group test of Intelligence.

Performance Test:

- Requires the subject to manipulate objects to perform the test.

- Written language is not necessary for answering the items.

- Example: Kohs's Block designs test. Here the subject is asked to arrange the blocks in a specified period to produce a given design, Bhatia's Battery performance test.

- Can be administered to persons from different cultures and reduce culture biases.

- Example: Draw a Man Test by Pramila Pathak, Kohs Block designs test.

Culture Biased or Culture Fair Tests based on Nature of Items used:

- Psychological tests that show a bias toward the culture in which they are developed are Culture Biased Tests.

- Tests developed-in-America and Europe represent an urban and middle class cultural ethos. (Middle class white subjects perform well on these tests). The items do not consider favourably to Asians and Africans.

- Culture Fair Tests: One does not discriminate against as individuals belong to different cultures.

- Non-verbal and Performance Tests reduce cultural influences.

To overcome the limitation of Culture biased tests, Culture fair tests were developed, e.g. non-verbal and performance tests are called so because people of any culture could take them. For e.g. Standard progressive Matrices and Bhatia's Battery Performance Test.

NCERT Questions

Q.1. How do psychologists characterize and define intelligence?

Ans. Psychological motion of intelligence is quite different from the common sensed motion of intelligence.

Generally people saw intelligence as mental alertness, ready art, quickness in learning and ability to understand relationships.

Oxford dictionary explained intelligence as the power of perceiving, learning understanding and knowing.

Accordingly Alfred Binet also used these attributes and defined intelligence as ability to judge well, understand well and reason well. Later Wechsler gave a comprehensive definition in terms of its functionality, i.e., its value for adaptation to environment. He defined intelligence as "the global and aggregate capacity of an individual to think rationally, act purposefully and to deal effectively with his/her environment."

Present day psychologists such as Gardner and Sternberg emphasized that "Intelligent individual not only adapts to the environment, but actively modifies or shapes it."

Sternberg views intelligence as " the ability to adapt, to shape and select environment to accomplish ones goals and those of ones society and culture."

Q.2. What extent is our intelligence the result of heredity (nature) and environment (nurture)? Discuss.   **(CBSE 2014)**

Ans. **(i)** Whether intelligence is evolved or it is developed due to the environment, is a question of debate.

(ii) Lot of studies have been done to determine the role of nature and nurture.

(iii) Here we will discuss the controversy with the help of various twin studies, adoption studies and environmental studies.

On the basis of twin studies co-relation results are as follows:

(i) Identical twins reared together correlate 0.90

(ii) Identical twins reported early in childhood and reared in different environments correlate 0.72

(iii) Fraternal twins reared together correlate 0.60

(iv) Siblings reared together correlate 0.50

(v) Siblings reared apart correlate 0.25

- **Adoption Studies before the Age of 6-7 Years**

These studies of adopted children show that children's intelligence is more similar to their biological parents.

These studies provide evidence that intelligence is determined because of nature.

- **Adoption Studies after the Age of 6-7 Years**

   According to these studies as children grew older tends to more closer to that of their adoptive parents.

Environmental Studies

Evidence for the influence of environment **(Nurture) on the basis of Twin studies.**

(i) The intelligence score of twins reared apart as they grew older, tends to more closer to that of their adoptive parents.

(ii) On the basis of differences in environment, children from disadvantaged homes adopted into families with higher, socio-economic status exhibit an increase in their intelligence scores.

(iii) Environmental deprivation lowers intelligence. Factors such **as nutrition, good family background and quality schooling** increase growth rate of intelligence.

(iv) There is general consensus among psychologists that intelligence is a product of complex interaction of heredity (Nature) and environment (Nurture).

(v) Heredity provides the potentials and sets a range of growth whereas environment facilitates the development of intelligence.

Q.3. Explain briefly the multiple intelligences identified by Gardner.   **(CBSE 2008)**

Ans. **Gardner's theory** based on information processing approaches functions on three basic principles:

(i) Intelligence is not a single entity, there exist multiple intelligences.

(ii) The intelligences are independent from each other.

(iii) Different types of intelligences work together to provide a solution of problem. Gardner has so far proposed eight intelligences, however all individuals do not possess them in equal proportion. The particular situation or the context decides the prominence of one type of intelligence over the others.

Following are the eight types of intelligence:

1. **Linguistic:** This is related to reading, writing, listening, talking, understanding etc. Poets exhibit this ability better than others.

2. **Logical-Mathematical:** This type of intelligence deals with abstract reasoning and manipulation of symbols involved in numerical problems. It is exhibited in scientific work.

3. **Spatial:** This type of intelligence is involved in perceiving third dimension formation of images. It is used while navigating in space, forming, transforming and using mental images. Sailors, engineers, surgeons, pilots, care drivers, sculptors and painters have highly developed spatial intelligence.

4. **Musical:** Persons with musical intelligence show sensitivity to pitch and tone required for singing, playing and instrument, composing and appreciating music etc.

5. **Bodily Kinesthetic:** It requires the skills and dexterity for fine coordinated motor movements, such as those required for dancing, athletics, surgery, craft making etc.

6. **Inter-personal:** It requires understanding of motives, feelings and behaviours of other people.sales people, politicians, teachers, clinicians and religious readers have high degree of inter-personal intelligence.

7. **Intra-personal:** It is related to understanding one's self and developing a sense of identity, e.g., philosophers and spiritual leaders.

8. **Naturalistic:** It is related to recognizing the flora and fauna, i.e., natural world and making a distinction in the natural world. It is more possessed by hunters, farmers, tourists, students of biological sciences etc.

Q.4. How does the Triarchic theory help us to understand intelligence?   **(CBSE 2012-13)**

Ans. 1. Robert J. Sternberg proposes a theory of intelligence based on information processing approach in 1985 known as the Triarchic theory of intelligence.

2. According to Sternberg, intelligence is an ability to adapt, to shape and select environment to accomplish ones goals and those of ones society and culture.

3. This theory attempts to understand the cognitive processes involved in problem solving.

4. According to him there are three types of intelligences:

(i) **Componential intelligence (Analytical):** This dimension specifies the cognitive processes that underlie an intelligent behaviour.

This dimension serves three different functions:

(a) **Knowledge acquisition components:** These are the processes used in learning, encoding, combining and comparing information.

(b) **Metacomponents:** 'Meta' means higher. These are executive processes. They control monitor and evaluate cognitive processing.

(c) **Performance components:** These components execute strategies prepared by metacomponents to perform a task.For example, While studying students plan the lesson chapterwise, they make schedules, categories the learning material and do integrate the information to comprehend well.

(ii) **Experiential intelligence (Creative):** This dimension specifies how experiences effect intelligence and how intelligence effects a person's experiences.

(a) Experiential intelligence refers to an individual's ability to make use of one's past experiences to deal with novel situations creatively and effectively.

(b) This intelligence is mostly high among scientists and creative people.

(c) For example if a person is trapped in a room, he finds out a way of coming out of the room using rope or ladder etc. in a creative way. He had some knowledge of getting out from this situation by watching out a movie few years back.

(iii) **Contextual intelligence (Practical):** This dimension specifies the ability to deal with environmental demands on daily basis.

(a) It is individual's ability to make use of his/her potential to deal with day-to-day life.

(b) It may be called street smartness or 'business sense'.

(c) People high in this ability are successful in life.

- It deals with the ways people handle effectively their environmental demands and adapt to different contexts with available resources.

Q.5. Any intellectual activity involves the independent functioning of three 'neurological systems'. Explain with reference to PASS model.

Ans. According to PASS model, theory based on information processing approach, intellectual activity involves the interdependent functioning of the three neurological systems called the **functional units of the brain.**

These units are responsible for:

- the arousal and attention.

- the simultaneous and successive processing.

- the planning.

Arousal and Attention

(i) State of arousal helps in attending to the stimuli.

(ii) Arousal and attention enable a person to process information.

(iii) Optimal level of arousal focuses our attention on relevant aspects of a problem.

(iv) Too much or too little arousal interferes with attention and performance. **Example:** Arousal helps the individual to focus ones attention on reading, learning and revising the contents of the material to be learnt.

Simultaneous and Successive Processing:

Simultaneous Processing refers to **perceiving relations amongst various concepts and integrate them into meaningful patterns for comprehension!**

For e.g., in Raven's standard progressive matrices (RSPM Test) choosing appropriate pattern by comprehending relationship.

Successive Processing refers to recalling information serially so that one recall leads to another recall. For example, learning of digits and letters and multiplication tables.

Planning:

1. After the information is attended to and processed, planning is activated.

2. Planning involves reaching to the target and evaluating their effectiveness. Planning allows us to think of possible courses of action and implementing them.

3. If a plan does not work, it is modified to suit the requirements of the task or the situation.

4. For example, to take a test scheduled by your teacher, you'd have to set goals, plan a time schedule of studies, get clarifications in case of problems or think of other ways to meet your goals.

Q.6. Are there cultural differences in the conceptualisation of intelligence?

Ans. Yes, culture, which is a set of beliefs, customs, attitudes and achievements in art of literature, affects the process of intellectual development.

- According to Sternberg, intelligence is a product of culture.

- Vyotsky believes that while elementary7 mental operations are common, higher mental activities like problem-solving and thinking are culturally produced.

- **Technological Intelligence**

(i) Promotes an individualistic pattern of action.

(ii) Individuals in technologically educated western societies possess this kind of intelligence.

(iii) They are well versed in skills of attention, observation, analysis, speed, moves abstraction, generalisation, creativity, Minimum moves etc.

- **Integral Intelligence**

(i) Intelligence in the Indian tradition is integral intelligence.

(ii) It views intelligence from a holistic perspective.

(iii) It gives equal attention to cognitive and non-cognitive processes, as well as their integration.

(iv) 'Buddhi' is the knowledge of one's own self based on conscience, will and desire.

(v) It has effective, motivational as well as cognitive components. .

It includes:

(i) Cognitive competence (discrimination, problem-solving).

(ii) Social competence (respect for elders, concern for others, respecting opinions of others).

(iii) Emotional competence (self regulation, self monitoring). '

(iv) Entrepreneurial competence commitment, persistence, patience).

Q.7. What is IQ? How do psychologists classify people on the bases of their IQ scores?

Ans. (i) IQ is an index of brightness.

(ii) It is the ratio of mental age to chronological age.

(iii) The concept of IQ was given by William. Stern w7ho gave the formula to calculate IQ i.e.,

- MA/CA ×100

  If MA > CA   Above average

  MA < CA   Below average

  MA = CA   Average

- IQ is relatively stable.

- It is a good predictor of potential.

- IQ scores are distributed in a population in such a way that most people tend to fall in the middle range of the distribution.

- This can be shown in the form of following table.

Classification of People on the Basis of IQ		
IQ Range	Descriptive Label	Per cent in the Population
Above 130	Very superior	2.2
120-130	Superior	6.7
110-119	High average	16.1
90-109	Average	50
80-89	Low average	16.1
70-79	Borderline	6.7
Below 70	Mentally challenged/reatarded	2.2

Q.8. Discuss various types of intelligence tests.

Or

How can you differentiate between verbal and performance tests of intelligence?

(CBSE 2008, 2014)

Ans. Types of Intelligence Tests:
Individual or group tests based on contact:.

Individual Test:

(i) Administered to one individual at a time.

(ii) Requires the administrator to establish a rapport with the subject and be sensitive to his/her feelings, mood and expressions during the testing sessions which provides understanding of other aspects of subjects personality.

(iii) Allows people to answer orally or in written form or manipulate the objects as per the tester's instructions.

- Example: Stanford Binet intelligence scale, WAIS, WISSC, Alexander Pass along test.

Group Test:

(i) Administered to several individuals at a time simultaneously.

(ii) Do not allow an opportunity to be familiar with the subjects' feelings.

(iii) Seek answers in a Multiple-choice format.

(iv) It is relatively economical and less time consuming.

(v) Example: Group Test of Intelligence by Prayag Mehta, Group Test on Intelligence by S. Jalota.

Verbal, Non-verbal and Performance Tests based on Mode of Administration: Verbal Tests:

(i) Requires subject to give verbal responses either orally or in written form.

(ii) Can be administered to literates only. ,

(iii) Example: CIE, Verbal Group Test, Stanford Binet Intelligence Scale.

Non-verbal Test:

- Has pictures or illustrations as test items.

- Example: Ravens progressive matrices. In this test the subject examines an incomplete pattern and chooses a figure from the alternatives that will complete the pattern.

- Reduces culture biases.

- Example: SRPM, CIE Non-verbal group test of Intelligence.

Performance Test:

- Requires the subject to manipulate objects to perform the test.

- Written language is not necessary for answering the items.

- Example: Kohs's Block designs test. Here the subject is asked to arrange the blocks in a specified period to produce a given design, Bhatia's Battery performance test.

- Can be administered to persons from different cultures and reduce culture biases.

- Example: Draw a Man Test by Pramila Pathak, Kohs Block designs test.

Culture Biased or Culture Fair Tests based on Nature of Items used:

- Psychological tests that show a bias toward the culture in which they are developed are Culture Biased Tests.

- Tests developed-in-America and Europe represent an urban and middle class cultural ethos. (Middle class white subjects perform well on these tests). The items do not consider favourably to Asians and Africans.

- Culture Fair Tests: One does not discriminate against as individuals belong to different cultures.

- Non-verbal and Performance Tests reduce cultural influences.

To overcome the limitation of Culture biased tests, Culture fair tests were developed, e.g. non-verbal and performance tests are called so because people of any culture could take them. For e.g. Standard progressive Matrices and Bhatia's Battery Performance Test.

Q.9. Discuss how interplay of Nature and Nurture influences intelligence.

Or

All persons do not have the same intellectual capacity. How do individuals vary in their intellectual ability? Explain. **(CBSE 2014)**

Ans. All persons do not have the same intellectual capacity. They vary in their intellectual ability. Some are exceptionally bright and some are below average. Some possess high IQ range while others have average or below average.

All the scores gradually and symmetrically decline towards both the sides but never touch the X-axis.

(i) The frequency distribution for the IQ scores tends to approximate a bell-shaped curve, called the **normal curve**. This type of distribution is symmetrical around the central value, called the **mean**.

(ii) On the basis of IQ, people are classified in different groups. It is clear that only 2.2 percent people who possess above 130 IQ range are very intelligent or very superior, their IQ score is more than 130.

(iii) People falling between 90-109 IQ range are considered as average. The mean IQ score in a population is 100. People with IQ scores in the range of 90-110 have normal intelligence.

(iv) Those with IQ below 70 are suspected to have 'mental retardation'. Mental retardation refers to sub-average intellectual functioning. The behaviour is maladaptive and manifest in four forms i.e., mild, moderate, severe and profound mental retardation.

The extreme right also lie to 2.2 percent population which are known as gifted i.e., they enjoy exceptional intelligence, exceptional talent and exceptional creativity.

Classification of People on the Basis of IQ		
IQ Range	Descriptive Label	Per cent in the Population
Above 130	Very superior	2.2
120-130	Superior	6.7
110-119	High average	16.1
90-109	Average	50
80-89	Low average	16.1
70-79	Borderline	6.7
Below 70	Mentally challenged/reatarded	2.2

Q.10. Which of the two lQ or EQ, do you think would be more related to success in life and Why?

Ans. (i) IQ is a good predictor of potential.

(ii) EQ is a good predictor of success.

-Researchers had proved that—EQ helps in dealing with students who are stressed and face challenges of the outside world.

-It improves the academic performance.

-It is very useful in preparing students to face the challenges of life outside the classroom.

-They are less anti-social and more co-operative.

Q.11. How is 'Aptitude' different from 'interest1 and intelligence?

Ans. Aptitude:

(i) Aptitude refers to combination of characteristics indicative of an individual's potential to acquire some specific skills with training.

(ii) It is specific mental ability or teach ability of an individual to learn a particular skill.

(iii)It is the potentiality to perform a particular activity.

(iv)Aptitude is a determiner to learn a particular skill.

Interest:

(i) Interest refers to preference for a particular activity or what one enjoys doing.

(ii) Interest are acquired/learnt.

(iii)Interest is a facilitator.

An individual with high scientific aptitude having strong interest in mechanical activities is more likely to be successful mechanical engineer.

(i) Intelligence is a global and aggregate capacity of an individual to think rationally, act purposefully and to deal effectively with her/his environment.

(ii) Intelligence is a general mental ability.

(iii)It is product of heredity and environment.

(iv)It does not require training for the growth.

Q.12. How is creativity related to intelligence?

(Delhi Board 2010)

Or

How creativity and creativity tests are related but different from each other?

Ans. Creativity and intelligence are positively correlated because high ability is component of creativity, A highly intelligent person may not be creative but all the creative persons are definitely high in intelligence.

(i) Creativity is the ability to produce ideas, objects, or problem solutions that are novel, appropriate and useful.

(ii) Intelligence is subset of creativity.

(iii)Terman found that persons with high IQ were not necessarily creative. The same time, creative ideas could come from persons who did not even one of those identified as gifted, followed up through out their adult life, had become well known for creativity in some field.

(iv)Researchers have found that both high and low level of creativity can be found in highly intelligent children and also children of average intelligence. The same person can be creative as well as intelligent but it is not necessary that intelligent once must be creative.

Creative tests are different from intelligence tests:

(i) Creative tests measure creative thinking ability whereas intelligence tests measure general mental ability.

(ii) Creative tests measure convergent and divergent thinking whereas intelligence test measure convergent thinking only.

(iii)Creative tests measure imagination and spontaneous expression to produce new ideas, to see new relationship, to guess causes and consequences and ability to put things in a new context. Intelligence tests measure potential.

(iv)In creative tests questions are open-ended that have no specified answers whereas intelligence tests mostly use close-ended questions.

Chapter Practice

Multiple Choice Questions   [1 Mark]

Q.1. _______________ the ability to adapt, to shape and select environment to accomplish one's goals and those of one's society and culture.

(a) Intelligence   (b) Parabolic

(c) Self   (d) Personality

Q.2. Raju have IQ score 120 – 130 he have which descriptive label ?

(a) Very superior   (b) superior

(c) High average   (d) Average

Q.3. _________________ refers to an individual's underlying potential for acquiring skills.

(a) Aptitude   (b) Intelligence

(c) Cognitive   (d) Contextual

Q.4. Athletes, dancers, actors, sportspersons, gymnasts, and surgeons are likely to have which type of intelligence ?

(a) Logical   (b) Linguistic

(c) Bodily-Kinaesthetic   (d) Interpersonal

Very Short Answer Type   [1 Mark]

Q.5. What is Assessment as per Psychology?

Q.6. Triarchic theory of intelligence was proposed by _________.

Short Answer Type - I   [2 Marks]

Q.7. Mention any two characteristics of emotionally intelligent persons.

Q.8. Mention any two points of multiple intelligences identified by Gardner?

Short Answer Type - II   [3 Marks]

Q.9. Differentiate between psychometric and information-processing approaches to intelligence.

Q.10. Explain the relationship between creativity and intelligence.

Long Answer Type   [5 Marks]

Q.11.. Explain how intelligence is the result of heredity and environment.

Q.12. Explain briefly the multiple intelligences identified by Gardner?

CHAPTER 2

Self and Personality

Summary

Introduction

Self and personality refer to the characteristic ways in which we define our existence.

Self refers to the totality of an individual's conscious experiences, ideas, thoughts and feelings with regard to herself or himself.

Personal identity refers to those attributes of a person that make him/her different from others.

Self can be understood as a subject as well as an object. When you say, "I know who I am", the self is being described as a 'knower' as well as something that can be 'known'. As a subject (actor) the self actively engages in the process of knowing itself. As an object (consequence) the self gets observed and comes to be known. This dual status of self should always be kept in mind.

Kinds of Self

The personal self leads to an orientation in which one feels primarily concerned with oneself.

The social self emerges in relation with others and emphasises such aspects of life as cooperation, unity, affiliation, sacrifice, support or sharing.

This self values family and social relationships. Hence, it is also referred to as familial or relational self.

Q.1. Stable pattern of behaviour represents the ____________ of that person.

(a) Self   (b) Personality

(c) Opinion   (d) Self esteem

Ans. (b)

Q.2. ____________ refers to those attributes of a person that make her/him different from others.

(a) Self

(b) Personal identity

(c) Trait

(d) Habbit

Ans. (b)

Q.3. Which of the following best define 'Personal self'?

(a) value judgment of a person about herself/ himself

(b) an orientation in which one feels primarily concerned with oneself

(c) attributes of a person that make her/him different from others

(d) aspects of a person that link her/him to a social or cultural group or are derived from it.

Ans. (b)

Very Short Answer Type   [1 Mark]

Q.1. Define Self.

Ans. self refers to the totality of an individual's conscious experiences, ideas, thoughts and feelings with regard to herself or himself.

Q.2. Define Personality of a person.

Ans. A relatively stable pattern of behaviour represents the "personality" of that person

Short Answer Type - I   [2 Marks]

Q.1. Distinguish Self as subject and Self as object.

Ans. As a subject (actor) the self actively engages in the process of knowing itself. As an object (consequence) the self gets observed and comes to be known.

Short Answer Type - II   [3 Marks]

Q.1. Discuss the kind of self?

Ans. There are several kinds of self.

  i.   The personal self leads to an orientation in which one feels primarily concerned with oneself.

  ii.   The social self emerges in relation with others and emphasises such aspects of life as cooperation, unity, affiliation, sacrifice, support or sharing.

  iii.   Biological self in the context of socio-cultural environment modifies itself.

Topic 2

Summary

Cognitive and Behavioural Aspects of Self

The way we perceive ourselves and the ideas we hold about our competencies and attributes is also called self-concept.

Self-esteem is an important aspect of our self. As persons we always make some judgment about our own value or worth. This value judgment of a person about herself/himself is called self-esteem.

Self-efficacy is the extent to which a person believes they themselves control their life outcomes or the outcomes are controlled by luck or fate or other situational factors.

Self-regulation refers to our ability to organise and monitor our own behavior.

Self-control is learning to delay or refer the gratification of needs.

Techniques of self-control:

1. Observation of own behaviour: provides necessary information that may be used to change, modify or strengthen certain aspects of self.

2. Self-instruction: instructs ourselves to do something and behave the way we want to.

3. Self-reinforcement: rewards behaviours that have pleasant outcomes.

Multiple Choice Questions   [1 Mark]

Q.4. Value judgment of a person about herself/himself is called____________.

  (a) Self-esteem   (b) Personal self

  (c) Self concept   (d) Self regulation

Ans. (a)

Q.5. A person who believes that s/he has the ability or behaviours required by a particular situation demonstrates high__________________.

  (a) Self regulation   (b) Self esteem

  (c) Self efficacy   (d) Self control

Ans. (c)

Q.6. ______________ refers to our ability to organise and monitor our own behavior.

  (a) Self-esteem   (b) Personal self

  (c) Self concept   (d) Self regulation

Ans. (d)

Q.7. Which of the following play a key role in fulfillment of long term goal?

  (a) Self-esteem   (b) Personal self

  (c) Self control   (d) Self regulation

Ans. (c)

Q.8. If Puja is going to see a movie with her friends, as she have done well in an examination. This technique of self control is called______.

(a) Self-instruction

(b) Self-reinforcement

(c) Observation of own behavior

(d) Self regulation

Ans. (b)

Very Short Answer Type [1 Mark]

Q.1. Define Self esteem.

Ans. Self-esteem is an important aspect of our self. As persons we always make some judgment about our own value or worth. This value judgment of a person about herself/himself is called self-esteem.

Q.2. What was Bandura's social learning theory?

Ans. The notion of self-efficacy is based on Bandura's social learning theory. Bandura's initial studies showed that children and adults learned behaviour by observing and imitating others.

Short Answer Type - I [2 Marks]

Q.3. Define Self regulation with examples

Ans. Self-regulation refers to our ability to organise and monitor our own behaviour. People, who are able to change their behaviour according to the demands of the external environment, are high on selfmonitoring.

Q.4. What is meant by delay of gratification?

Ans. Delay of gratification, the act of resisting an impulse to take an immediately available reward in the hope of obtaining a more-valued reward in the future. The ability to delay gratification is essential to self-regulation, or self-control.

Short Answer Type - II [3 Marks]

Q.5. Define self-control. What are techniques for sel control?

Ans. Learning to delay or defer the gratification of needs is called self-control.

A number of psychological techniques of self-control have also been suggested.

i. Observation of own behaviour is one of them. This provides us with necessary information that may be used to change, modify, or strengthen certain aspects of self.

ii. Self-instruction is another important technique. We often instruct ourselves to do something and behave the way we want to. Such instructions are quite effective in self-regulation.

iii. Self-reinforcement is the third technique. This involves rewarding behaviours that have pleasant outcomes.

Q.6. How does the Indian notion of self differ from the Western notion?

Ans. Indian Concept of Self

- Self is characterized by the shifting nature of the boundaries.

- The Indian view does not make rigid dichotomies.

- It is based on collectivistic Indian society.

Western Concept of Self

- The boundaries between self and the group are rigid.

- It holds clear dichotomies between self and group.

- It is based on individualistic society of the West.

Q.1. What is self? How does the Indian notion of self differ from the Western notion?

Ans. Self is an organized cognitive structure. It can be understood in terms of subject and object or I and Me. It refers to the totality of one's conscious thoughts, and feelings which pertain to one's own self. .

Indian Concept of Self

- Self is characterized by the shifting nature of the boundaries.
- The Indian view does not make rigid dichotomies.
- It is based on collectivistic Indian society.

Western Concept of Self

- The boundaries between self and the group are rigid.
- It holds clear dichotomies between self and group.
- It is based on individualistic society of the West.

TOPIC 3

Summary

Concept of Personality

In psychological terms, personality refers to our characteristic ways of responding to individuals and situations.

Features of Personality:

1. Personality has both physical and psychological components.
2. Its expression in terms of behaviour is fairly unique in a given individual.
3. Its main features do not easily change with time.
4. It is dynamic in the sense that some of its features may change due to internal or external situational demands; adaptive to situations.

Personality-related Terms

- Temperament: Biologically based characteristic way of reacting.
- Trait: Stable, persistent and specific way of behaving.
- Disposition: Tendency of a person to react to a given situation in a particular way.
- Character: The overall pattern of regularly occurring behaviour.
- Habit: Over learned modes of behaving.
- Values: Goals and ideals that are considered important and worthwhile to achieve

Major Approaches to the Study of Personality

Psychologists distinguish between type and trait approaches to personality.

The type approaches attempts to comprehend human personality by examining certain broad patterns in the observed behavioural characteristics of individuals. In contrast, the trait approach focuses on the specific psychological attributes along which individuals tend to differ in consistent and stable ways. For example, one person may be less shy, whereas another may be more; or one person may be less friendly, whereas another may be more.

The interactional approach holds that situational characteristics play an important role in determining our behaviour.

Type Approaches

India also, Charak Samhita, a famous treatise on Ayurveda, classifies people into the categories of vata, pitta and kapha on the basis of three humoural elements called tridosha.

Apart from this, there is also a typology of personality based on the trigunas, i.e. sattva, rajas, and tamas. Sattva guna includes attributes like cleanliness, truthfulness, dutifulness, detachment, discipline, etc.

The personality types given by Sheldon are fairly wellknown. Using body build and temperament as the main basis, Sheldon proposed the Endomorphic, Mesomorphic, and Ectomorphic typology. The endomorphs are fat, soft and round. By temperament they are relaxed and sociable. The mesomorphs have strong musculature, are rectangular with a strong body build. They are energetic and courageous. The ectomorphs are thin, long and fragile in body build. They are brainy, artistic and introvert.

Five-Factor Model of Personality:

- Openness to experience :
- Extraversion :
- Agreeableness :
- Neuroticism :
- Conscientiousness :

Multiple Choice Questions [1 Mark]

Q.1. _______________ refers to our characteristic ways of responding to individuals and situations.

(a) Personality   (b) Self

(c) Self esteem   (d) Ego

Ans. (a)

Q.2. One person may be less shy, whereas another may be more; or one person may be less friendly, whereas another may be more is an example of _____________.

(a) Type approach

(b) Trait approach

(c) Interactional approach

(d) Ectomorphic

Ans. (b)

Q.3. The overall pattern of regularly occurring behavior_____________________.

(a) Temperament

(b) Character

(c) Values

(d) Trait

Ans. (b)

Q.4. Which of the following is not a one types of Personality as given Sheldon?

(a) Endomorphic,

(b) Mesomorphic,

(c) Ectomorphic

(d) Extraverts

Ans. (d)

Q.5. Which of the following is not the part of triguna?

(a) Sattva,

(b) Rajas,

(c) Tamas.

(d) All of the above

Ans. (d)

Very Short Answer Type [1 Mark]

Q.1. Define Personality.

Ans. In psychological terms, personality refers to our characteristic ways of responding to individuals and situations.

Q.2. _____________ refers to those attributes of a person that make her/him different from others.

Ans. Personal identity

Q.3. ___________ refers to our characteristic ways of responding to individuals and situations.

Ans. Personality

Short Answer Type - I [2 Marks]

Q.1. Distinguish between type and trait approaches to personality

Ans. i. The type approaches attempts to comprehend human personality by examining certain broad patterns in the observed behavioural characteristics of individuals.

ii. In contrast, the trait approach focuses on the specific psychological attributes along which individuals tend to differ in consistent and stable ways. For example, one person may be less shy, whereas another may be more

Q.2. Define the following terms.

Ans. (a) Temperament: Biologically based characteristic way of reacting.

(b) Values: Goals and ideals that are considered important and worthwhile to achieve

Short Answer Type - II   [3 Marks]

Q.1. List the features that characterize personality.

Ans. Personality is characterised by the following features:

- It has both physical and psychological components.

- Its expression in terms of behaviour is fairly unique in a given individual.

- Its main features do not easily change with time.

- It is dynamic in the sense that some of its features may change due to internal or external situational demands. Thus, personality is adaptive to situations.

Q.2. State techniques of self regulation.

Ans. Following are the techniques suggested for self-control:

- Observation of own behaviour : helps to change, modify, or strengthen certain aspects of self.

- Self-instruction :We often instruct ourselves to do something and behave the way we want to. Such instructions are quite effective in self-regulation.

- Self-reinforcement : This involves rewarding behaviours that have pleasant outcomes. For example, you may go to see a movie with friends, if you have done well in an examination.

Long Answer Type   [5 Marks]

Q.1. How do you define personality? How does it trait differ from type approach?

Ans. The word 'personality' is derived from the Latin word 'persona', which means a mask or false face which Greek actors used to wear when acting on stage. According to **Gordon Allport** "Personality is the dynamic organization within the individual of those psychological systems thqt determine his unique adjustments to his environment."

Trait approach psychologists explain personality on the basis of specific psychological characteristics.

Type approach psychologists believe that personality can be classified into broad categories.

Traits are relatively stable, persistent and characteristic patterns of behaviour which makes the individual different from others.

(i) These are overlapping, i.e., inclusive in nature.

(ii) Traits are specific psychological characteristics, e.g., shy or timid.

Types are cluster of similar traits.

(i) These are broad categories. .

(ii) These do not overlap, i.e., exclusive in nature, e.g., extrovert or introvert.

NCERT Questions

Q.1. What is meant by delay of gratification? Why is it considered important for adult development?

(Delhi board 2011, 2014)

Ans. Learning to delay or defer the gratification of needs is called self-control. Self-control plays a key role in the fulfilment of long-term goals. Indian cultural tradition provides us with certain effective mechanisms (e.g., fasting in vrata or roza and nonattachment with worldly things) for developing self-control.

Psychological techniques to develop **self-control** are:

(a) **Observation of Own Behaviour:** it provides us with necessary information that may be used to change, modify, or strengthen certain concepts of self. '

(b) **Self-instruction:** We often instruct ourselves to do something and behave the way we want.

(c) **Self-reinforcement:** It involves rewarding behaviours that have pleasant outcomes (like going to see a-movie with friends if we do well in exams).

— Self-control is important for the development of mature personality. This is the reason that all cultures emphasise the self-control. It helps in the fulfilment of long-term goals. Indian cultural tradition provide us with certain effective mechanisms, e.g., fasting in varta or roja and know attachment with worldly things for developing self-control.

— Self-control is also important for effective functioning of social network.

TOPIC 4

Summary

Allport's Trait Theory

Gordon Allport is considered the pioneer of trait approach. He proposed that individuals possess a number of traits, which are dynamic in nature.

Allport argued that the words people use to describe themselves and others provide a basis for understanding human personality.

Allport considered traits more like intervening variables that occur between the stimulus situation and response of the person. This meant that any variation in traits would elicit a different response to the same situation.

Cattell: Personality Factors

Raymond Cattell believed that there is a common structure on which people differ from each other. This structure could be determined empirically. He tried to identify the primary traits from a huge array of descriptive adjectives found in language. He applied a statistical technique, called factor analysis, to discover the common structures. He found 16 primary or source traits.

The source traits are stable, and are considered as the building blocks of personality. Besides these, there are also a number of surface traits that result out of the interaction of source traits.

Cattell described the source traits in terms of opposing tendencies. He developed a test, called Sixteen Personality Factor Questionnaire (16PF), for the assessment of personality. This test is widely used by psychologists.

Eysenck's Theory

H.J. Eysenck proposed that personality could be reduced into two broad dimensions.

(1) Neuroticism vs. emotional stability : It refers to the degree to which people have control over their feelings.

(2) Extraversion vs. introversion : It refers to the degree to which people are socially outgoing or socially withdrawn.

(3) Psychoticism vs. Sociability, which is considered to interact with the other two dimensions mentioned above. A person who scores high on psychoticism dimension tends to be hostile, egocentric, and antisocial. Eysenck Personality Questionnaire is the test which is used for studying these dimensions of personality.

Psychodynamic Approach

This is a highly popular approach to studying personality. Freud used free association (a method in which a person is asked to openly share all the thoughts, feelings and ideas that come to her/his mind), dream analysis, and analysis of errors to understand the internal functioning of the mind.

Levels of Consciousness

Freud's theory considers the sources and consequences of emotional conflicts and the way people deal with these. In doing so, it visualises the human mind in terms of three levels of consciousness.

Structure of Personality

According to Freud's theory, the primary structural elements of personality are three, i.e. id, ego, and superego.

Id : It is the source of a person's instinctual energy. It deals with immediate gratification of primitive needs, sexual desires and aggressive impulses. It works on the pleasure principle, which assumes that people seek pleasure and try to avoid pain.

Ego : It grows out of id, and seeks to satisfy an individual's instinctual needs in accordance with reality. It works by the reality principle, and often directs the id towards more appropriate ways of behaving. For example, the id of a boy, who wants an ice-cream cone, tells him to grab the cone and eat it. His ego tells him that if he grabs the cone without asking, he may be punished.

Superego : The best way to characterise the superego is to think of it as the moral branch of mental functioning. The superego tells the id and the ego whether gratification in a particular instance is ethical.

Freud also assumed that id is energised by two instinctual forces, called life instinct and death instinct.

Ego Defence Mechanisms

According to Freud, much of human behaviour reflects an attempt to deal with or escape from anxiety. Thus, how the ego deals with anxiety largely determines how people behave.

Multiple Choice Questions [1 Mark]

Q.1. Mahatma Gandhi's non-violence and Hitler's Nazism are examples of______________.

(a) Cardinal traits   (b) central traits

(c) secondary traits   (d) Non of the above

Ans. (a)

Q.2. Who among the following developed a test, called Sixteen Personality Factor Questionnaire (16PF)?

(a) Gordon Allport

(b) Raymond Cattell

(c) H.J. Eysenck

(d) Sheldon

Ans. (b)

Q.3. The___________ are stable, and are considered as the building blocks of personality.

(a) source traits

(b) surface traits

(c) cardinal traits

(d) central traits

Ans. (a)

Q.3. Which of the following is not a primary structural elements of personality?

(a) id,

(b) ego,

(c) superego

(d) Weak ego

Ans. (d)

Very Short Answer Type [1 Mark]

Q.1. What was Allport's Trait Theory?

Ans. Gordon Allport is considered the pioneer of trait approach. He proposed that individuals possess a number of traits, which are dynamic in nature.

Q.2. What is Eysenck Personality Questionnaire?

Ans. Eysenck Personality Questionnaire is the test which is used for studying these dimensions of personality.

Short Answer Type - I [2 Marks]

Q.1. Discuss two broad dimensions of personality as suggested by H.J. Eysenck.

Ans. H.J. Eysenck proposed that personality could be reduced into two broad dimensions.

   i. Neuroticism vs. emotional stability : It refers to the degree to which people have control over their feelings.

   ii. Extraversion vs. introversion : It refers to the degree to which people are socially outgoing or socially withdrawn.

Q.2. Write a short notes on Psychoticism vs. Sociability.

Ans. In a later work Eysenck proposed a third dimension, called Psychoticism vs. Sociability, which is considered to interact with the other two dimensions mentioned above. A person who scores high on psychoticism dimension tends to be hostile, egocentric, and antisocial. Eysenck Personality Questionnaire is the test which is used for studying these dimensions of personality.

Short Answer Type - II [3 Marks]

Q.1. Mention three levels of consciousness as given by freud.

Ans. i. The first level is conscious, which includes the thoughts, feelings and actions of which people are aware.

ii. The second level is preconscious, which includes mental activity of which people may become aware only if they attend to it closely.

iii. The third level is unconscious, which includes mental activity that people are unaware of

Q.2. Mention the primary structural elements of personality.

Ans. According to Freud's theory, the primary structural elements of personality are three, i.e. id, ego, and superego.

I. Id : It is the source of a person's instinctual energy. It deals with immediate gratification of primitive needs, sexual desires and aggressive impulses

II. Ego : It grows out of id, and seeks to satisfy an individual's instinctual needs in accordance with reality. It works by the reality principle, and often directs the id towards more appropriate ways of behaving. For example, the id of a boy, who wants an ice-cream cone, tells him to grab the cone and eat it.

III. Superego : The best way to characterise the superego is to think of it as the moral branch of mental functioning.

Long Answer Type [5 Marks]

Q.1. What is meant by structured personality tests? Which are the two most widely used structured personality tests? **(Delhi Board 2010 Part)**

Ans.

Structured personality tests are self-report measures that have the following features:

- Questions are direct and structured.

- They are called self-report because the examinee has to respond objectively to the items of the measure and his/her response are accepted as they are.

- They are objective in nature and they deal with the present state of mind.

— Self-report measures use inventories and questionnaires to assess conscious part of personality.

— Goal of the test may be revealed.

— These tests assess only conscious part of personality

- Their results depend on motivation and emotional state of the examinee; they are non-projective and direct inferences are made. _

Some of the self-report measures are:

1. **Eysenck Personality Questionnaire (EPQ):** This test was developed by Eysenck to assess two basic dimensions of personality namely introverted—extroversion and emotionally stable—emotionally unstable (Neuroticism).

2. **MMPI:** Minnesota Multiphasic Personality Inventory. This test was developed by Hathaway and Mckinely.

- It has been found very effective in detecting psycho-pathology like hypochondriasis, depression, hysteria etc.

- The test is divided into 10 sub scales. This test helps in clinical diagnosis of various mental disorders like hypochondriasis, depression, hysteria, etc.

- It has two sets'MMPI-I and MMPI-II. Now-a-days, MMPI-II is being used.

- It has 567 items in the form of affirmative statements. The subject judges each item 'statements' as true or false.

- MMPI is one of the very good tests for clinical purposes (diagnosis).

- Indian version of MMPI is also available named as Jodhpur Multiphasic Personality Inventory (JMPI) by Malik and Joshi.

16-PF Questionnaire (Delhi board 2010)

- It is developed by Cattell.

- It identifies large set of personality descriptions—subjected to factor analysis to identify basic personality structure.

- Subject responds to situation by choosing from alternatives.

- This test is being used with high school level students in India for career guidance and counselling. '

Problems Faced by self-report Measures

- **Social Desirability:** It is a tendency on part of the respondent to endorse items in a socially desirable manner.

- **Acquiescence:** It is a tendency of the subject to agree with items/questions irrespective of contents.

- Testing and understanding personality require great skill and training.

- People become self-aware and conscious, hesitate to share thoughts and feelings and motivation. If they do it, it is done in a socially desirable manner. So, the real personality characteristics are not manifested.

TOPIC 5

Summary

Stages of Personality Development

Freud claims that the core aspects of personality are established early, remain stable throughout life, and can be changed only with great difficulty. He proposed a five-stage theory of personality (also called psychosexual) development. Problems encountered at any stage may arrest development, and have long-term effect on a person's life. A brief description of these stages is given here

- **Oral Stage :** A newborn's instincts are focused on the mouth. This is the infant's primary pleasure seeking centre

- **Anal Stage :** It is found that around ages two and three the child learns to respond to some of the demands of the society.

- **Phallic Stage :** This stage focuses on the genitals. At around ages four and five children begin to realise the differences between males and females.

During this stage, the male child experiences the Oedipus Complex, which involves love for the mother, hostility towards the father, and the consequent fear of punishment or castration by the father (Oedipus was a Greek king who unknowingly killed his father and then married his mother).

For girls, the Oedipus complex (called the Electra Complex after Electra, a Greek character, who induced her brother to kill their mother) follows a slightly different course.

- **Latency Stage :** This stage lasts from about seven years until puberty. During this period, the child continues to grow physically, but sexual urges are relatively inactive.

- **Genital Stage :** During this stage, the person attains maturity in psychosexual development. The sexuality, fears and repressed feelings of earlier stages are once again exhibited.

Post-Freudian Approaches

Carl Jung : Aims and Aspirations Jung worked with Freud in his early stages of career, but later on he broke away from Freud. Jung saw human beings guided as much by aims and aspirations as by sex and aggression.

Jung claimed that there was a collective unconscious consisting of archetypes or primordial images. These are not individually acquired, but are inherited.

Karen Horney : Optimism Horney was another disciple of Freud who developed a theory that deviated from basic Freudian principles. She adopted a more optimistic view of human life with emphasis on human growth and selfactualisation.

Horney's major contribution lies in her challenge to Freud's treatment of women as inferior. According to her, each sex has attributes to be admired by the other, and neither sex can be viewed as superior or inferior.

Alfred Adler : Lifestyle and Social Interest

Adler's theory is known as individual psychology. His basic assumption is that human behaviour is purposeful and goaldirected. Each one of us has the capacity to choose and create. Our personal goals are the sources of our motivation. The goals that provide us with security and help us in overcoming the feelings of inadequacy are important in our personality development.

Erich Fromm : The Human Concerns In contrast to Freud's biological orientation, Fromm developed his theory from a social orientation. He viewed human beings as basically social beings who could be understood in terms of their relationship with others. He argued that psychological qualities such as growth and realisation of potentials resulted from a desire for freedom, and striving for justice and truth.

Erik Erikson : Search for Identity Erikson's theory lays stress on rational, conscious ego processes in personality development. In his theory, development is viewed as a lifelong process, and ego identity is granted a central place in this process. His concept of identity crisis of adolescent age has drawn considerable attention. Erikson argues that young people must generate for themselves a central perspective and a direction that can give them a meaningful sense of unity and purpose.

Behavioural Approach

This approach does not give importance to the internal dynamics of behaviour. The behaviourists believe in data, which they feel are definable, observable, and measurable. Thus, they focus on learning of stimulus-response connections and their reinforcement. According to them, personality can be best understood as the response of an individual to the environment.

Cultural Approach

This approach attempts to understand personality in relation to the features of ecological and cultural environment. It proposes that a group's 'economic maintenance system' plays a vital role in the origin of cultural and behavioural variations. The climatic conditions, the nature of terrain of the habitat and the availability of food (flora and fauna) in it determine not only people's economic activities, but also their settlement patterns, social structures, division of labour, and other features such as childrearing practices.

Humanistic Approach

The humanistic theories are mainly developed in response to Freud's theory. Carl Rogers and Abraham Maslow have particularly contributed to the development of humanistic perspective on personality.

The most important idea proposed by Rogers is that of a fully functioning person. He believes that fulfilment is the motivating force for personality development. People try to express their capabilities, potentials and talents to the fullest extent possible. There is an inborn tendency among persons that directs them to actualise their inherited nature.

Assessment of Personality

A formal effort aimed at understanding personality of an individual is termed as personality assessment.

Assessment refers to the procedures used to evaluate or differentiate people on the basis of certain characteristics. The goal of assessment is to understand and predict behaviour with minimum error and maximum accuracy.

The Minnesota Multiphasic Personality Inventory (MMPI)

This inventory is widely used as a test in personality assessment. Hathaway and McKinley developed this test as a helping tool for psychiatric diagnosis, but the test has been found very effective in identifying varieties of psychopathology. . In India, Mallick and Joshi have developed the Jodhpur Multiphasic Personality Inventory (JMPI) along the lines of MMPI.

Eysenck Personality Questionnaire (EPQ)

Developed by Eysenck this test initially assessed two dimensions of personality, called introverted-extraverted and emotionally stable-emotionally unstable. These dimensions are characterised by 32 personality traits. Later on, Eysenck added a third dimension, called psychoticism. A person scoring high on this dimension tends to be hostile, egocentric, and antisocial. This test is also widely used.

Sixteen Personality Factor Question- naire (16 PF)

This test was developed by Cattell. On the basis of his studies, he identified a large set of personality descriptors, which were subjected to factor analysis to identify the basic personality structure.

Projective Techniques

The techniques of personality assessment described so far are known as direct techniques, because they tend to rely on information directly obtained from the person who clearly knows that her/his personality is being assessed.

The Rorschach Inkblot Test

This test was developed by Hermann Rorschach. The test consists of 10 inkblots. Five of them are in black and white, two with some red ink, and the remaining three in some pastel colours. The blots are symmetrical in design with a specific shape or form. Each blot is printed in the centre of a white cardboard of about 7"×10" size.

The Thematic Apperception Test (TAT)

This test was developed by Morgan and Murray. It is a little more structured than the Inkblot test. The test consists of 30 black and white picture cards and one blank card. Each picture card depicts one or more people in a variety of situations. Each picture is printed on a card. Some cards are used with adult males or females. Others are used with boys or girls.

Rosenzweig's Picture-Frustration Study (P-F Study)

This test was developed by Rosenzweig to assess how people express aggression in the face of a frustrating situation. The test presents with the help of cartoon like pictures a series of situations in which one person frustrates another, or calls attention to a frustrating condition.

Sentence Completion Test

This test makes use of a number of incomplete sentences. The starting part of the sentence is first presented and the subject has to provide an ending to the sentence. It is held that the type of endings used by the subjects reflect their attitudes, motivation and conflicts.

A few sample items of a sentence completion test are given below.

   1. My father———————————————.

   2. My greatest fear is ——————————.

   3. The best thing about my mother is ————
       —————————.

   4. I am proud of ————————————
       ——————————.

   Draw-a-Person Test

   It is a simple test in which the subject is asked to draw a person on a sheet of paper. A pencil and eraser is provided to facilitate drawing. After the completion of the drawing, the subject is generally asked to draw the figure of an opposite sex person.

Behavioural Analysis

An observer's report may contain data obtained from interview, observation, ratings, nomination, and situational tests.

Interview Interview is a commonly used method for assessing personality. This involves talking to the person being assessed and asking specific questions.

Observation Behavioural observation is another method which is very commonly used for the assessment of personality.

Behavioural Ratings Behavioural ratings are frequently used for assessment of personality in educational and industrial settings.

Nomination This method is often used in obtaining peer assessment. It can be used with persons who have been in long-term interaction and who know each other very well.

Situational Tests A variety of situational tests have been devised for the assessment of personality. The most commonly used test of this kind is the situational stress test.

Multiple Choice Questions   [1 Mark]

Q.1. The Thematic Apperception Test (TAT) was developed by ________

   (a) Morgan and Murray

   (b) Hathaway and McKinley

   (c) Hermann Rorschach and Cattel

   (d) H.J. Eysenck

Ans. (a)

Q.2. Which of the following is not the part of Five-Factor Model of Personality?

   (a) Conscientiousness (b) Neuroticism

   (c) Agreeableness   (d) Preconscious

Ans. (d)

Q.3. Which of the following test consists of 10 inkblots?

   (a) Rorschach Test

   (b) Thematic Apperception Test

   (c) Self esteem Test

   (d) Draw-a-Person Test

Ans. (a)

Q.4. Sixteen Personality Factor (16 PF) Questionnaire was developed by ___________.

(a) Hathaway   (b) McKinley

(c) Cattell   (d) Eysenck

Ans. (c)

Q.5. P-F Study was developed by_________?

(a) Mckinley

(b) Rosenzweig

(c) Morgan and Murray

(d) Cattell

Ans. (b)

Q.6. Who among the following developed Client-centred therapy?

(a) Rogers   (b) Alfred Adler

(c) Erik Erikson   (d) Erich Fromm

Ans. (a)

Q.7. Analytical psychology one of the theory of personality is developed by_______?

(a) Carl Jung

(b) Karen Horney

(c) Erich Fromm

(d) Erik Erikson

Ans. (a)

Q.8. The Minnesota Multiphasic Personality Inventory (MMPI) is developed by_________?

(a) Hathaway and McKinley

(b) Eysenck

(c) Cattell

(d) Morgan and Murray

Ans. (a)

Q.9. Five-stage theory of personality developed by_______?

(a) Erik Erikson   (b) Mckinley

(c) Murray   (d) Freud

Ans. (d)

Q.10. Which of the following is not one of the stage of Stages of Personality development?

(a) Oral   (b) Anal

(c) Mature   (d) Phallic

Ans. (c)

Very Short Answer Type [1 Mark]

Q.1. What is halo effect?

Ans. Raters often display certain biases that colour their judgments of different traits. For example, most of us are greatly influenced by a single favourable or unfavourable trait. This often forms the basis of a rater's overall judgment of a person. This tendency is known as the halo effect.

Q.2. What is the meaning of omission in a drawn a person test ?

Ans. Omission of facial features suggests that the person tries to evade a highly conflict-ridden interpersonal relationship.

Q.3. Define Acquiescence.

Ans. Acquiescence is another one. It is a tendency of the subject to agree with items/questions irrespective of their contents. It often appears in the form of saying 'yes' to items. These tendencies render the assessment of personality less reliable.

Q.4. What was the main idea proposed by Rogers in Humanistic approach ?

Ans. The most important idea proposed by Rogers is that of a fully functioning person. He believes that fulfilment is the motivating force for personality development.

Q.5. Who had given the concept of concept of identity crisis?

Ans. Erikson's theory lays stress on rational, conscious ego processes in personality development. In his theory, development is viewed as a lifelong process, and ego identity is granted a central place in this process. His concept of identity crisis of adolescent age has drawn considerable attention.

Short Answer Type - I   [2 Marks]

Q.1. Differentiate between personal self and relational self.

Ans.

Personal self	Relational self
The personal self leads to an orientation in which one feels primarily concerned with oneself.	Relational self or social self mostly is concerned with relation with others.
Personal self relates only to their personal freedom, personal responsibility, personal achievement, or personal comforts.	Relational self type relates to cooperation, unity, affiliation, sacrifice, support or sharing. This self values family and social relationships.

Q.2. How are extroverts different from introverts according to Jung?

Ans. Jung has proposed another important typology by grouping people into introverts and extraverts. According to Jung,

- Introverts are people who prefer to be alone, tend to avoid others, withdraw themselves in the face of emotional conflicts, and are shy.

- Extraverts, on the other hand, are sociable, outgoing, drawn to occupations that allow dealing directly with people, and react to stress by trying to lose themselves among people and social activity.

Short Answer Type - II   [3 Marks]

Q.1. Analyse Alfred Adler's approach to Personality.

Ans. Alfred Adler's theory is known as individual psychology.

- His basic assumption is that human behaviour is purposeful and goal directed.

- Our personal goals are the sources of our motivation. The goals that provide us with security and help us in overcoming the feelings of inadequacy are important in our personality development.

- In Adler's view, every individual suffers from the feelings of inadequacy and guilt, i.e. inferiority complex, which arise from childhood. Overcoming this complex is essential for optimal personality development.

Q.2. Differentiate between self-esteem and self-efficacy.

Ans.

Self-Esteem	Self-Efficacy
In this an individual makes some judgment about our own value or worth.	In this an individual believes they themselves control their life outcomes or the outcomes are controlled by luck or fate or other situational factors, e.g. passing an examination.
In order to understand self-esteem of an individual they are presented with a variety of statements (for example :s "I am good at homework", or "I am the one usually chosen for the games", or "I am highly liked by my peers") and asked to indicate the extent to which those statements are true for her or him.If they are reported as true the individual is having a high self -esteem.	A person who believes that s/he has the ability or behaviours required by a particular situation demonstrates high self-efficacy.

Long Answer Type [5 Marks]

Q.1. State in common features of projective techniques. Describe anyone projective technique.

Or

Explain how projective techniques assess personality. Which projective tests of personality are widely used by psychologists?

(CBSE 2013, 2010, 2007)

Ans
- Projective tests of personality are widely used by psychologists.

- Projective techniques are most **indirect method** to assess personality.

- Psycho analytic theory proposed that behaviour is also determined by unconscious forces.

- The projective techniques were developed to assess unconscious motives and feelings.

— The stimulus material is relative or fully unstructured and poorly defined.

— The person being assessed is usually not told the purpose and the method of scoring and interpretation before the administration of test.

— The person is informed that there are no right or wrong responses.

— Each response is considered to reveal a true and significant aspect of personality.

— The scoring and interpretation in projective assessment are lengthy and subjective.

Projective Techniques

— Developed to assess unconscious motives, feelings and conflicts.

— A less structured or unstructured stimulus or situation will allow the individual to project his/her feelings, desires and needs on to that situation,

— Projections are interpreted by experts.

— Cannot be scored objectively, require qualitative analysis for which a rigorous training is needed.

1. **The Rorschach Inkblot Test (Hermann Rorschach)**

   - Consists of 10 inkblots—5 black and white, 2 with red ink, 3 in pastel colours.

   - Blots are symmetrical in design with a specific shape or form, made by dropping ink on a piece of paper and then folding the paper in half (hence called inkblot test).

   - The cards are administered individually in two phases:

   — **Performance proper:** The subjects are shown the cards and are asked to tell what they see in each of them.

   — **Inquiry:** A detailed report of the response is prepared by asking the subject to tell where, how, and on what basis was a particular response made.

   - Fine judgment is necessary to place the subject's responses in a meaningful context. Use and interpretation of this test requires extensive training

2. **The Thematic Apperception Test (TAT) Morgan and Murray**

   - This test consists of 30 black and white picture cards and one blank card—each picture card depicts one or more people in a variety of situations.

   - Some cards are used specifically with adult males or females, boys or girls—have been modified for the children and the aged.

   - The cards are presented one at a time and the subject is asked to tell a story describing the situation presented in the picture—what led up to the situation, what is happening at the moment, what will happen in the future, what the characters are feeling and thinking?

   - **Uma Chaudhury's** Indian adaptation of TAT is also available.

3. **Rosenzweig's Picture-Frustration Study (P-F Study)**

   - This study assesses how people express aggression in the face of a frustrating situation.

- Presents with the help of cartoon-like pictures a series of situations in which one person frustrates another, or calls attention to a frustrating condition.

- The subject is asked to tell what the other (frustrated) person will say or do.

- The analysis of responses is based on the type and direction of aggression—examine whether the focus is on the frustrating object (environment), or on protection of the frustrated person (oneself), or on constructive solution of the problem.

- **Pareek** has adapted this test for the Indian population

4. **Sentence Completion Test**

- This test makes use of a number of incomplete sentences—the starting part of the sentence is first presented and the subject has to provide an ending to the sentence.

- The type of endings used by the subjects reflect their attitudes, motivation and conflicts.

- The test provides subjects with several opportunities to reveal their underlying unconscious motivations.

5. **Draw-a-Person Test**

- In this test, the subject is asked to draw a person on a sheet of paper and then a figure of an opposite sex person.

- Finally, the subject is asked to make a story about the person as if he/she was a character in a novel or play.

- Some examples of interpretations are as follows:

— Omission of facial features suggests that the person tries to evade a highly conflict-ridden interpersonal relationships.

— Graphic emphasis on the neck suggests lack of control over impulses.

— Disproportionately large head suggests organic brain disease and pre-occupation with headaches. ..

Limitations

- Interpretation of the responses requires sophisticated skills and specialized training.

- There are problems associated with the reliability of scoring and validity of interpretations.

Chapter Practice

Multiple Choice Questions [1 Mark]

Q.1. Hardworking and self-controlled persons belong to _____________ intelligence.

(a) Self-efficacy
(b) Self-regulation
(c) Conscientiousness
(d) Self-instruction

Q.2. Which of the following work on the pleasure principle?

(a) Ego
(b) ID
(c) Super ego
(d) Self-reinforcement

Q.3. Which of the following is indirect method of assessment of personality?

(a) Projective technique
(b) Stimuli
(c) Schema technique
(d) Behavioural stress technique

Q.4. Who among the following is given trait approach theory?

(a) H.J. Eysenck
(b) Gordon Allport
(c) Gandhian
(d) Peter start

Very Short Answer Type [1 Mark]

Q.5. Define Self-esteem.

Q.6. What is the main objective of Humanistice approach?

Short Answer Type - I [2 Marks]

Q.7. What is psychoanalytic theory? How it is different from Projective techniques ?

Q.8. Mention any two criticism of Psychodynamic theories.

Short Answer Type - II [3 Marks]

Q.9. Explain the interactional approach to understand personality.

Q.10. Discuss structural elements of personality.

NCERT Questions

Q.11. Discuss the main observational methods used in personality assessment. What problems do we face in using these methods?

Q.12. Arihant wants to become a singer even though he belongs to a family of doctors. Though his family members claim to love him but strongly disapprove his choice of career. Using Carl Rogers' terminology, describe the attitudes shown by Arihant's family.

Meeting Life Challenges

Nature, Types and Sources of Stress

Summary

All the challenges, problems, and difficult circumstances put us to stress. It is important to remember that not all stress is inherently bad or destructive. Stress is like electricity. It gives energy, increases human arousal and affects performance. However, if the electric current is too high, it can fuse bulbs, damage appliances, etc. High stress too can produce unpleasant effects and cause our performance to deteriorate.

Stress Have Two Levels

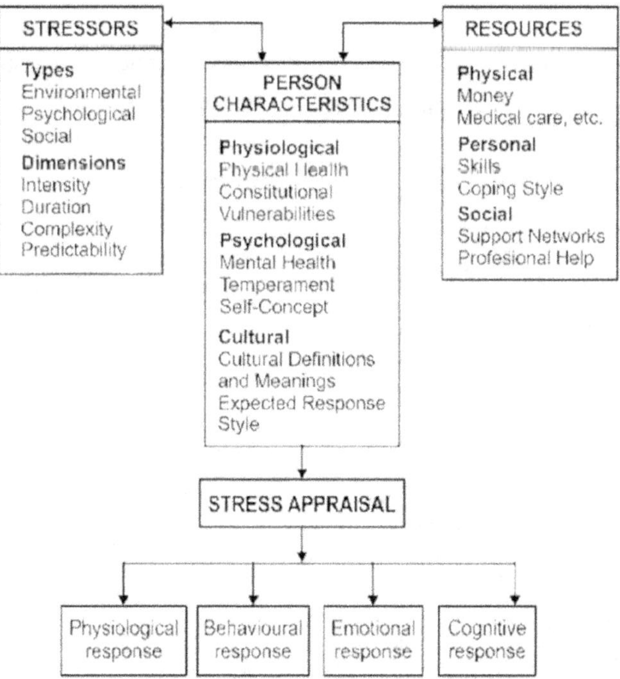

Fig. : A general Model of the Stress Process

'Eustress' is the term used to describe the level of stress that is good for you and is one of a person's best assets for achieving peak performance and managing minor crisis.

Distress : It is negative, unhealthy demotivating and causes our body's wear and tear. Thus, stress can be described as the pattern of responses an organism makes to stimulus event that disturbs the equilibrium and exceeds a person's ability to cope.

Nature of stress : The word stress has its origin in the Latin word 'strictus', meaning tight or narrow and stringer, the verb meaning to tighten. These root words reflect the internal feelings of tightness and constriction of the muscles and breathing reported by many people under stress.

Psychological characteristics like mental health, temperament, and self-concept are relevant to the experience of stress. The reaction to external stressors is called 'strain'.

Signs and Symptoms of Stress : Symptoms of stress can be physical, emotional and behavioral. Any of the symptoms can indicate a degree of stress which, if left unresolved, might have serious implications.

Types of Stress

Physical and Environmental Stress : Physical stresses are demands that change the state of our body. Environmental stresses are aspects of our surroundings that are often unavoidable such as air pollution, crowding, noise, heat of the summer, winter cold, disasters.

Psychological Stress

Some of the important sources of psychological stress are frustration, conflicts, internal and social pressures, etc.

Frustration results from the blocking of needs and motives by something or someone that hinders us from achieving a desired goal.

Conflicts may occur between two or more incompatible needs or motives, e.g. whether to study dance or psychology.

Internal pressures stem from beliefs based upon expectations from inside us to ourselves such as, 'I must do everything perfectly'.

Social pressures may be brought about from people who make excessive demands on us. This can cause even greater pressure when we have to work with them.

Social Stress : These are induced externally and result from our interaction with other people. Social events like death or illness in the family, strained relationships, trouble with neighbours are some examples of social stresses.

Sources of Stress : Among the most important of these are major stressful life events, such as death of a loved one or personal injury, the annoying frequent hassles of everyday life and traumatic events that affect our lives.

Life Events Changes, both big and small, sudden and gradual affect our life from the moment we are born. We learn to cope with small, everyday changes but major life events can be stressful, because they disturb our routine and cause upheaval.

Hassles These are the personal stresses we endure as individuals, due to the happenings in our daily life, such as noisy surroundings, commuting, quarrelsome neighbours, electricity and water shortage, traffic snarls, and so on.

Traumatic Events These include being involved in a variety of extreme events such as a fire, train or road accident, robbery, earthquake, tsunami, etc. The effects of these events may occur after some lapse of time and sometimes persist as symptoms of anxiety, flashbacks, dreams and intrusive thoughts, etc.

Multiple Choice Questions   [1 Mark]

Q. 1. What is the meaning of the word 'strictus' ?

    (a) Stress   (b) Strain

    (c) Eustress   (d) Distress

Ans. (a)

Q. 2. The reaction to external stressors is called ____.

    (a) Eustress   (b) Distress

    (c) Strain   (d) Stimulus

Ans. (c)

Q. 3. ____________ results from the blocking of needs and motives by something or someone that hinders us from achieving a desired goal.

(a) Social Pressure (b) Internal Pressure

(c) Conflict (d) Frustration

Ans. (d)

Q. 4. Which of the following is not the dimension of stressors?

(a) Intensity (b) Duration

(c) Complexity (d) Flexibility

Ans. (d)

Q. 5. ____________may occur between two or more incompatible needs or motives.

(a) Conflict (b) Internal Pressure

(c) Social pressure (d) Frustration

Ans. (a)

Very Short Answer Type [1 Mark]

Q. 1. What is Eustress?

Ans. 'Eustress' is the term used to describe the level of stress that is good for you and is one of a person's best assets for achieving peak performance and managing minor crisis. Eustress, however, has the potential of turning into 'distress'.

Q. 2. Who developed life event measure of stress?

Ans. Holmes and Rahe developed a life event measure of stress. A measure of stressful life events based on the above scale known as the Presumptive Stressful Life Events Scale has been developed for the Indian population by Singh, Kaur and Kaur.

Q. 3. Define Stress.

Ans. The pattern of responses an organism makes to stimulus event that disturbs the equilibrium and exceeds a person's ability to cope is called as stress.

Q. 4. What is Frustration?

Ans. Frustration results from the blocking of needs and motives by something or someone that hinders us from achieving a desired goal. There could be a number of causes of frustration such as social discrimination, interpersonal hurt, low grades in school, etc.

Short Answer Type - I [2 Marks]

Q. 1. Discuss the difference between Frustration and conflict?

Ans. Frustration results from the blocking of needs and motives by something or someone that hinders us from achieving a desired goal. There could be a number of causes of frustration such as social discrimination, interpersonal hurt, low grades in school, etc.

Conflicts may occur between two or more incompatible needs or motives, e.g. whether to study dance or psychology.

Q. 2. Explain social stress as a type of stress.

Ans. Social stress is induced externally and result from our interaction with other people.

- Death, illness in family, issues with neighbors are examples of social stress.

- Stress differs from person to person. For example a quiet person will find it stressful to attend parties who is more interested is spending a quiet evening at home, whereas for an outgoing person staying at home will be very stressful.

Q. 3. What are sign and symptom of stress?

Ans. Everyone has their own pattern of stress response. So the warning signs may vary, as may their intensity. Some of us know our pattern of stress response and can gauge the depth of the problem by the nature and severity of our own symptoms or changes in behaviour.

These symptoms of stress can be physical, emotional and behavioural. Any of the symptoms can indicate a degree of stress which, if left unresolved, might have serious implications.

Q. 4. Discuss any two psychological stress .

Ans. Psychological Stress are stresses that we generate ourselves in our minds. These are personal and unique to the person experiencing them and are internal sources of stress. We worry about problems, feel anxiety, or become depressed.

(i) Internal pressures stem from beliefs based upon expectations from inside us to ourselves such as, 'I must do everything perfectly'. Such expectations can only lead to disappointment. Many of us drive ourselves ruthlessly towards achieving unrealistically high standards in achieving our goals.

(ii) Social pressures may be brought about from people who make excessive demands on us. This can cause even greater pressure when we have to work with them.

Short Answer Type - II   [3 Marks]

Q. 1. Discuss Life events and Hassles as sources of stress.

Ans. Life Events:

- Changes either big or small effect our lives right from the moment we are born.

- We learn to cope up with small changes happening in our life but major life events can be very stressful because they destroy our routine and cause sudden change.

- If several life events that are planned ie moving in a new house or unplanned events like break up of marriage occur in a short span of time , we find it difficult to manage and cause a lot of stress in our life.

Hassles:

- Hassles mainly refer to daily happenings in our life that cause stress example crowded environment, electricity issues, water shortage, quarrelsome neighbours, noisy surroundings, traffic jams etc.

- Attending to various emergencies are hassles to a house wife.

- These daily hassles may have damaging consequences for the individual who is often the one coping alone with them as others may not even be aware of them as outsiders.

- The more stress people report as a result of daily hassles, the poorer is their psychological well-being.

Q. 2. Describe the sources of psychological stress.

Ans. Psychological stress are the ones we generate in our minds and they are like worrying about problems, anxiety, or getting depressed. These problems are unique to the person experiencing it.

Some of the important sources of psychological stress are **frustration, conflicts, internal and social pressures**.

Frustration : is resulted when we block our needs and motives from something or someone that comes in between achieving our desired goal. There could be a number of causes of frustration such as social discrimination, interpersonal hurt, low grades in school, etc.

Conflicts : can occur between two or more incompatible needs or motives for example whether to study dance or pshychology. You may want to take up a job or study further. There may be conflict when you are pressurized to take any action which is against your values.

Internal Pressures : they come up from beliefs based upon expectations from inside us to ourselves such as, "I must do everything perfectly". Such expectations can only lead to disappointment. Many of us drive ourselves ruthlessly towards achieving unrealistically high standards in achieving our goals.

Social Pressures : can come up from people who make excessive demands on us. This can cause even greater pressure when we have to work with them. Also, there are people with whom we face interpersonal difficulties, "a personality clash".

Long Answer Type   [5 Marks]

Q. 1. Explain the concept of stress. Give examples from daily life.

Ans. The pattern of responses an organism makes to stimulus event that disturbs the equilibrium and exceeds a person's ability to cope. Origin in the Latin word 'strictus', meaning tight/narrow and 'stringere' (to tighten). Stress may get manifested in two forms :

(a) Eustress : The level qf stress that is good for you and is one of a person's best assets for achieving peak performance and managing minor crises. This is positive, healthy and inspiring.

(b) Distress : Manifestation of stress that causes our body's wear and tear. It is negative, unhealthy and demotivating.

Stressors : Events that cause our body to give the stress response. Whatever causes stress is known as stressor.

Strain : Reaction to external stressors is known as strain.Hans Selye (Father of modem stress research) defined stress as a non-specific response of the body to any demands.

Basic Features of Stress :

1. Different stressors may produce different patterns of stress reaction.

2. Stress is embedded in the ongoing process that involves individuals interacting ' with their social and cultural environment. Stress is a dynamic mental/cognitive state. It is a disruption in homeostasis/imbalance that gives rise to resolution of the imbalance/ restoration of homeostasis.

Perception of stress is dependent on an individual's cognitive appraisal of events and the resources available to deal with them.

Q. 2. State the symptoms and 'sources of stress.

Ans. • Everyone has higher own pattern of stress response. So the warning signs may vary, as may their intensity.

• Some of us know our pattern of stress response and can understand the depth of the

• problem by the nature and severity of our own symptoms or changes in behaviour.

• These symptoms of stress can be physical, emotional and behavioural.

A wide range of events and conditions can generate stress; among the most important of these are major stressful life events such as death of a loved one or personal injury, the annoying frequent hassles of everyday life and traumatic events that affect our lives.

(i) Recent Life Events:

• Changes, both big and small, sudden and gradual affect our life from the moment we are born.

• We learn to cope with small, everyday changes but major life events can be stressful because they disturb our routine and cause trouble.

• If several of these life events that are planned (e.g., moving into a new house) or unpredicted (e.g., break-up of a long-term relationship) occur within a short period of timer we find it difficult to cope with them and will be more prone to the symptoms of stress.

(ii) Daily Hassles : There are daily hassles from which we have to cope like noisy surroundings, quarrelsome neighbours, electricity and water shortage, traffic jams,and so on.

The more stressed people report as a result of daily hassles, the poorer is" the | psychological well-being.

(iii) Traumatic Events:

• These include being involved in a variety of extreme events such as fire, train or road accident, robbery, earthquake, tsunami, etc.

• The effects of these events may occur after some lapse of time and sometimes persist as symptoms of anxiety, flashbacks, dreams and intrusive thoughts etc.

• Severe trauma can also strain relationships.

TOPIC 2

Effects of Stress on Psychological Functioning and Health

▌ Summary

There are four major effects of stress associated with the stressed state, viz. emotional, physiological, cognitive, and behavioural.

Emotional Effects : Those who suffer from stress are far more likely to experience mood swings, and show erratic behaviour that may alienate them from family and friends. In some cases this can start a vicious circle of decreasing confidence, leading to more serious emotional problems. Some examples are feelings of anxiety and depression, increased physical tension, increased psychological tension and mood swings.

Physiological Effects : When the human body is placed under physical or psychological stress, it increases the production of certain hormones, such as adrenaline and cortisol. These hormones produce marked changes in heart rate, blood pressure levels, metabolism and physical activity.

Cognitive Effects : If pressures due to stress continue, one may suffer from mental overload. This suffering from high level of stress can rapidly cause individuals to lose their ability to make sound decisions. Faulty decisions made at home, in career, or at workplace may lead to arguments, failure, financial loss or even loss of job.

Behavioural Effects : Stress affects our behaviour in the form of eating less nutritional food, increasing intake of stimulants such as caffeine, excessive consumption of cigarettes, alcohol and other drugs such as tranquillisers etc.

When stress is prolonged, it affects physical health and impairs psychological functioning. People experience exhaustion and attitudinal problems when the stress due to demands from the environment and constraints are too high and little support is available from family and friends.

General Adaptation Syndrome

Selye studied this issue by subjecting animals to a variety of stressors such as high temperature, X-rays and insulin injections, in the laboratory over a long period of time. He also observed patients with various injuries and illnesses in hospitals. Selye noticed a similar pattern of bodily response in all of them. He called this pattern the General Adaptation Syndrome (GAS). According to him, GAS involves three stages: alarm reaction, resistance, and exhaustion

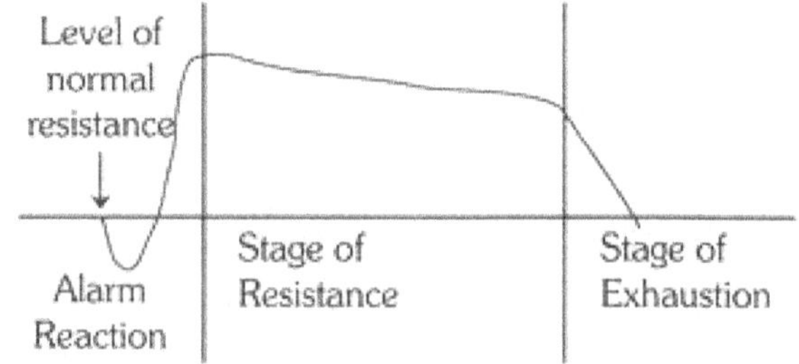

Fig. : The General Adaptation Syndrome

1. **Alarm reaction stage :** The presence of a noxious stimulus or stressor leads to activation of the adrenalpituitary-cortex system. This triggers the release of hormones producing the stress response. Now the individual is ready for fight or flight.

2. **Resistance stage :** If stress is prolonged, the resistance stage begins. The parasympathetic nervous system calls for more cautious use of the body's resources. The organism makes efforts to cope with the threat, as through confrontation.

3. **Exhaustion stage :** Continued exposure to the same stressor or additional stressors drains the body of its resources and leads to the third stage of exhaustion. The physiological systems involved in alarm reaction and resistance become ineffective and susceptibility to stress-related diseases such as high blood pressure becomes more likely.

Stress and the Immune System

Psychoneuroimmunology focuses on the links between the mind, the brain and the immune system.

Stress can affect natural killer cell cytotoxicity, which is of major importance in the defence against various infections and cancer. Reduced levels of natural killer cell cytotoxicity have been found in people who are highly stressed, including students facing important examinations, bereaved persons, and those who are severely depressed.

Lifestyle

Stress can lead to unhealthy lifestyle or health damaging behaviour. Lifestyle is the overall pattern of decisions and behaviours that determine a person's health and quality of life. Stressed individuals may be more likely to expose themselves to pathogens, which are agents causing physical illness.

Coping With Stress

Coping is a dynamic situation-specific reaction to stress. It is a set of concrete responses to stressful situations or events that are intended to resolve the problem and reduce stress.

The three coping strategies given by Endler and Parker are:

Task-oriented Strategy : This involves obtaining information about the stressful situation and about alternative courses of action and their probable outcome; it also involves deciding priorities and acting so as to deal directly with the stressful situation. For example, schedule my time better, or think about how I have solved similar problems.

Emotion-oriented Strategy : This can involve efforts to maintain hope and to control one's emotions; it can also involve venting feelings of anger and frustration, or deciding that nothing can be done to change things. For example, tell myself that it is not really happening to me, or worry about what I am going to do.

Avoidance-oriented Strategy : This involves denying or minimising the seriousness of the situation; it also involves conscious suppression of stressful thoughts and their replacement by self- protective thoughts. Examples of this are watching TV, phone up a friend, or try to be with other people.

Stress Management Techniques

Some of these techniques are: Relaxation Techniques , Meditation Procedures, Biofeedback.

Relaxation Techniques : It is an active skill that reduces symptoms of stress and decreases the incidence of illnesses such as high blood pressure and heart disease.

Meditation Procedures : The yogic method of meditation consists of a sequence of learned techniques for refocusing of attention that brings about an altered state of consciousness.

Biofeedback : It is a procedure to monitor and reduce the physiological aspects of stress by providing feedback about current physiological activity and is often accompanied by relaxation training.

Creative Visualisation : It is an effective technique for dealing with stress. Creative visualisation is a subjective experience that uses imagery and imagination. Before visualising one must set oneself a realistic goal, as it helps build confidence. It is easier to visualise if one's mind is quiet, body relaxed and eyes are closed.

Cognitive Behavioural Techniques : These techniques aim to inoculate people against stress. Stress inoculation training is one effective method developed by Meichenbaum. The essence of this approach is to replace negative and irrational thoughts with positive and rational ones.

Exercise : Exercise can provide an active outlet for the physiological arousal experienced in response to stress. Regular exercise improves the efficiency of the heart, enhances the function of the lungs, maintains good circulation, lowers blood pressure, reduces fat in the blood and improves the body's immune system.

Promoting Positive Health and Well-Being

When we find ways of managing these pressures and can use the energy to create something positive out of the situation, then we will have learned to survive healthily and this will leave us more stress fit for future crises. It is like being immunised against the dangers of unhealthy stress.

Stress Resistant Personality : Recent studies by Kobasa have shown that people with high levels of stress but low levels of illness share three characteristics, which are referred to as the personality traits of hardiness. It consists of 'the three Cs', i.e. commitment, control, and challenge.

Life Skills Life skills are abilities for adaptive and positive behaviour that enable individuals to deal effectively with the demands and challenges of everyday life. Our ability to cope depends on how well we are prepared to deal with and counterbalance everyday demands, and keeps equilibrium in our lives.

Assertiveness : Assertiveness is a behaviour or skill that helps to communicate, clearly and confidently, our feelings, needs, wants, and thoughts. It is the ability to say no to a request, to state an opinion without being self-conscious, or to express emotions such as love, anger, etc.

Time Management : The way you spend your time determines the quality of your life. Learning how to plan time and delegate can help to relieve the pressure. The major way to reduce time stress is to change one's perception of time.

Rational Thinking : Many stress-related problems occur as a result of distorted thinking. The way you think and the way you feel are closely connected.

Improving Relationships : The key to a sound lasting relationship is communication. This consists of three essential skills: listening to what the other person is saying, expressing how you feel and what you think, and accepting the other person's opinions and feelings, even if they are different from your own.

Self-care : If we keep ourselves healthy, fit and relaxed, we are better prepared physically and emotionally to tackle the stresses of everyday life.

Overcoming Unhelpful Habits : Unhelpful habits such as perfectionism, avoidance, procrastination, etc. are strategies that help to cope in the short-term but which make one more vulnerable to stress.

Diet : A balanced diet can lift one's mood, give more energy, feed muscles, improve circulation, prevent illness, strengthen the immune system and make one feel better to cope with stresses of life.

Exercise : A large number of studies confirm a consistently positive relationship between physical fitness and health. Also, of all the measures an individual can take to improve health, exercise is the lifestyle change with the widest popular approval.

Positive Attitude : Positive health and well-being can be realised by having a positive attitude. Some of the factors leading to a positive attitude are: having a fairly accurate perception of reality; a sense of purpose in life and responsibility.

Positive Thinking : The power of positive thinking has been increasingly recognised in reducing and coping with stress. Optimism, which is the inclination to expect favourable life outcomes, has been linked to psychological and physical wellbeing.

Multiple Choice Questions   [1 Mark]

Q. 1. Which one of the following are not the effects of stress?

    (a) Emotional   (b) Behavioral

    (c) Cognitive   (d) Social

Ans. (d)

Q. 2. General Adaptation Syndrome(GAS) was studied by____________?

    (a) Selye   (b) Endler

    (c) Parker   (d) Kobasa

Ans. (a)

Q. 3. Stress Resistant Personality studied is done by________?

    (a) Endler   (b) Kobasa

    (c) Parker   (d) Selye

Ans. (b)

Q. 4. Which of the following techniques aim to inoculate people against stress?

    (a) Stress Resistant Personality

    (b) Creative Visualisation

    (c) Cognitive Behavioural Techniques

    (d) Assertiveness

Ans. (b)

Q. 5. The state of physical, emotional and psychological exhaustion is known as :

    (a) Resistance   (b) Stress

    (c) Burnout   (d) coping

Ans. (c)

Q. 6. _______ are abilities for adaptive and positive behaviour that enable individuals to deal effectively with the demands and challenges of everyday life.

    (a) Assertiveness   (b) Life Skill

    (c) Self-care   (d) Time management

Ans. (b)

Q. 7. Coping concept is conceptualized by_____?

    (a) Lazarus   (b) Folkman

    (c) Both (a) and (b)   (d) None

Ans. (c)

Q. 8. Which of the following is not the part of personality traits of hardiness?

    (a) Conflict   (b) Commitment

    (c) Control   (d) Challenge

Ans. (a)

Very Short Answer Type   [1 Mark]

Q. 1. Define Coping.

Ans. Coping is a dynamic situation-specific reaction to stress. It is a set of concrete responses to stressful situations or events that are intended to resolve the problem and reduce stress.

Q. 2. What is Psychoneuroimmunology?

Ans. Psychoneuroimmunology focuses on the links between the mind, the brain and the immune system. It studies the effects of stress on the immune system.

Q. 3. What is Assertiveness?

Ans. Assertiveness is a behaviour or skill that helps to communicate, clearly and confidently, our feelings, needs, wants, and thoughts. It is the ability to say no to a request, to state an opinion without being self-conscious, or to express emotions such as love, anger, etc

Short Answer Type - I   [2 Marks]

Q. 1. Analyse the role of the following techniques to manage stress :

    (a) Creative visualization

    (b) Exercise

Ans. **(a) Creative Visualization**

- Creative Visualization is an effective technique for dealing with stress.
- Creative visualisation is a subjective experience that uses imagery and imagination.
- Before visualizing one must set a realistic goal, as it helps build the confidence.
- It is easier to visualise if one's mind is quiet, body relaxed and eyes are closed.
- This reduces the risk of interference from unbidden thoughts and provides the creative energy needed for turning an imagined scene into reality.

(b) Exercise

- Exercise can provide an active outlet for the physiological arousal experienced in response to stress.
- Regular exercise improves heart , lungs functioning, maintains blood pressure, reduces fat and improves immune system.
- Exercise like swimming, walking, running, cycling, skipping, etc. help to reduce stress.
- Exercise should be done with commitment at least 4 times a week for 30 minutes.
- Each session must have a warm-up, exercise and cool down phases.

Q. 2. How does stress affect the immune system?

(NCERT)

Ans. Stress can cause illness by impairing the workings of the immune system. The immune system guards the body against attackers, both from within and outside.

The white blood cells (leucocytes) within the immune system identify and destroy foreign bodies (antigens) such as viruses. It also leads to the production of antibodies. There are several kinds of white blood cells or leucocytes within the immune system, including T cells, B cells and natural killer cells. T cells destroy invaders, and T-helper cells increase immunological activity. It is these T-helper cells that are attacked by the Human Immuno Deficiency Virus (HIV), the virus causing Acquired Immuno Deficiency Syndrome (AIDS). B cells produce antibodies. Natural killer cells are involved in the fight against both viruses and tumours.

Short Answer Type - II   [3 Marks]

Q. 1. Give the three coping strategies given by Endler and Parker ?

Ans. The three coping strategies given by Endler and Parker are:

(i) **Task-oriented Strategy :** This involves obtaining information about the stressful situation and about alternative courses of action and their probable outcome; it also involves deciding priorities and acting so as to deal directly with the stressful situation. For example, schedule my time better, or think about how I have solved similar problems.

(ii) **Emotion-oriented Strategy :** This can involve efforts to maintain hope and to control one's emotions; it can also involve venting feelings of anger and frustration, or deciding that nothing can be done to change things. For example, tell myself that it is not really happening to me, or worry about what I am going to do.

(iii) Avoidance-oriented Strategy : This involves denying or minimising the seriousness of the situation; it also involves conscious suppression of stressful thoughts and their replacement by self- protective thoughts. Examples of this are watching TV, phone up a friend, or try to be with other people.

Long Answer Type   [5 Marks]

Q. 1. Describe the GAS model and illustrate the relevance of this model with the help of an example.

Ans. **Hans Selye's** GAS Model explains the influence of stress on the body.

- From his studies, he found that there was a similar pattern of bodily responses in animals to a variety of stressors.

- According to **Hans Selye**, stress refer to non-specific bodily reactions. He believed that stresses may be many but responses are only physiological reactions. Selye is known as 'father of modern stress researches'. He did many experiments on animals in extreme climatic conditions as well as he observed chronic patients and concluded that reaction of stress is the same.

- On the basis of his experimental conclusions, he gave a pattern of stress reactions. He called this pattern the **General Adaptation Syndrome** and it involves three stages:

1. **Alarm Reaction :** The presence of a harmful stimulus or stressor leads to activation of the adrenal-pituitary-cortex system.

   This triggers the release of hormones which produces the stress response and prepares the individual for fight or flight.

2. **Resistance :** If stress is prolonged, the parasympathetic nervous system calls for more cautious use of the body's resources.

   During this stage, an individual makes an effort to cope with the threat.

3. **Exhaustion :** Continued exposure to the same stressor or additional stressors drains the body of its resources and leads to burn out.

The physiological systems involved in the first two stages become ineffective and susceptibility to stress-related diseases like high blood-pressure increases.

This model is widely criticized because it focuses only on physiological aspects of stress and ignores the psychological dimension of stress.

Q. 2. Explain Behavioural effects of stress.

(CBSE 2013)

Or

Explain the effect of stress on psychological functioning.

Ans. Physiological Effects : When the human body is placed under physical or psychological stress, it increases the production of certain hormones such as adrenaline and cortisol. It causes:

- Changes in heart-rate, blood-pressure levels, metabolism and physical activity.
- Slowing down of digestive system.
- Constriction of blood vessels.

Cognitive Effects : High levels of stress can lead to:

- Mental overload.
- Impairment in the ability to make sound decision.
- Poor concentration.
- Reduced short term memory.

Emotional Effects : Those who suffer from stress are more likely to experience:

- Mood swings.
- Erratic behaviour.
- Maladjustment with family and friends.
- Feeling of anxiety and depression.

- Increased physical and psychological tension.
- Intolerance.
- Impatience.

Behavioural Effects : Stress affects our behaviour in the form of:

- Eating less nutritional food.
- Increasing intake of stimulants such as caffeine or excessive consumption of cigarettes, alcohol and drugs.
- Disrupted sleep pattern.
- Reduced work performance.

Q. 3. Describe how life skills can help meet life's challenges.

Ans. Life skills are abilities for adaptive and positive behaviour that enables individual to deal effectively with stressful situations.

Few such skills are as follows :

(i) Assertiveness:

- It helps to communicate, clearly and confidently, our feelings, needs, wants and thoughts.
- It is ability of an individual to say 'no' to a request which is against his wishes.
- If one is assertive then he or she feels confident high self-esteem and maintains his/her identity. '

(ii) Time Management:

- Learning time management determines quality of life.
- It is setting the priorities, goals and values in life.

Each day making list of things one wants to accomplish:

- Arranging work schedule.
- Changing perception of time.
- Setting aside time in schedule for exercise and leisure activities
- Learning to plan time.

(iii) Rational Thinking:

- It is challenging the distorted thinking and irrational beliefs.
- Deriving the anxiety provoking thoughts.
- Making positive statements.
- It is learning to ignore negative thoughts and images.

(iv) Improving Relationship : It consists following essential skills: ,

- (a) Listening to what the other person is saying.
- (b) Expressing what one feels and thinks.
- (c) Accepting the other person's opinions and feelings, even if they are different from your own.
- (d) Avoiding jealously and sulking behaviour.

(v) Self-care : Healthy mind in healthy body.

- Learning right pattern of breathing i.e., relaxed, slow, stomach-centered breathing from diaphragm.
- Avoiding environmental stress like pollutions, because it affects our mood.

(vi) Overcoming Unhelpful Habits : Perfectionism, avoidance, procrastination and our strategies which provides short-term gain but makes the individual vulnerable to stress.

Perfectionists want to get everything just as they want which is not always possible. Avoidance is ignoring the issue and refusal to face it or accept it.

Procrastination means putting off what we know we need to do, i.e., postponing the things like 'I will do it later' just to avoid confrontation due to the fear of failure.

Q. 4. Describe briefly four factors which facilitate development of positive health.   **(CBSE 2013)**

Or

Discuss the factors that lead to positive health and well-being.

Ans. Factors facilitating positive health and well-being are:

1. **Diet :** Diet can affect health independently or may enhance or modify the effects of stress in combination with other factors:

- (a) How much nutrition one needs depends on one's activity level, genetic structure,climate and health history. In fact, there is no one diet, which is ideal for everyone, in all situations.
- (b) Stress is supposed to affect diet and weight in many wrays. People, who are under stress or in a negative moods are often seen eating more. They seek 'comfort foods' or foods that make them feel better.
- (c) Stress may increase consumption of less healthy foods. Such people gain weight and loose stamina to fight stress.
- (d) Obesity and weight gain is a problem for a section of the society. A much larger section of the society, which is below the poverty line, suffer from malnutrition.
- (e) In the condition of poverty, women are the one who are most malnourished. Studies have shown that in India diets of female children and women are inadequate due to discriminatory practices.

2. **Exercise:**

- Exercise is directly related to promoting positive health.
- Two kinds of physical exercises essential for good health are 'stretching exercises' such as yogic asanas and 'aerobic exercises' such as jogging, swimming and cycling.
- Stretching exercises have a calming effect.
- Aerobic exercises increase the arousal level of the body.

- Yogic asanas provide systematic stretching to all the muscles and joints of the body and massages the glands and other body organs.

- Regular exercise reduces stress because it improves efficiency of vital body organs and improves immune system.

- Positive health and well-being come through a positive attitude of the mind.

- Positive health is the state of complete physical, mental, social and spiritual well¬being. It is not merely the absence of disease.

- Positive health comprises high quality of personal relationships, a sense of purpose in life, self regard, mastery of life skills and resilience to stress, trauma and change.

3. **Positive Attitude:**

Positive health and well-being can be realized by:

- Perceiving the reality fairly accurately.

- Tolerating and understanding different points of view.

- Having a sense of purpose in life.

- Having a sense of responsibility, accepting blame for failures and taking credit for success.

- Being open to new ideas, activities, or ways of doing things.

- Having a good sense of humour, to be able to laugh at oneself and absurdities of life helps to see things in their proper perspective.

4. **Positive Thinking:**

- Positive thinking leads to a belief that adversity can be handled successfully whereas negative thinking and pessimism anticipate disaster.

- Optimism, which is the inclination to expect favourable life outcomes is directly linked to psychological and physical well-being.

- Optimists use more problem-focused coping and seek advice and help from others. This optimism function helps the individual to cope up stress effectively.

Q. 5. Reflect on the environmental factors that have (a) a positive impact on the being and (b) a negative effect.

Ans. Until recently, catastrophic events were not studied systematically, because of their infrequent and unpredictable occurrence. However, because the survivors of these devastating events often experience the severe psychological aftermath termed 'post-traumatic stress disorder'.

Whether large-scale natural disasters produce lasting psychological effects, however, remains a source of controversy. Some research shows evidence of long-term psychological effects, whereas other studies show that the psychological impact of natural disasters is minimal.

In certain respects, the psychological trauma that results from human-produced disasters can be more dramatic and long term in its scope than natural disasters. Several factors seem to contribute to this phenomenon. One important factor seems to be control. Human-produced disasters are usually the result of human error; but we expect that adequate precautions will be taken to prevent human error. Thus, when disaster strikes, our expectations are violated, leading to a loss of control. In contrast, we do not expect to have control over hurricanes, earthquakes, or other types of natural disasters and accept them as fate.

A second factor has to do with the consequences associated with each type of disaster.

Natural disasters, while large in scope, tend to be clearly marked and limited in time. In contrast, human-produced disasters—such as the contamination of ground water with toxic chemicals—can, potentially exert their effects for many years. For example, exposure to toxic chemicals can increase people's risk of developing cancer or produce genetic damage. Moreover, the psychological trauma combined with the uncertainty regarding when or if these consequences will appear can produce chronic stress-related problems.

Q. 6. Given what you know about coping strategies, what suggestions would you give to your friends to avoid stress in their everyday fives?

Ans. High school students these days avoid extremely stressful fives, with increasing completion, expectations and demands. Therefore, I would suggest 'task-oriented strategy' as explained by **Endler** and **Parker**, to be an effective means in coping with stress.

Task-oriented coping involves :

1. Obtaining information about a stressful situation.

2. Deciding our priorities.

3. Dealing directly with the stressful situation.

Such an approach helps during exams and project deadlines.

I would also suggest the adoption of positive attitude and thinking which promotes health and well-being.

A positive attitude where the individual has a fairly accurate perception of reality; ability to take credit for success and blame for failure; acceptance and tolerance for other's view points.

Positive thinking interns of being optimistic. Optimism points towards the inclination to expect favourable life outcomes. An optimist will always use problem-focused coping and try and find the source of stress. Relaxation Techniques, Exercise, Balanced Diet all contribute significantly to stress reduction.

Chapter Practice

Multiple Choice Questions [1 Mark]

1. _________ It is this latter manifestation of stress that causes our body's wear and tear.
   - (a) Hassles
   - (b) Distress
   - (c) Strain-oriented Strategy
   - (d) Social Pressure

2. _______ The parasympathetic nervous system calls for more cautious use of the body's resources.
   - (a) Alarm reaction stage
   - (b) Exhaustion stage
   - (c) Resistance stage
   - (d) Both (a) and (b)

3. _________ are agents causing physical illness.
   - (a) Social Pressure
   - (b) Pathogenes
   - (c) Conflict
   - (d) Frustration

4. _______ It is a procedure to monitor and reduce the physiological aspects of stress by providing feedback about current physiological activity.
   - (a) Conflict
   - (b) Commitment
   - (c) Control
   - (d) Biofeedback

Very Short Answer Type [1 Mark]

5. Define Eustress.

Short Answer Type - I [2 Marks]

6. Discuss two types of appraisal as given by Lazarus.

7. Discuss any two stress management technique?

Short Answer Type - II [3 Marks]

8. Discuss any three psychological stress.

9. What are the three different sources of stress?

Long Answer Type [5 Marks]

10. Explain Behavioural effects of stress.

Or

Explain the effect of stress on psychological functioning.

11. Describe briefly four factors which facilitate development of positive health.

Or

Discuss the factors that lead to positive health and well-being.

Psychological Disorders

Summary

Concepts of Abnormality and Psychological Disorders

Although many definitions of abnormality have been used over the years, none has won universal acceptance.

Still, most definitions have certain common features, often called the 'four Ds': deviance, distress, dysfunction and danger. That is, psychological disorders are deviant (different, extreme, unusual, even bizarre), distressing (unpleasant and upsetting to the person and to others), dysfunctional (interfering with the person's ability to carry out daily activities in a constructive way), and possibly dangerous (to the person or to others).

Since the word 'abnormal' literally means "away from the normal", it implies deviation from some clearly defined norms or standards.

The first approach views abnormal behaviour as a deviation from social norms. The stigma attached to mental illness means that people are hesitant to consult a doctor or psychologist because they are ashamed of their problems.

The second approach views abnormal behaviour as maladaptive. The stigma attached to mental illness means that people are hesitant to consult a doctor or psychologist because they are ashamed of their problems. Well-being is not simply maintenance and survival but also includes growth and fulfilment, i.e. the actualisation of potential, which you must have studied in Maslow's need hierarchy theory.

Classification Of Psychological Disorders

The American Psychiatric Association (APA) has published an official manual describing and classifying various kinds of psychological disorders.

The current version of it, the Diagnostic and Statistical Manual of Mental Disorders, 5th Edition (DSM-5), presents discrete clinical criteria which indicate the presence or absence of disorders.

The classification scheme officially used in India and elsewhere is the tenth revision of the International Classification of Diseases (ICD-10), which is known as the ICD-10 Classification of Behavioural and Mental Disorders.

Factors Underlying Abnormal Behaviour

We will examine some of the approaches which are currently being used to explain abnormal behaviour.

Biological factors influence all aspects of our behaviour. A wide range of biological factors such as faulty genes, endocrine imbalances, malnutrition, injuries and other conditions may interfere with normal development and functioning of the human body. When an electrical impulse reaches a neuron's ending, the nerve ending is stimulated to release a chemical, called a neuro-transmitter.

Genetic factors have been linked to bipolar and related disorders, schizophrenia, intellectual disability and other psychological disorders. Researchers have not, however, been able to identify the specific genes that are the culprits. It appears that in most cases, no single gene is responsible for a particular behaviour or a psychological disorder.

There are several psychological models which provide a psychological explanation of mental disorders. The psychological models include the psychodynamic, behavioural, cognitive, and humanistic-existential models. The psychodynamic model is the oldest and most famous of the modern psychological models. Psychodynamic theorists believe that behaviour, whether normal or abnormal, is determined by psychological forces within the person of which s/he is not consciously aware. These internal forces are considered dynamic, i.e. they interact with one another and their interaction gives shape to behaviour, thoughts and emotions.

Another model that emphasises the role of psychological factors is the behavioural model. This model states that both normal and abnormal behaviours are learned and psychological disorders are the result of learning maladaptive ways of behaving. The model concentrates on behaviours that are learned through conditioning and proposes that what has been learned can be unlearned.

Multiple Choice Questions [1 Mark]

Q.1. ___________________ removing the evil that resides in the individual through countermagic and prayer, is still commonly used.

(a) Exorcism

(b) Magical forces

(c) Deviance

(d) Distress

Ans. (a)

Q.2. When an electrical impulse reaches a neuron's ending, the nerve ending is stimulated to release a chemical, called a_____________________.

(a) Neuro-transmitter

(b) Cognitive pulse

(c) Schema

(d) Stigma

Ans. (a)

Q.3. _______________ is the term used when people develop a fear of entering unfamiliar situations.

(a) Phobia (b) Agoraphobia

(c) Anxiety (d) Social phobia

Ans. (b)

Q.4. Psychological conflict and disturbed interpersonal relationships as causes of psychological disorders is said by_____________________?

(a) Johann Weyer

(b) Hippocrates

(c) Plato

(d) Socrates

Ans. (a)

Q.5. The seventeenth and eighteenth centuries were known as the_____________________.

(a) Renaissance Period

(b) Reform Movement

(c) Age of Reason and Enlightenment

(d) Deinstitutionalisation

Ans. (c)

Q.6. _______________ defined as a diffuse, vague, very unpleasant feeling of fear and apprehension.

(a) Phobia

(b) Anxiety

(c) Conversion disorder

(d) Dissociative disorder

Ans. (b)

Very Short Answer Type [1 Mark]

Q.1. What is diathesis-stress model?

Ans. This model states that psychological disorders develop when a diathesis (biological predisposition to the disorder) is set off by a stressful situation. This model has three components. The first is the diathesis or the presence of some biological aberration which may be inherited. The second component is that the diathesis may carry a vulnerability to develop a psychological disorder.

Q.2. What is Psychodynamic model?

Ans. The psychological models include the psychodynamic, behavioural, cognitive, and humanistic-existential models. The psychodynamic model is the oldest and most famous of the modern psychological models.

Short Answer Type - I [2 Marks]

Q.1. Differentiate between norms and culture?

Ans. Each society has norms, which are stated or unstated rules for proper conduct. Behaviours, thoughts and emotions that break societal norms are called abnormal.

A society's norms grow from its particular culture — its history, values, institutions, habits, skills, technology, and arts.

Q.2. Discuss the two biological factors that affect abnormal behavior.

Ans. i. A wide range of biological factors such as faulty genes, endocrine imbalances, malnutrition, injuries and other conditions may interfere with normal development and functioning of the human body.

ii. Biological researchers have found that psychological disorders are often related to problems in the transmission of messages from one neuron to another.

Short Answer Type - II [3 Marks]

Q.1. Mention any three models that provide a psychological explanation of mental disorders.

Ans. (a) The behavioural model states that both normal and abnormal behaviours are learned and psychological disorders are the result of learning maladaptive ways of behaving.

(b) Another psychological model is the humanistic-existential model which focuses on broader aspects of human existence.

(c) According to the socio-cultural model, abnormal behaviour is best understood in light of the social and cultural forces that influence an individual.

NCERT Questions

Q.1. "Physicians make diagnosis looking at a person's physical symptoms." How are psychological disorders diagnosed?

Ans. Psychological disorders are diagnosed on the basis of two classifications, i.e., DSM or IV and ICD-X.

* Classification of psychological disorders consists of a list of categories of specific psychological disorders grouped into various classes on the basis of some shared characteristics.

* International Classification of Diseases (ICD-10) is classification of behavioural and mental disorders.

* **ICD-10** refers to international classification of diseases and its 10th revision is being used.

* It is developed by **WHO** under one broad heading 'Mental Disorders' which is based on symptoms.

(The classification scheme is officially used in India)

* The **American Psychiatric Association (APA)** has published an official manual of psychological disorders:

The Diagnostic and Statistical Manual of Mental Disorders, IVth Edition (DSM-IV).

* It Evaluates the patient on five axes or dimensions rather than just one broad aspect of 'mental disorder'.

* These dimensions relate to biological, psychological, social and other aspects.

Uses of Classification:

* Classifications are useful because they enable psychologists, psychiatrists and social workers to communicate with each other about the disorders.

* Helps in understanding the causes of psychological disorders and the processes involved in their development.

* It helps in Clinical diagnosis.

TOPIC 2

Summary

Major Psychological Disorders

The term anxiety is usually defined as a diffuse, vague, very unpleasant feeling of fear and apprehension. The anxious individual also shows combinations of the following symptoms: rapid heart rate, shortness of breath, diarrhoea, loss of appetite, fainting, dizziness, sweating, sleeplessness, frequent urination and tremors.

A panic attack denotes an abrupt surge of intense anxiety rising to a peak when thoughts of a particular stimuli are present. Such thoughts occur in an unpredictable manner. The clinical features include shortness of breath, dizziness, trembling, palpitations, choking, nausea, chest pain or discomfort, fear of going crazy, losing control or dying.

People who have phobias have irrational fears related to specific objects, people, or situations. Phobias often develop gradually or begin with a generalised anxiety disorder. Phobias can be grouped into three main types, i.e. specific phobias, social phobias, and agoraphobia.

Specific phobias are the most commonly occurring type of phobia. Intense and incapacitating fear and embarrassment when dealing with others characterises social anxiety disorder (social phobia).

Agoraphobia is the term used when people develop a fear of entering unfamiliar situations.

Separation anxiety disorder (SAD) is another type of anxiety disorder. Individuals with separation anxiety disorder are fearful and anxious about separation from attachment figures to an extent that is developmentally not appropriate.

Obsessive-Compulsive and Related Disorders

People affected by obsessivecompulsive disorder are unable to control their preoccupation with specific ideas or are unable to prevent themselves from repeatedly carrying out a particular act or series of acts that affect their ability to carry out normal activities.

Obsessive behaviour is the inability to stop thinking about a particular idea or topic. The person involved, often finds these thoughts to be unpleasant and shameful. Compulsive behaviour is the need to perform certain behaviours over and over again. Many compulsions deal with counting, ordering, checking, touching and washing.

Trauma- and Stressor-Related Disorders

Very often people who have been caught in a natural disaster (such as tsunami) or have been victims of bomb blasts by terrorists, or been in a serious accident or in a war-related situation, experience post-traumatic stress disorder (PTSD). PTSD symptoms vary widely but may include recurrent dreams, flashbacks, impaired concentration, and emotional numbing.

Somatic Symptom and Related Disorders

Somatic symptom disorder involves a person having persistent body-related symptoms which may or may not be related to any serious medical condition. People with this disorder tend to be overly preoccupied with their symptoms and they continually worry about their health and make frequent visits to doctors.

Illness anxiety disorder involves persistent preoccupation about developing a serious illness and constantly worrying about this possibility.

The symptoms of conversion disorders are the reported loss of part or all of some basic body functions. Paralysis, blindness, deafness and difficulty in walking are generally among the symptoms reported.

Dissociative Disorders

Dissociation involves feelings of unreality, estrangement, depersonalisation, and sometimes a loss or shift of identity. Conditions included in this are Dissociative Amnesia, Dissociative Identity Disorder, and Depersonalisation/ Derealisation Disorder.

Dissociative amnesia is characterised by extensive but selective memory loss that has no known organic cause (e.g., head injury).

Dissociative identity disorder, often referred to as multiple personality, is the most dramatic of the dissociative disorders. It is often associated with traumatic experiences in childhood.

Depersonalisation/Derealisation disorder involves a dreamlike state in which the person has a sense of being separated both from self and from reality. In depersonalisation, there is a change of self-perception, and the person's sense of reality is temporarily lost or changed.

Depressive Disorders

One of the most widely prevalent and recognised of all mental disorders is depression. Depression covers a variety of negative moods and behavioural changes. Depression can refer to a symptom or a disorder.

Major depressive disorder is defined as a period of depressed mood and/or loss of interest or pleasure in most activities, together with other symptoms which may include change in body weight, constant sleep problems, tiredness, inability to think clearly, agitation, greatly slowed behaviour, and thoughts of death and suicide.

Factors Predisposing towards Depression : Genetic make-up, or heredity is an important risk factor for major depression and other depressive disorders.

Bipolar and Related Disorders

Bipolar I disorder involves both mania and depression, which are alternately present and sometimes interrupted by periods of normal mood. Manic episodes rarely appear by themselves; they usually alternate with depression. Bipolar mood disorders were earlier referred to as manic-depressive disorders. Some examples of types of bipolar and related disorders include Bipolar I Disorder, Bipolar II disorder and Cyclothymic Disorder.

The stigma surrounding suicide continues despite recent advances in research in this field. Due to this, many people who are contemplating or even attempting suicide do not seek help thus, preventing timely help from reaching them.

Suicides are preventable. There is a need for comprehensive multi-sectoral approach where the government, media and civil society all play important role as stakeholders. Some measures suggested by WHO include:

- limiting access to the means of suicide;
- reporting of suicide by media in a responsible way;
- bringing in alcohol-related policies;
- early identification, treatment and care of people at risk;
- training health workers in assessing and managing for suicide;
- care for people who attempted suicide and providing community support.

Schizophrenia Spectrum and Other Psychotic Disorders

Schizophrenia is the descriptive term for a group of psychotic disorders in which personal, social and occupational functioning deteriorate as a result of disturbed thought processes, strange perceptions, unusual emotional states, and motor abnormalities.

Symptoms of Schizophrenia

The symptoms of schizophrenia can be grouped into three categories, viz. positive symptoms (i.e. excesses of thought, emotion, and behaviour), negative symptoms (i.e. deficits of thought, emotion, and behaviour), and psychomotor symptoms.

Positive symptoms are 'pathological excesses' or 'bizarre additions' to a person's behaviour. Delusions, disorganised thinking and speech, heightened perception and hallucinations, and inappropriate affect are the ones most often found in schizophrenia.

Many people with schizophrenia develop delusions. Delusions of persecution are the most common in schizophrenia. People with this delusion believe that they are being plotted against, spied on, slandered, threatened, attacked or deliberately victimised.

People with schizophrenia may not be able to think logically and may speak in peculiar ways. These formal thought disorders can make communication extremely difficult.

People with schizophrenia may have hallucinations, i.e. perceptions that occur in the absence of external stimuli.

Auditory hallucinations are most common in schizophrenia. Patients hear sounds or voices that speak words, phrases and sentences directly to the patient (second-person hallucination) or talk to one another referring to the patient as s/he (third-person hallucination).

People with schizophrenia also show psychomotor symptoms. They move less spontaneously or make odd grimaces and gestures. These symptoms may take extreme forms known as catatonia. People in a catatonic stupor remain motionless and silent for long stretches of time. Some show catatonic rigidity, i.e. maintaining a rigid, upright posture for hours.

Neurodevelopmental Disorders : A common feature of the neurodevelopmental disorders is that they manifest in the early stage of development. Often the symptoms appear before the child enters school or during the early stage of schooling.

We will now discuss several disorders like Attention-Deficit/Hyperactivity Disorder (ADHD), Autism Spectrum Disorder, Intellectual Disability, and Specific Learning Disorder.

The two main features of ADHD are inattention and hyperactivityimpulsivity. Children who are inattentive find it difficult to sustain mental effort during work or play.

Hyperactivity also takes many forms. Children with ADHD are in constant motion. Sitting still through a lesson is impossible for them. The child may fidget, squirm, climb and run around the room aimlessly. Parents and teachers describe them as 'driven by a motor', always on the go, and talk incessantly.

Autism Spectrum Disorder is characterised by widespread impairments in social interaction and communication skills, and stereotyped patterns of behaviours, interests and activities.

Children with autism spectrum disorder experience profound difficulties in relating to other people. They are unable to initiate social behaviour and seem unresponsive to other people's feelings.

Disruptive, Impulse-Control and Conduct Disorders

The disorders included under this category are Oppositional Defiant Disorder, Conduct Disorder and others.

Children with Oppositional Defiant Disorder (ODD) display age-inappropriate amounts of stubbornness, are irritable, defiant, disobedient, and behave in a hostile manner. Individuals with ODD do not see themselves as angry, oppositional, or defiant and often justify their behaviour as reaction to circumstances/demands.

Feeding and Eating Disorders

Another group of disorders which are of special interest to young people are eating disorders. These include anorexia nervosa, bulimia nervosa, and binge eating. In anorexia nervosa, the individual has a distorted body image that leads her/ him to see herself/himself as overweight. Often refusing to eat, exercising compulsively and developing unusual habits such as refusing to eat in front of others, the person with anorexia may lose large amounts of weight and even starve herself/himself to death

Substance-Related and Addictive Disorders: Addictive behaviour, whether it involves excessive intake of high calorie food resulting in extreme obesity or involving the abuse of substances such as alcohol or cocaine, is one of the most severe problems being faced by society today.

Alcohol

People who abuse alcohol drink large amounts regularly and rely on it to help them face difficult situations. Alcoholism destroys millions of families, social relationships and careers. Intoxicated drivers are responsible for many road accidents. It also has serious effects on the children of persons with this disorder.

Heroin

Heroin intake significantly interferes with social and occupational functioning. Most abusers further develop a dependence on heroin, revolving their lives around the substance, building up a tolerance for it, and experiencing a withdrawal reaction when they stop taking it.

Cocaine

Regular use of cocaine may lead to a pattern of abuse in which the person may be intoxicated throughout the day and function poorly in social relationships and at work. It may also cause problems in short-term memory and attention.

Q.1. Paralysis, blindness, deafness and difficulty in walking are generally among the symptoms of _______?

(a) Dissociative disorder

(b) Anxiety

(c) Conversion disorder

(d) Phobia

Ans. (c)

Q.2 _________________ is a false belief that is firmly held on inadequate grounds.

(a) Schizophrenia   (b) Delusions

(c) Avolition   (d) Alogia

Ans. (b)

Q.3. Perceptions that occur in the absence of external stimuli is called ________?

(a) Hallucinations   (b) Alogia

(c) Delusions   (d) Avolition

Ans. (a)

Q.4. In ______________ there are frequent episodes of out-of-control eating.

(a) Binge Eating   (b) Bulimia nervous

(c) Anorexia nervosa (d) Hyperactivity

Ans. (a)

Q.5. Which of the following is not Commonly Abused Substances?

(a) Caffeine   (b) Tobacco

(c) Stimulants   (d) Neem

Ans. (d)

Q.6. _______________ is characterized by extensive but selective memory loss that has no known organic cause.

(a) Dissociative amnesia

(b) Dissociative fugue

(c) Dissociative identity disorder

(d) None of the above

Ans. (a)

Q.7. _________________ is the term used when people develop a fear of entering unfamiliar situations.

(a) Social phobias   (b) Agoraphobia

(c) Specific phobias   (d) None of the above

Ans. (b)

Q.1. What is separation anxiety disorder?

Ans. Separation anxiety disorder (SAD) is another type of anxiety disorder. Individuals with separation anxiety disorder are fearful and anxious about separation from attachment figures to an extent that is developmentally not appropriate. Children with SAD may have difficulty being in a room by themselves, going to school alone, are fearful of entering new situations, and cling to and shadow their parents' every move.

Q.2. Define Agoraphobia.

Ans. Agoraphobia is the term used when people develop a fear of entering unfamiliar situations. Many people with agoraphobia are afraid of leaving their home. So their ability to carry out normal life activities is severely limited.

Q.3. What is Schizophrenia?

Ans. Schizophrenia is the descriptive term for a group of psychotic disorders in which personal, social and occupational functioning deteriorate as a result of disturbed thought processes, strange perceptions, unusual emotional states, and motor abnormalities.

Q.1. Mention any two approaches to foster positive self-esteem in children?

Ans. Children the following approaches can be useful:

i. Accentuating positive life experiences to develop positive identity. This increases confidence in self.

ii. Providing opportunities for development of physical, social and vocational skills.

Q.2. Difference between Panic Disorder and Specific Phobia.

Ans. i. **Panic Disorder :** frequent anxiety attacks characterised by feelings of intense terror and dread; unpredictable 'panic attacks' along with physiological symptoms like breathlessness, palpitations, trembling, dizziness, and a sense of loosing control or even dying.

ii. **Specific Phobia :** irrational fears related to specific objects, interactions with others, and unfamiliar situations.

Q.3. Mention any two measures suggested by WHO for prevention for suicides.

Ans. Some measures suggested by WHO include:

- limiting access to the means of suicide;
- reporting of suicide by media in a responsible way;
- bringing in alcohol-related policies;
- early identification, treatment and care of people at risk;
- training health workers in assessing and managing for suicide;

Short Answer Type - II [3 Marks]

Q.1. What is Schizophrenia? What are the Symptoms of Schizophrenia?

Ans. Schizophrenia is the descriptive term for a group of psychotic disorders in which personal, social and occupational functioning deteriorate as a result of disturbed thought processes, strange perceptions, unusual emotional states, and motor abnormalities. It is a debilitating disorder.

Symptoms of Schizophrenia

i. positive symptoms (i.e. excesses of thought, emotion, and behaviour),

ii. negative symptoms (i.e. deficits of thought, emotion, and behaviour), and

iii. psychomotor symptoms

Q.2. Mention three difference between Somatic Symptom and Related Disorders and Dissociative Disorders?

Ans. Salient Features of Somatic Symptom and Related Disorders and Dissociative Disorders

Somatic Symptom and Related Disorders	Dissociative Disorders
Somatic Symptom Disorder : The person experiences body-related symptoms in the absence of any medical condition (or even if medical condition is present, it is not as serious as the symptoms presented).	Dissociative amnesia : The person is unable to recall important, personal information often related to a stressful and traumatic report. The extent of forgetting is beyond normal.
Illness Anxiety Disorder : The person experiences worry about the possibility of developing a serious medical condition.	Depersonalisation/Derealisation Disorder : The person experiences a change in the person's sense of reality and perception of self.
Conversion : The person suffers from a loss or impairment of motor or sensory function (e.g., paralysis, blindness, etc.) that has no physical cause but may be a response to stress and psychological problems.	Dissociative identity (multiple personality) Disorder : The person exhibits two or more separate and contrasting personalities, generally associated with a history of abuse.

Q.3. Mention any three Substance-Related and Addictive Disorders?

Ans. Addictive behaviour, whether it involves excessive intake of high calorie food resulting in extreme obesity or involving the abuse of substances such as alcohol or cocaine, is one of the most severe problems being faced by society today.

i. Alcohol

People who abuse alcohol drink large amounts regularly and rely on it to help them face difficult situations. Alcoholism destroys millions of families, social relationships and careers. Intoxicated drivers are responsible for many road accidents. It also has serious effects on the children of persons with this disorder.

ii. Heroin

Heroin intake significantly interferes with social and occupational functioning. Most abusers further develop a dependence on heroin, revolving their lives around the substance, building up a tolerance for it, and experiencing a withdrawal reaction when they stop taking it.

iii. Cocaine

Regular use of cocaine may lead to a pattern of abuse in which the person may be intoxicated throughout the day and function poorly in social relationships and at work. It may also cause problems in short-term memory and attention.

NCERT Questions

Q.1. Identify the symptoms associated with depression and mania.

Ans. Depression and Mania are mood disorders. These are characterized by disturbances in mood or prolonged maladaptive emotional state.

The main types of mood disorders include:

1. Major Depression disorders

2. Mania

3. Biopolar Disorders

Depression may get manifested as a symptom of a disorder or a major disorder in itself.

1. **Major depressive disorders,** are defined as a period of depressed mood and/or loss of interest or pleasure in most activities, together with other symptoms which may include.

Symptoms of Depression:

- Loss of energy, great fatigue.

- Change in body weight,

- Constant sleep problems.

- Tiredness.

- Inability to think clearly.

- Agitation

- Greatly slowed behaviour.

- Thoughts of death and suicide.

- Breakup in relationship.

- Negative self-concept.

- No interest in pleasurable activities.

- Other symptoms include excessive quilt or feelings of worthlessness.

Factors Predisposing towards Depression:

- **Genetic make-up**

  Heredity is an Important risk factor for major depression and bipolar disorders.

- **Age** is also a risk factor. For instance, women are particularly at risk during young adulthood, while for men the risk is highest in early middle age.

- **Gender** also plays a great role in this differential risk addition. For example, women in comparison to men are more likely to report a depressive disorder.

- **Situational factors** like negative life event, lack of social support and not able to live up to expectations etc. are few examples.

2. **Mania:**

Symptoms of mania.

- Increase in activity level.

- Euphoric.

- Excessively talkative

- Easily distracted.

- Impulsive.

- Less than usual amount of sleep.

- Inflated self esteem.

- Excessive involvement in pleasurable activities.

3. Biopolar Disorders:

Mood disorder, in which both mania and depression are alternately present, is sometimes interrupted by periods of normal mood. This is known **as bipolar mood disorder.** (Bipolar mood disorders were earlier referred to as **manicdepressive disorders.**)

- It is cyclic in nature.

- In bipolar disorders, depression alternates with periods of mania, and shows behaviour that is quite opposite to depression.

- In the manic state, the individual turns megalomaniac. Person develops grandiose cognitions and doesn't consider the negative consequences before acting on these grandiose plans.

- Speech is often rapid, as if she has to say as many words as possible in the time allotted.

- The risk of a suicide attempt is highest in ease of bipolar mood disorders.

Q.2. What do you understand by substance abuse and dependence?

(Outside Delhi 2009, Delhi Board 2014)

Ans. Disorders relating to maladaptive behaviours resulting from regular and consistent use of the substance involved are called **substance abuse disorders.**

These disorders include problems associated with using and abusing such drugs as alcohol, cocaine and which alter the way people think, feel and behave. There are **two sub-groups of substance-use disorders:**

(a) Substance Dependence refers **to intense craving for the substance** to which the person is addicted.

The person shows tolerance, withdrawal symptoms and compulsive drug taking. Tolerance means that the person has to use more and more of a substance to get the same effect.

Withdrawal refers to physical symptoms that occur when a person stops or cuts down on the use of a psychoactive substance, i.e., a substance that has the ability to change an individual's consciousness, mood and thinking processes.

(b) Substance Abuse refers to recurrent and significant adverse consequences related to the use of substances.

People, who regularly consume drugs, damage their family and social relationships, perform poorly at work, and create physical hazards.

Substance abuse disorders are a joint result of physiological dependence and psychological dependence. **Physiological dependence** refers to withdrawal symptoms, i.e., the excessive dependence of the body on drugs. **Psychological dependence**, on the other hand, refers to the strong craving for a drug because of its pleasurable effects.

The three most common forms of substance abuse:

- Alcohol abuse and dependence

- Heroin abuse and dependence

- Cocaine abuse and dependence

Alcohol Abuse and Dependence:

- People, who abuse alcohol, drink large amounts regularly and rely on it to help them face difficult situations.

- Eventually, the drinking interferes with their social behaviour and ability to think and work.

- For many people the pattern of alcohol abuse extends to dependence. That is . their bodies build up a tolerance for alcohol and they need to drink even greater amounts to feel its effects.

- They also experience withdrawal responses when they stop drinking. Alcoholism destroys millions of families and careers.

- Intoxicated drivers are responsible for many road accidents.

- It also has serious effects in the children of persons with this disorder.

- These children have higher rates of psychological problems. Particularly anxiety.

- Depression phobias afid substance-related disorders.

- Excessive drinking can seriously damage physical health. Some of the ill effects of alcohol can be been on health and psychological functioning.

Heroin Abuse and Dependence:

- Heroin intake significantly interferes with social and occupational functioning.

- Most abusers further develop a dependence on heroin, revolving their lives around the substance, building up a tolerance for it, and experiencing a withdrawal reaction when they stop taking it.

- The most direct danger of heroin abuse is an overdose, which slows down the respiratory centres in the brain, almost paralyzing breathing, arid in many cases causing death.

- Regular use of cocaine may lead to a pattern of abuse in which the person may be intoxicated throughout the day and function poorly in social relationships and at work.

- It may also cause problem in short-term memory and attention.

- Dependence may develop, so that cocaine dominates the person's life, more of the drug is needed to get the desired effects and stopping it results in feeling of depression, fatigue, sleep problems, irritability and anxiety.

- Cocaine poses serious dangerous effects on psychological functioning and physical well-being.

Q.3. What do you understand by the term 'dissociation'? Discuss its various forms.

(Delhi Board 2008, 2010)

Ans. • According to **Freud**, the anxiety and conflicts were believed to be converted into physical symptoms.

- Dissociation can be viewed as **severance of the connections between ideas and emotions.**

- Dissociation involves amnesia, feelings of unreality, estrangement, depersonalization and sometimes a loss or shift of identity.

- Sudden temporary alterations of consciousness that blot out painful experiences are a defining characteristic of dissociative disorders.

Four conditions are included in this group—Dissociative amnesia, Dissociative fugue, disseminative identity disorder and depersonalization.

1. **Dissociative Amnesia:** is characterized by **extensive but selective memory loss** that has no organic cause (e.g., head injury). Some people cannot remember anything about their past. Others can no longer recall specific events, people, places, or objects, while their memory for other events remains intact.

- This disorder is often associated with an over-whelming stress.

2. **Dissociative Fugue:**

Symptoms:

- Unexpected **travel away from home or workplace.**

- The **assumption of a new identity.**

- Inability to recall the previous identity.

- The fugue usually ends when the person suddenly 'wakes up' with no memory of the events that occurred during the fugue.

3. **Dissociative identity disorder,** often referred to as multiple personality, is the most dramatic of the dissociative disorders.

- It is often associated with traumatic experiences in childhood.

- The person assumes **alternate personalities** that may or may not be aware of each other.

4. **Depersonalization** involves a dreamlike state in which the person has a sense of being separated both from self and from reality.

- In depersonalization, there is a change of self-perception.
- The person's sense of reality is temporarily lost or changed.
- The patient experiences change in his body parts.

Q.4. What are phobias? If someone had an intense fear of snakes, could this simple phobia be a result of faulty learning? Analyse how this phobia could have developed.

Ans. An intense, persistent irrational fear of something that produces conscious avoidance of the feared subject, activity or situation is called a **phobia.**

- Phobias can vary in degree and how much they interfere with healthy adaptation to the environment. Some otherwise normal and well-adjusted persons also have phobias.

Phobias are mainly of three types :

1. **Specific phobias** are those directed towards specific objects and situations and can be varied, e.g., acrophobia (fear of heights), pyrophobia (fear of fire), and hydrophobia (fear of water).

2. **Social phobia** is a fear of social situations, and people with this phobia may avoid a wide range of situations in which they fear they will be exposed to, scrutinized and possibly humiliated by other people.

3. **Agoraphobia:** is the term used when people developed a fear of entering unfamiliar situations.

   Social learning theories work on the principle that our experience be it positive or negative such as phobia of lizards/cockroaches are the result of learning process which start early in life. Small children can play with snakes; they are not aware of the danger involved. For them it is just another play object, as they grow up the fear of these things are instilled by their parents and society which is reinforced and accounts for reactions like phobia.

   A psychoanalytical account for the same could involve attribution to some unconscious >

or/and repressed experiences. For example, suppose in your childhood you watched a group of roudy boys brutally torturing a cockroach/snake, which eventually died, although you going about the incidence after some days, but it might remain in back of your mind forever, which might explain your phobia to cockroaches which might remind you of the incidence and disturbs you emotionally.

Q.5. Describe the characteristics of children with hyperactivity.

Ans. **Achenbach** has identified two factors in behavioural disorders:

- Externalizing Factors
- Internalizing Factors

These disorders must manifest before the age of 18.

On the basis of these two factors he classified children's disorders in two categories:

- **The externalizing disorders or undercontrolled emotions:** Behaviours that are disruptive and often aggressive and aversive to others in the child's environment.
- **The Internalizing disorders or over-controlled emotions:** Those conditions where the child experiences depression, anxiety, and discomfort that may not be evident to others.

1. **Externalizing Disorders:**

   (a) Attention-deficit Hyperactivity Disorder (ADHD).

   (b) Oppositional Defiant Disorder (ODD).

   (c) Conduct Disorder.

   (a) **Attention-deficit Hyperactivity Disorder (ADHD):**

   The two main features of ADHD are:

   (i) Inattention (ii) Hyperactivity-impulsivity.

   Inattention:

   - Children who are inattentive find it difficult to sustain mental effort during work or play.
   - They have a hard time keeping their minds on any one thing or in following instructions.

Common complaints are that

- The child does not listen, **cannot concentrate**, does not follow instructions, is disorganized, easily distracted forgetful, does not finish assignments, and is quick to lose interest in boring activities.

- Children who are **impulsive**, unable to control their immediate reactions or to think before they act.

- They find it difficult to wait or take turns, have **difficulty resisting immediate temptations** or delaying gratification.

- **Minor mishaps** such as knocking things are common whereas more serious accidents and injuries can also occur.

- **Hyperactivity** also takes many forms. Children with ADHD are in constant notion. Sitting still for some time through a lesson is impossible for them. The child may fidget, squirm, climb and run around the room aimlessly.

- Parents and teachers describe them as 'driven by a motor', always on the go, and talk a lot.

- Boys are four times more prone for this diagnosis than girls.

(b) Children with Oppositional Defiant Disorder (ODD):

- Age-inappropriate amounts of stubbornness,

- Irritable,

- Defiant, disobedient, and

- Behave in a hostile manner.

  Unlike ADHD, the rates of ODD in boys and girls are not very different.

(c) Conduct Disorder and Antisocial Behaviour refer to age-inappropriate actions and attitudes that violate family expectation, societal norms, and the personal or property rights of other.

The behaviours typical of conduct disorder include:

- Aggressive actions that cause or threaten harm to people or animals,

- Non-aggressive conduct that causes property damage,

- Major dishonesty,

- Theft and

- Serious rule violations.

Children show many different types of aggressive behaviour, as:

1.
   - Verbal aggression (i.e., name-calling, swearing),

   - Physical aggression (i.e., hitting, fighting),

   - Hostile aggression (i.e., directed at inflicting injury to others),

   - Proactive aggression (i.e., dominating and bullying others without provocation).

2. **Internalizing disorders**

   (a) Separation Anxiety Disorder (SAD)

   (b) Depression

   (a) Separation anxiety disorder is an internalizing disorder unique to children. Its most prominent symptom is—

   - Excessive anxiety or even panic experienced by children at being separated from their parents.

   - Have difficulty being in a room by themselves, going to school alone, are fearful of entering new situations, and cling to and shadow their parents' every move.

   - **To avoid separation**, children with SAD may fuss, scream, throw severe tantrums, or make suicidal gestures.

   (b) Depression:

   - An **infant** may show sadness by being **passive** and **unresponsive; a preschooler** may appear withdrawn and inhibited; **a school-age child** may be **argumentative** and **combative;** and **a teenager** may express feelings of guilt and hopelessness.

Chapter Practice

Multiple Choice Questions   [1 Mark]

Q.1. "I can control the weather according to my moods." This is a statement made by a person suffering from delusion of _________________.

(a) Persecution   (b) Reference

(c) Grandeur   (d) Control

Q.2. When the person has to use more and more of a substance to get the same effect, is called _________ .

(a) Substance dependence   (b) Substance abuse

(c) Tolerance   (d) Withdrawal

Q.3. _____________________ was marked by increased humanism and curiosity about behaviour.

(a) psychodynamic model   (b) Renaissance Period

(c) Exorcism   (d) Maladaptive

Q.4. Dissociation involves feelings of unreality, estrangement, depersonalisation, and sometimes a loss or shift of identity are symptom of which disorder?

(a) Panic Disorder   (b) Generalised Anxiety Disorder

(c) Conversion disorder   (d) Dissociative Disorders

Very Short Answer Type   [1 Mark]

Q.5. Explain the term phobias.

Q.6. What is humanistic-existential model ?

Short Answer Type - I   [2 Marks]

Q.7. State two symptoms of Suicide which can be prevented if one is alert to.

Q.8. State the symptoms of Panic Disorders.

Short Answer Type - II   [3 Marks]

Q.9. Analyse heroin abuse and dependence.

Q.10. State the symptoms of Hypochondriasis and Conversion disorder.

Long Answer Type   [5 Marks]

Q.11. Describe Dissociative Disorders.

Q.12. Explain the negative symptoms of Schizophrenia.

Therapeutic Approaches

Summary

Psychotherapy is a voluntary relationship between the one seeking treatment or the client and the one who treats or the therapist. The purpose of the relationship is to help the client to solve the psychological problems being faced by her or him.

The relationship is conducive for building the trust of the client so that problems may be freely discussed. Psychotherapies aim at changing the maladaptive behaviours, decreasing the sense of personal distress, and helping the client to adapt better to her/his environment.

All psychotherapies aim at a few or all of the following goals :

- (i) Reinforcing client's resolve for betterment.
- (ii) Lessening emotional pressure.
- (iii) Unfolding the potential for positive growth.
- (iv) Modifying habits.
- (v) Changing thinking patterns.
- (vi) Increasing self-awareness.
- (vii) Improving interpersonal relations and communication

Therapeutic Relationship

The special relationship between the client and the therapist is known as the therapeutic relationship or alliance. Two components of the therapeutic relationship are:

- Contractual nature of the relationship in which two willing individuals, the client, and the therapist, enter into a partnership that is propelled by the aim of resolving the problems of the client

- Limited duration of the psychotherapy

The high level of trust enables the client to unburden herself/himself to the therapist and confide her/his psychological and personal problems to the latter. The therapist encourages this by being accepting, empathic, genuine and warm to the client.

This is the unconditional positive regard which the therapist has for the client. The therapist has empathy for the client.

Empathy is different from sympathy and intellectual understanding of another person's situation. In sympathy, one has compassion and pity towards the suffering of another but is not able to feel like the other person.

Types of Therapies

The following sections explain representative therapies from each of the three major systems of psychotherapy mentioned earlier.

Psychodynamic Therapy

Psychodynamic therapy is considered as the oldest form of therapy which was given by Dr. Sigmund Freud and this therapy explained the sources of psychological distress, conceptualized the structure of the psyche, dynamics between different components of the psyche and the source of psychological distress. The method of treatment, steps in the treatment, nature of the therapeutic relationship, and the expected outcome from the psychodynamic therapy are explained below.

Methods of Eliciting the Nature of Intrapsychic Conflict: Psychoanalysis has invented free association and dream interpretation as two important methods for eliciting the intrapsychic conflicts. The free association method is the main method for understanding the client's problems.

The images of the dreams are symbols which signify intrapsychic forces. Dreams use symbols because they are indirect expressions and hence would not alert the ego.

Modality of Treatment

Transference and Interpretation are the means of treating the patient. As the unconscious forces are brought into the conscious realm through free association and dream interpretation described above, the client starts identifying the therapist with the authority figures of the past, usually childhood.

A full-blown transference neurosis is helpful in making the therapist aware of the nature of intrapsychic conflicts suffered by the client. There is the positive transference in which the client idolises, or falls in love with the therapist, and seeks the therapist's approval. Negative transference is present when the client has feelings of hostility, anger, and resentment towards the therapist.

Duration of Treatment

Psychoanalysis lasts for several years, with one hour session for 4–5 days per week. It is an intense treatment. There are three stages in the treatment. Stage one is the initial phase. The client becomes familiar with the routines, establishes a therapeutic relationship with the analyst, and gets some relief with the process of recollecting the super ficial materials from the consciousness about the past and present troublesome events.

Multiple Choice Questions   [1 Mark]

Q.1. Which of the following are two important methods for eliciting the intrapsychic conflicts?

    (a) Free Association

    (b) Dream interpretation

    (c) Empathy

    (d) Both (a) and (b)

Ans. (d)

Q.2. Transference and ____________ are the means of treating the patient.

    (a) Interpretation   (b) Resistance

    (c) Confrontation   (d) None

Ans. (a)

Q.3. ____________ is the case in which the client idolises, or falls in love with the therapist, and seeks the therapist's approval.

    (a) Transference neurosis

    (b) Positive transference

    (c) Negative transference

    (d) None of the above

Ans. (b)

Q.4. Which of the following are inventions for for eliciting the intrapsychic conflicts.?

    (a) Dream interpretation   (b) Transference

    (c) Psychodynamic   (d) Existential

Ans. (a)

Q.5. Who among the following invented Rational Emotive Therapy?

    (a) Aaron Beck   (b) Albert Ellis

    (c) Freiderick   (d) Simon hard

Ans. (b)

Q.6. Client-centred therapy was given by ____________.

    (a) Freiderick   (b) Victor Frankl

    (c) Carl Rogers   (d) None of the above

Ans. (c)

Very Short Answer Type   [1 Mark]

Q.1. Define Psychotherapy.

Ans. Psychotherapy is a voluntary relationship between the one seeking treatment or the client and the one who treats or the therapist. Psychotherapies aim at changing the maladaptive behaviours, decreasing the sense of personal distress, and helping the client to adapt better to her/his environment.

Q.2. What is therapeutic alliance?

Ans. The special relationship between the client and the therapist is known as the therapeutic relationship or alliance. It is neither a passing acquaintance, nor a permanent and lasting relationship. There are two major components of a therapeutic alliance.

Q.3. What is the duration of psychotherapies treatment?

Ans. The duration of classical psychoanalysis may continue for several years. However, several recent versions of psychodynamic therapies are completed in 10–15 sessions. Behaviour and cognitive behaviour therapies as well as existential therapies are shorter and are completed in a few months.

Short Answer Type - I   [2 Marks]

Q.1. Difference between empathy and Sympathy.

Ans. Empathy is different from sympathy and intellectual understanding of another person's situation.

In sympathy, one has compassion and pity towards the suffering of another but is not able to feel like the other person. Intellectual understanding is cold in the sense that the person is unable to feel like the other person and does not feel sympathy either.

Q.2. Mention any two characteristics of psychotherapeutic approaches ?

Ans. (i) there is systematic application of principles underlying the different theories of therapy,

(ii) persons who have received practical training under expert supervision can practice psychotherapy, and not everybody.

Q.3. What is the chief method of psychodynamic therapy treatment?

Ans. Psychodynamic therapy uses the methods of free association and reporting of dreams to elicit the thoughts and feelings of the client. This material is interpreted to the client to help her/him to confront and resolve the conflicts and thus overcome problems. Behaviour therapy identifies the faulty conditioning patterns and sets up alternate behavioural contingencies to improve behaviour. The cognitive methods employed in this type of therapy challenge the faulty thinking patterns of the client to help her/him overcome psychological distress.

Short Answer Type - II   [3 Marks]

Q.1. Discuss the Steps in the Formulation of a Client's Problem?

Ans. Clinical formulation refers to formulating the problem of the client in the therapeutic model being used for the treatment. The clinical formulation has the following advantages:

1. Understanding of the problem : The therapist is able to understand the full implications of the distress being experienced by the client.

2. Identification of the areas to be targetted for treatment in psychotherapy : The theoretical formulation clearly identifies the problem areas to be targetted for therapy. Thus, if a client seeks help for inability to hold a job and reports inability to face superiors, the clinical formulation in behaviour therapy would state it as lack of assertiveness skills and anxiety. The target areas have thus been identified as inability to assert oneself and heightened anxiety.

3. Choice of techniques for treatment : The choice of techniques for treatment depends on the therapeutic system in which the therapist has been trained. However, even within this broad domain, the choice of techniques, timing of the techniques, and expectations of outcome of the therapy depend upon the clinical formulation.

Long Answer Type [5 Marks]

Q.1. Describe the nature and scope of psychotherapy. Highlight the importance of therapeutic relationship in psychotherapy.

(CBSE 2013, 2014)

Ans. Psychotherapy is a voluntary relationship between two people, one who seeks help and the other who is ready to provide the help, i.e., the therapist. It is given under therapeutic conditions.

Various psychotherapeutic approaches have the following characteristics:

1. All psychotherapies are systematic application of some theory or principle of different therapies.

2. Only trained professionals can practise psychotherapy.

3. Therapeutic situation is a two-way process in which therapist as well as client actively interact.

4. Psychotherapy functions under formation of therapeutic relationship which is confidential, interpersonal and dynamic in nature.

   Psychotherapy has very broad scope to deal with disorders which are as follows:

   • Reinforcing client's resolve for betterment.

   • Lessening emotional pressure.

   • Unfolding the potential for positive growth.

   • Modifying habits.

   • Changing thinking patterns.

   • Increasing self-awareness.

   • Improved interpersonal relations and communication.

   • Facilitating decision-making.

   • Becoming aware of ones preferences in life.

   • Development of adaptive behaviour.

Therapeutic Relationship:

The special professional relationship between the client and the therapist is known as therapeutic relationship or alliance.

There are two major components of this relationship:

1. **The Contractual Nature of the Relationship** in which two willing individuals, the client and the therapist, enter into a partnership which aims at helping the client overcome his problems.

2. **Limited Duration of the Therapy:** This alliance lasts until the client becomes able to deal with his problems and take control of his life.

Through therapeutic relationship the therapist wins the trust of the client. The quality of this relationship/alliance determines early healing in psychotherapy.

Q.2. What are the different types of psychotherapy? On what basis are they classified?

Ans. Following are the main psychotherapies:

   • Psychodynamic Therapy

   • Behaviour Therapy

   • Humanistic Therapy or Existential Therapy

   Parameters of classification are as follows :

1. What is the cause of the problem?

   (a) Psychodynamic therapy-Intrapsychic conflicts (id, ego and super ego) causes problems.

   (b) Behaviour therapy-Faulty learning of behaviours and unrealistic cognition , (thinking process) cause problems.

   (c) Existential therapy-Ansviev about the meaning of one's life and existence is not available.

2. How did the cause come into existence?

   (a) Psychodynamic therapy-Intrapsychic conflicts are caused due to unfulfilled desires of childhood or unresolved fears which cause fixation and repression during psycho-sexual stages of life.

   (b) Behaviour therapy-Faulty conditioning patterns, faulty learning through improper rewards, faulty thinking and beliefs.

   (c) Existential therapy-Current feelings of loneliness, aimless life or meaningless existence.

3. What is the chief method of treatment?

   (a) Psychodynamic therapy-Free association and reporting of dream to make the person confront and resolve the conflict.

   (b) Behaviour therapy-To identify faulty conditioning patterns and faulty learning and to challenge the faulty thinking patterns.

   (c) Existential therapy-Providing positive, non-judgmental and accepting therapeutic environment. Therapist acts as a facilitator helping client solve his own problems and arrive at solution through personal growth.

4. What is the nature of the therapeutic relationship?

   (a) Psychodynamic therapy-Therapist under-stands the client and is more capable in interpreting his thoughts and feelings.

   (b) Behaviour therapy-Therapist is able to identify faulty behaviour and thought patterns and is capable of finding out correct behaviour and realistic thought patterns.

   (c) Existential therapy-Therapist provides warm and emphatic relationship helping the client feel secured to explore the causes of his problems himself and herself.

5. What is the chief benefit to the client?

   (a) Psychodynamic therapy-Emotional insight to resolve problems.

   (b) Behaviour therapy-Adaptive and healthy behaviour and thought pattern to reduce stress.

   (c) Existential therapy-Personal growth by increasing understanding of one's aspirations, emotions and motives.

6. What is the duration of treatment?

   (a) Psychodynamic therapy-Classical psychoan-alysis lasts for several years. New version? 10-15 sessions.

   (b) Behaviour therapy-Short and completed within few months.

   (c) Existential therapy-Short and completed within few month

Q.3. A therapist asks the client to reveal all his/her thoughts including early childhood experiences. Describe the technique and type of therapy being used.

Ans. Psychoanalysis is a method of treatment of neurotic patients which emphasized the thoughts and experiences of childhood. It was developed by Dr. Sigmund Freud.

The whole modality of treatment occurs in three phases:

1. **Initial Phase:** The client becomes making client familial with the routines.

   • Establishment of a therapeutic relationship with the analyst,

   • Relief with the process of recollecting the superficial materials from the unconscious about the past and present troublesome events.

2. **Middle Phase: Transference** and **interpretation** are the means of treating the patient.

   • **Transference:** The client starts identifying positively or negatively to the therapist with other significant people often with father and mother, in his childhood.

   • Parent-child relationships are often replayed in this way.

   • The therapist may be seen as the punitive father or as negligent mother or vice-versa.

   • The therapist maintains a non-judgmental yet permissive attitude towards the client and overcomes the resistance showed by the client.

   • This whole process is known as **transference** and when the therapist becomes a substitute for the client in the present is known as **transference neurosis.**

Stage of Transference Neurosis:

In the process of transference the client acts out his/her frustrations, anger, fear and depression that he/she carried toward that person in the past, but could not express at that time.

   • The therapist becomes a substitute for that person in the present.

This substitution which is known as transference neurosis is helpful in making the therapist aware of the nature of intrapsychic conflicts suffered by the client.

The transference neurosis may develop in two forms:

(i) **Positive Transference:** Here the client may fall in love with the therapist and seeks the therapist's approval.

(ii) **Negative Transference:** When the client develops feeling of hostility, anger and resentment towards the therapist.

- **Stage of Resistance:** During the process of transference an individual may develop resistance. Since process of transference exposes the unconscious wishes and conflicts, client's distress level increases and so the client resists transference.

(i) **Conscious Resistance:** It is present when the client intentionally hides some information.

(ii) **Unconscious Resistance:** It is present when the client becomes silent during the therapy session or starts coming late for the sessions, flight into sickness or show unwillingness-to talk about certain things, sudden blocks forgetting and so on.

- According to Freud, resistance is patient's unconscious struggle to prevent painful material from being brought to the surface and faced directly.

- Interpretation: Interpretation is the fundamental mechanism to bring change in the client. **Interpretation is done through two analytical techniques:**

(i) **Confrontation:** The therapist points out to the client an aspect of his psyche that must be faced by the client. It is a subtle process and considered to be the pinnacle of psychoanalysis. .

(ii) **Clarification:** It is the process by which the therapist brings a vague or confusing event into clarity.

Both the process are done by sharpening and pruning of the material which is brought from unconscious to conscious level.

- The therapist highlights certain important aspects and deletes the unimportant ones.

Working Through: The repeated process of using confrontation, clarification and interpretation is known as working through.

- This process helps the patient to understand himself and the source of the problem.

- It integrates the uncovered material into his ego.

- **Insight:** The end product of working through is insight.

It is a gradual process wherein the unconscious memories are again and again integrated into conscious awareness.

As this process continues, the client starts to understand himself better at an intellectual and emotional level and gains insight into his/her conflicts and problems. The insight is of two types:

(i) **Intellectual Insight:** It is intellectual understanding of the event.

(ii) **Emotional Insight:** The emotional understanding, acceptance of one's irritations due to unpleasant events of the past and the willingness to change emotionally is known as emotional insight.

3. **Third Phase:**

- **Termination:** Insight is the end part of therapy. Now the client is supposed to gain new understanding of himself. Conflicts of the past, excessive usage of defence mechanism and physical symptoms are no longer present and he/she becomes a healthy person.

TOPIC 2

Summary

Behavior Therapy

Behaviour therapies postulate that psychological distress arises because of faulty behaviour patterns or thought patterns. It is, therefore, focused on the behaviour and thoughts of the client in the present. The past is relevant only to the extent of understanding the origins of the faulty behaviour and thought patterns.

The foundation of behaviour therapy is on formulating dysfunctional or faulty behaviours, the factors which reinforce and maintain these behaviours, and devising methods by which they can be changed.

Method of Treatment

Malfunctioning behaviours are those behaviours which cause distress to the client. Antecedent factors are those causes which predispose the person to indulge in that behaviour. Maintaining factors are those factors which lead to the persistence of the faulty behaviour.

Various techniques of behavioral therapy are discussed below:

1. Aversive Conditioning – Here an association is made between an undesirable response and an unfavorable consequence and this Technique is used in rehabilitation centers

2. Positive Reinforcement- When the adaptive Behaviour occurs rarely, positive reinforcement is used to cover up the deficit

3. Negative Reinforcement- It is provided in order to escape the painful stimulus in the environment.

4. Modeling – In order to bring the desired change in the behavior, the client will try to imitate or shadow the movements of the person whom they consider as their role model

5. Other techniques of behavioural therapy are token economy, differential reinforcement, principle of reciprocal inhibition, and systematic desensitisation

Albert Ellis formulated rational-emotive therapy. The first step in this therapy is ABC (Antecedent-Behaviour-Consequence) analysis where Antecedent events are the causal factors of Psychological distress, Irrational beliefs are found out by interviewing the client and these beliefs distort the reality.

Cognitive Therapy

Cognitive therapies locate the cause of psychological distress in irrational thoughts and beliefs. Albert Ellis formulated the Rational Emotive Therapy (RET). The central thesis of this therapy is that irrational beliefs mediate between the antecedent events and their consequences. This distorted perception of the antecedent event due to the irrational belief leads to the consequence, i.e. negative emotions and behaviours. Irrational beliefs are assessed through questionnaires and interviews.

Another cognitive therapy is that of Aaron Beck. His theory of psychological distress characterised by anxiety or depression, states that childhood experiences provided by the family and society develop core schemas or systems, which include beliefs and action patterns in the individual.

Cognitive Behaviour Therapy

The most popular therapy presently is the Cognitive Behaviour Therapy (CBT). Research into the outcome and effectiveness of psychotherapy has conclusively established CBT to be a short and efficacious treatment for a wide range of psychological disorders such as anxiety, depression, panic attacks, and borderline personality, etc. CBT adopts a biopsychosocial approach to the delineation of psychopathology. It combines cognitive therapy with behavioural techniques.

Humanistic-Existential Therapy

The main cause of Psychological distress is feelings of loneliness, alienation, and inability to find meaning and responsibility in life. Human beings are motivated by the desire for personal growthand self-actualisation, and an innate need to grow emotionally. When these needs are curbed by society and family, human beings experience psychological distress.

Self-actualisation is defined as an innate or inborn force that moves the person to become more complex, balanced, and integrated, i.e. achieving the complexity and balance without being fragmented.

Healing occurs when the client is able to perceive the obstacles to selfactualisation in her/his life and is able to remove them. Self-actualisation requires free emotional expression. The family and society curb emotional expression, as it is feared that a free expression of emotions can harm society by unleashing destructive forces. The chief aim of the therapy is to expand the client's awareness. Healing takes place by a process of understanding the unique personal experience of the client by herself/himself. The client initiates the process of selfgrowth through which healing takes place.

Existential Therapy

Victor Frankl, a psychiatrist and neurologist propounded the Logotherapy. Logos is the Greek word for soul and Logotherapy means treatment for the soul. Frankl calls this process of finding meaning even in life-threatening circumstances as the process of meaning making. The basis of meaning making is a person's quest for finding the spiritual truth of one's existence.

Frankl emphasised the role of spiritual anxieties in leading to meaninglessness and hence it may be called an existential anxiety, i.e. neurotic anxiety of spiritual origin. The goal of logotherapy is to help the patients to find meaning and responsibility in their life irrespective of their life circumstances.

Client-Centered Therapy

This Therapy was given by Carl Rogers. The main focus is to provide a warm relationship so that the client can reconnect and understand his/her disintegrated feelings. In client-centered therapy, the Therapist provides unconditional positive regard which means total acceptance of what the client actually is, empathy which means understanding the client's problems from their perspective, and that helps clients feel secure.

Gestalt Therapy

The German word gestalt means 'whole'. This therapy was given by Freiderick (Fritz) Perls together with his wife Laura Perls. The goal of gestalt therapy is to increase an individual's self-awareness and selfacceptance. The client is taught to recognise the bodily processes and the emotions that are being blocked out from awareness.

Biomedical Therapy

In some cases, medicines are used to treat mental Disorders and these medicines can be given by professional doctors called Psychiatrists. They are medical doctors who have specialised in the understanding, diagnosis and treatment of mental disorders. The nature of medicines used depends on the nature of the disorders. Severe mental disorders such as schizophrenia or bipolar disorder require anti-psychotic drugs.

Electro-convulsive Therapy (ECT) is another form of biomedical therapy. Mild electric shock is given via electrodes to the brain of the patient to induce convulsions. The shock is given by the psychiatrist only when it is necessary for the improvement of the patient. ECT is not a routine treatment and is given only when drugs are not effective in controlling the symptoms of the patient.

Factors Contributing to Healing in Psychotherapy

The technique adopted by the therapist and its execution is a major factor that contributes to healing in Psychotherapy. Factors contributing to healing in Psychotherapy are given as follows:

1. The therapeutic alliance between the Therapist and client is also an important factor as the healing of the client depends on warmth and empathy provided by the Therapist.

2. The process of complete emotional expression which is called catharsis is important for healing.

3. Some non-specific factors like patient variables like motivation for change, the expectation of improvement due to therapy, and therapist variables like warmth, positive nature, etc

Ethics in Psychotherapy

Just like every job role, psychotherapy also has some ethics to be followed by every individual. Ethical standards that need to be adhered to by psychologists are mentioned below:

1. Informed Consent needs to be taken

2. Respect for human rights and dignity

3. Confidentiality of the client's problem must be maintained

4. Professional competence and skills are musts

5. Alleviating the personal distress of the client must be the goal of therapy

6. The integrity of the practitioner-client relationship must be there

Multiple Choice Questions [1 Mark]

Q.1. Which of the following therapy is used for the treatment of soul?

(a) Existential anxiety

(b) Gestalt Therapy

(c) Logotherapy

(d) Biomedical Therapy

Ans. (c)

Q.2. The central thesis of this therapy is that irrational beliefs mediate between the antecedent events and their consequences. Name the therapy.

(a) Cognitive Behaviour Therapy (CBT)

(b) Rational Emotive Therapy (RET)

(c) Humanistic-existential Therapy(HET)

(d) None of the above

Ans. (b)

Q.3. The repeated process of using confrontation, clarification, and interpretation is known as________

(a) Working through. (b) Insight

(c) Resistance (d) Confrontation

Ans. (a)

Q.4. __________________ are those causes which predispose the person to indulge in that behaviour.

(a) Malfunctioning behaviours

(b) Antecedent factors

(c) Maintaining factors

(d) Consequent operations

Ans. (b)

Q.5. Who among the following given theory Psychological distress ?

(a) Freiderick

(b) Victor Frankl

(c) Carl Rogers

(d) Aaron Beck

Ans. (d)

Q.6. The goal of______________ is to increase an individual's self-awareness and selfacceptanc.

(a) Gestalt therapy

(b) Biomedical Therapy

(c) Client-centred Therapy

(d) Logotherapy

Ans. (a)

Very Short Answer Type [1 Mark]

Q.1. What is Aversive conditioning?

Ans. Aversive conditioning refers to repeated association of undesired response with an aversive consequence. For example, an alcoholic is given a mild electric shock and asked to smell the alcohol. With repeated pairings the smell of alcohol is aversive as the pain of the shock is associated with it and the person will give up alcohol.

Q.2. What is Systematic desensitization?

Ans. Systematic desensitisation is a technique introduced by Wolpe for treating phobias or irrational ears. The client is interviewed to elicit fearprovoking situations and together with the client, the therapist prepares a hierarchy of anxiety-provoking stimuli with the least anxiety-provoking stimuli at the bottom of the hierarchy.

Q.3. What is the central thesis of Rational Emotive Therapy?

Ans. Albert Ellis formulated the Rational Emotive Therapy (RET). The central thesis of this therapy is that irrational beliefs mediate between the antecedent events and their consequences.

Short Answer Type - I [2 Marks]

Q.1. Give an example of Negative reinforcement and positive reinforcement?

Ans. Responses that lead organisms to get rid of painful stimuli or avoid and escape from them provide negative reinforcement. For example, one learns to put on woollen clothes, burn firewood or use electric heaters to avoid the unpleasant cold weather.

If an adaptive behaviour occurs rarely, positive reinforcement is given to increase the deficit. For example, if a child does not do homework regularly, positive reinforcement may be used by the child's mother by preparing the child's favourite dish whenever s/he does homework at the appointed time.

Q.2. What is principle of reciprocal inhibition? Give an example.

Ans. The principle of reciprocal inhibition operates here. This principle states that the presence of two mutually opposing forces at the same time, inhibits the weaker force. Thus, the relaxation response is first built up and mildly anxiety-provoking scene is imagined, and the anxiety is overcome by the relaxation.

The client is able to tolerate progressively greater levels of anxiety because of her/his relaxed state. Modelling is the procedure wherein the client learns to behave in a certain way by observing the behaviour of a role model or the therapist who initially acts as the role model.

Q.3. What is the difference between Cognitive Behaviour Therapy and Humanistic-existential Therapy?

Ans. The most popular therapy presently is the Cognitive Behaviour Therapy (CBT).

CBT adopts a biopsychosocial approach to the delineation of psychopathology. It combines cognitive therapy with behavioural techniques.

The rationale is that the client's distress has its origins in the biological, psychological, and social realms.

Humanistic-existential Therapy

The humanistic-existential therapies postulate that psychological distress arises from feelings of loneliness, alienation, and an inability to find meaning and genuine fulfilment in life. Human beings are motivated by the desire for personal growth and self-actualisation, and an innate need to grow emotionally. When these needs are curbed by society and family, human beings experience psychological distress.

Q.4. Discuss the Client-centred Therapy.

Ans. Client-centred therapy was given by Carl Rogers. Rogers combined scientific rigour with the individualised practice of clientcentred psychotherapy. Rogers brought into psychotherapy the concept of self, with freedom and choice as the core of one's being. The therapist shows empathy, i.e. understanding the client's experience as if it were her/his own, is warm and has unconditional positive regard, i.e. total acceptance of the client as s/he is.

Empathy sets up an emotional resonance between the therapist and the client. Unconditional positive regard indicates that the positive warmth of the therapist is not dependent on what the client reveals or does in the therapy sessions.

Short Answer Type - II   [3 Marks]

Q.1. What is Biomedical therapy? How this is different from gestalt therapy?

Ans. Medicines may be prescribed to treat psychological disorders. Prescription of medicines for treatment of mental disorders is done by qualified medical professionals known as psychiatrists. They are medical doctors who have specialised in the understanding, diagnosis and treatment of mental disorders.

The medicines prescribed to treat mental disorders can cause side-effects which need to be understood and monitored.

Electro-convulsive Therapy (ECT) is another form of biomedical therapy. Mild electric shock is given via electrodes to the brain of the patient to induce convulsions. The shock is given by the psychiatrist only when it is necessary for the improvement of the patient.

Gestalt Therapy

The German word gestalt means 'whole'. This therapy was given by Freiderick (Fritz) Perls together with his wife Laura Perls. The goal of gestalt therapy is to increase an individual's self-awareness and selfacceptance.

The client is taught to recognise the bodily processes and the emotions that are being blocked out from awareness. The therapist does this by encouraging the client to act out fantasies about feelings and conflicts. This therapy can also be used in group settings.

Q.2. Mention any three Ethics in Psychotherapy?

Ans. Some of the ethical standards that need to be practiced by professional psychotherapists are:

   i. Alleviating personal distress and suffering should be the goal of all attempts of the therapist.

   ii. Integrity of the practitioner-client relationship is important.

   iii. Respect for human rights and dignity. Professional competence and skills are essential.

Long Answer Type   [5 Marks]

Q.1. Discuss the various techniques used in behaviour therapy. (CBSE 2012)

Ans. The techniques used in behaviour therapy are not based on any unified theory. These are developed on the basis of various principles particularly on classical conditioning, operant conditioning and modelling. The main objective of the techniques are to modify maladaptive behaviour. Negative reinforcement and aversive conditioning are the two major techniques of behaviour modification.

1. Reinforcement Techniques:

(a) Negative Reinforcement: It refers to following an undesired response with an outcome that is painful or not liked. For example, a mother may cover her son's thumb with a bitter NEEM paste so that he should not develop habit of thumb sucking. Due to the bitterness, the child tries to avoid or withdraw the bitterness of thumb and will leave the habit of thumb-sucking.

Aversive Conditioning:

- It is establishing relationship between undesirable behaviour and aversive consequences.

- Aversive therapy is a therapeutic technique which uses an unpleasant stimulus to change a deviant behaviour.

- It works by pairing together the stimulus that normally invites the deviant behaviour (such as an alcoholic drink or sexual image) with an unpleasant (aversive) stimulus such as an electric shock or a nausea-inducing drug, with repeated presentations.

- The two stimuli become associated and the person develops an aversion toward the stimulus that formerly gave rise to the deviant behaviour.

(b) Positive Reinforcement: If an adaptive behaviour occurs, positive reinforcement may be used by the therapist. For example, the child's mother may prepare child's favourite dish on the day when most of the time child was being observed not keeping his thumb in the mouth.

Token Economy: A behaviour therapy is based on positive reinforcement.

- A package or deal is being established between the therapist and the client.

- Persons with behavioural problems can be given a token as a reward every time a wanted behaviour occurs.

- The tokens are collected and exchanged with for a predetermined reward such as outing for the patient or a treat for the child.

- The technique is widely used in hospitals, schools and reformatory.

(c) Differential Reinforcement: In differential reinforcement, both positive and negative reinforcements are used together. By using this method, unwanted behaviour can be reduced and wanted behaviour can be increased simultaneously.

(d) Method of ignoring Unwanted Behaviour: In this method, the therapist positively reinforces the wanted behaviour and ignores the unwanted behaviour. For example, the parents are instructed to praise the child or give chocolate to him or to take him to cinema if the child does not suck the thumb,:

but ignore the unwanted behaviour that is sucking the thumb. This method is less painful and equally effective for modifying the unwanted behaviour.

2. **Systematic Desensitisation:** It is a technique introduced by **Wolpe,** for treating phobias or irrational fears. This technique is based on the principle of **reciprocal inhibition.** This principle states that the presence of two mutually opposing forces forces at the same time, inhibits the weaker force, e.g., distress, at the same time, relaxation, can not occur.

The technique follows four steps:

(i) Initial interview.

(ii) Training in relaxation exercises.

(iii) Preparation of hierarchy of anxiety-provoking situation. This is a subjective process and changes from problem to problem.

(iv) **Desensitization:** When the client becomes relaxed, he/she is exposed to least anxiety-provoking situation. Over sessions, the client is able to unique more severe fear-provoking situations while maintaining with relaxation. The client gets systematically desensitized to the fear.

3. **Modelling:** It is the procedure wherein the client learns to behave in a certain way by observing the behaviour of a role model or the therapist.

- It is role playing.

- Vicarious learning (learning by observing others) is used and through a process of rewarding small changes in the behaviour, the client gradually learns to acquire the behaviour of the model.

Q.2. Explain with the help of an example how cognitive distortions take place.   **(CBSE 2011)**

Ans. Aaron Beck devised cognitive therapy.

- It is also known as **cognitive restructuring therapy.**

- **Basic Assumption:** Negative thinking, irrational beliefs and faulty generalization caused disorder.

- This therapy believes that repeated cognitive distortions play significant role in causing disorder. Cognitive distortion means way of thinking which are general in nature but which distorts the reality in a negative manner, e.g., persistent negative and irrational thoughts such as: "Nobody loves me", "I am ugly", " I am stupid" etc.

Step I – Analysis of Core Schemata: Childhood experiences provided by the family and society develop core schemata or systems, which include beliefs and action patterns of the individual.

- A client, who was neglected by the parents as a child, develops the core schema of "I am not wanted." This may be validated by the teachers in the school.

- Such negative automatic thoughts cause cognitive distortions.

- Cognitive distortions are ways of thinking which are general in nature but which distort the reality in a negative manner. Their patterns are called **Dysfunctional cognitive structure.**

- Repeated occurrence of these distorted thoughts leads to the development of feelings of anxiety and depression.

Treatment Method:

- The therapist uses questioning, which is gentle, non-threatening and non- judgmental, non probing but thought proviking questions.

- The questions make the client to think deeper into her/his assumptions about his life and problems.

- These questions make the client to think in a direction opposite to his negative thoughts and gains insight of his dysfunctional schemas and able to restructure his thoughts in positive direction.

- **Beck's** cognitive approach does not attempt to disprove the ideas held by depressed persons, rather the therapist and client work together to identify the individual's assumptions, beliefs and expectations and to formulate ways of testing them.

Aim of the Therapy:

- Cognitive restructuring by helping people to recognize and reject the false assumptions that are central to their difficulties.

Q.3. Which therapy encourages the client to seek personal growth and actualise their potential? Write about the therapies which are based on this principle. **(2009, 2010)**

Ans. • The humanistic-existential therapies encourage personal growth and actualize the potential.

Fundamental Assumption:

- The client has the freedom and responsibility to control his/her own behaviour.

- Psychological distress arises from feeling of loneliness, alienation and an inability to find meaning and genuine fulfilment in life.

- All individuals have desire for personal growth and self-actualization and an innate need to grow emotionally.

Causes of Distress:

1. Obstacles created by the society and family to achieve personal growth.

2. Obstacles in attainment of self-actualization, because it requires free emotional expression.

Treatment Modalities:

- The therapist is merely facilitator and guide. It is the client who is responsible for the success of the therapy.

- The client initiates the process of self-growth through which healing takes place.

Therapies based on Humanistic-existential Approach:

Logo therapy is a form of existential therapy.

Victor Frankl, a psychiatrist and neurologist propounded logo therapy.

Basic Assumption: 'Logo' is the Greek word for 'soul' and "logo" therapy 'means treatment of the soul'.

- Person's desire of finding the spiritual truth of ones existence is the source of motivation.

- binding meaning of self even in life-threatening circumstances is process of meaning making.

- There is a spiritual unconscious, which is the store house of love, aesthetic awareness and values of life.

Aim of Therapy: To help the client to find meaning and responsibility in their life irrespective of their life circumstances.

Treatment Modality:

- The therapist emphasizes the unique nature of the patients life and encourages them to find meaning in their life.

- The therapist is open and shares his/her feelings, values and his/her own existence with the client.

- The emphasis is on here and now.

- In the therapy, transference is actively discouraged.

- The goal is to facilitate the client to find meaning of his/her being.

Gestalt Therapy:

- It is humanistic therapy developed by Fritz Pearl and his wife Laima Pearl.

- It helps the client to develop self-awareness and self-acceptance.

  The client is taught to bring his disowned thoughts, conflicts and anxieties to his awareness.

- The therapist does this by encouraging the client to act out or speak out his/her fantasies about feelings and conflicts.

- This therapy can also be used in group setting.

Client-Centered Therapy:

This kind of therapy is developed by Carl Rogers.

- It is based on non-directive approach.

- To understand individual, we must look at the way they experience events rather than at the events themselves.

- The therapy provides a warm relationship in which the client can reconnect with his/her disintegrated feeling.

Q.4. What are the factors that contribute to healing in psychotherapy? Enumerate some of the alternative therapies.   **(CBSE 2012)**

Ans. There are several factors which contribute to the healing process. Some of these factors are as follows:

- The techniques adopted by the therapist and the implementation of the same with the client.

- The quality of therapeutic alliance—the regular availability of the therapist, and the warmth and empathy provided by the therapist has its importance.

- The quality of emotional unburdening (catharsis) has significant impact on healing.

- Non-specific factors dre associated with psychotherapy. These are patient variable and therapist variable.

- Patient variable refers to attributed to the client, e.g., clients motivation for change and expectation of improvement due to the treatment etc. Therapist variable refers to his/her good mental health, absence of his/her unresolved emotional conflicts and expertise.

   Alternative therapies are so called, because they are alternative treatment possibilities to the conventional drug treatment or psychotherapy. There are many alternative therapies such as yoga, meditation, herbal remedies and so on.

1. Yoga is an ancient Indian technique detailed in the Ashtanga Yoga of Patanjali's Yoga Sutra. Yoga, as it is commonly called today either refers to only the asanas or body positive component or to breathing practices or pranayama or to a combination of the two.

2. Meditation refers to the practice of focusing attention on breath or an object or thought or a mantra.

3. Vipasana Meditation, also known as mindfulness-based meditation, has ,no fixed object or thought to hold the attention. The person possibly observes the various bodily sensation and thoughts that are passing through his awareness.

4. The rapid breathing techniques to induce hyperventilation as in Sudarshana Kriya Yoga (SKY) is found to be a beneficial, low-risk, low-cost, adjunct to the treatment of stress, anxiety, post-traumatic stress disorder (PTSD) depression, stress-related medical illness, substance abuse, and rehabilitations of criminal offenders.

5. Kundalini Yoga taught in USA has found to be effective in treating mental disorders, obsessive-compulsive disorder. It combines pranayama or breathing with chanting of mantras.

Q.5. What are the techniques used in the rehabilitation of the mentally ill?

Ans. Rehabilitation of the mentally ill is necessary to improve their quality of life once their active symptoms are reduced.

- In the case of milder disorders, such as generalized anxiety disorder, reduction of symptoms improves their quality of life and such patients need not to help rehabilitation.

- However in severe mental disorders, such as schizophrenic disorders, reduction of symptoms does not mean that patient is cured. Such patients develop negative symptoms like apathy or lack of motivation and their cognitive social and occupational skills get impaired. So they need rehabilitation.

- Rehabilitation provides:

1. **Social Skill Training:** It helps the patients to develop interpersonal skills through role play, imitation and instruction.

2. **Cognitive Retraining:** It helps the patients to improve the basic cognitive functions of attention, memory and executive functions.

3. **Occupational Therapy:** The patients are taught skills such as candle¬making, paper bag making and weaving to develop work discipline.

4. **Vocational Training:** When the patient becomes self-sufficient, vocational training is given wherein the patient is helped to gain skills necessary to undertake productive employment.

Q.6. How would a social learning theorist account for a phobic fear of lizards/cockroaches? How yvould a psychoanalyst account for the same phobia?

(CBSE 2013)

Ans. Social learning theories work on the principle that our experience—be it positive or negative—such as phobia of lizards/cockroaches are the result of learning process which start early in life. Small children can play with snakes, they sire not aware of the danger involved. For them it is just another play object, as they grow up the fear of these things are instilled by their parents and society which is reinforced and accounts for reactions like phobia.

A psychoanalytical account for the same could involve attribution to some unconscious or/and repressed experiences. For example, suppose in your childhood you watched a group of roudy boys brutally torturing a cockroach/snake, which eventually died, although you going about the incidence after some days, but it might remain in back of your mind forever, which might explain your phobia to cockroaches which might remind you of the incidence and disturbs you emotionally.

Q.7. Should Electro-convulsive Therapy (ECT) be used in the treatment of mental disorders?

Ans. Electro-convulsive Therapy (ECT):

- It is used to alleviate sudden and severe depression.

- In this method one electrode is placed on each side of the person's temples and a mild current is turned on for a very short period.

- In the beginning, it was done by injecting metrazol and other drugs in mental patients. These shocks are continued until the patient has a seizure, a muscle contraction of the entire body, lasting at least twenty to twenty-five seconds. ECT seems to work at least for some disorders.

- Unfortunately, there are hazardous risk connected with it. There is amnesia for the whole treatment and after several treatments. There is memory impairment, which may last for several weeks. However, no permanent loss of memory occurs. ECT use has declined since 1950.

- ECT is still used in various hospitals in India because it is economical and effective. In my opinion as a last resort this therapy should continue to be used in India.

Drug Therapy:

- It has been used mainly with four types of disorders—schizophrenia, mania, depression and anxiety.

- These drugs are referred as 'psychotropic drugs' because their main effect is on psychological behaviour.

- They are also called as 'antipsychotic drugs'.

- They are used for the treatment of schizophrenia. 'Antimanic drugs' are used to treat patients who are highly agitated, excited and at times unmanageable. 'Antidepressant drugs' are used for patients having depression and suicidal risk. 'Antianxiety drugs' are known to be minor tranquillisers.

Q.8. What kind of problems is cognitive behaviour therapy best suited for?

Ans. CBT is a short and effective treatment for a wide range of psychological disorders such as anxiety, depression, panic attacks and borderline personality, etc.

- It combines cognitive therapy and behavioural technique.

- According to CBT, the cause of client's distress is biological, psychological and social relations in combination.

- CBT focuses on the biological aspects through relaxation procedures and the psychological ones through behaviour therapy. Social aspects are dealt with environmental manipulations.

- This multi-axial approach makes CBT a comprehensive technique, which is easy to use, applicable to a varicty of disorders and has full potential to deal effectively with psychological disorders.

Chapter Practice

Multiple Choice Questions   [1 Mark]

Q.1. Who among the following oldest form of psychotherapy.?

   (a) Aaron Beck   (b) Albert Ellis

   (c) Freiderick   (d) Sigmund Freud

Q.2. Which of the following therapy is used for the treatment the concept of self?

   (a) Client-centred therapy   (b) Gestalt Therapy

   (c) Logotherapy   (d) Biomedical Therapy

Q.3. ________________________ principle states that the presence of two mutually opposing forces at the same time, inhibits the weaker force

   (a) Transference   (b) Principle of reciprocal inhibition

   (c) Interpretation   (d) Both (a) and (c)

Q.4. ______________and _________ as two important methods for eliciting the intrapsychic conflicts.

   (a) Free Association   (b) Dream association

   (c) Self-acceptance   (d) Both (a) and (b)

Very Short Answer Type   [1 Mark]

Q.5. What is the meaning of logotherapy?

Q.6. What is therapist variables ?

Short Answer Type - I   [2 Marks]

Q.7. State two psychological disorders in which cognitive behaviour therapy is used for treatment.

Q.8. What is occupational therapy ?

Short Answer Type - II   [3 Marks]

Q.9. State three characteristics of psychotherapeutic approaches.

Q.10. Explain the concept of "unconditional positive regard".

Long Answer Type   [5 Marks]

Q.11. Analyse the Behaviour Technique of Systematic Desensitisation.

Q.12. Analyse the Rehabilitation of the Mentally Ill.

CHAPTER 6

Attitude and Social Cognition

Summary

Social behaviour is a necessary part of human life, and being social means much more than merely being in the company of others.

Because of social influences, people form views, or attitudes about people, and about different issues in life, that exist in the form of behavioural tendencies.

When we meet people, we make inferences about their personal qualities. This is called impression formation.

Two such examples are social facilitation/ inhibition, i.e. the improvement/decline in performance in the presence of others, and helping, or pro-social behaviour, i.e. responding to others who are in need or distress.

When we meet people, we make inferences about their personal qualities. This is called impression formation.

Nature and Components of Attitudes

An attitude is a state of the mind, a set of views, or thoughts, regarding some topic (called the 'attitude object'), which have an evaluative feature (positive, negative or neutral quality).

The thought component is referred to as the cognitive aspect, the emotional component is known as the affective aspect, and the tendency to act is called the behavioural (or conative) aspect.

Attitudes have to be distinguished from two other closely related concepts, namely beliefs and values. Beliefs refer to the cognitive component of attitudes, and form the ground on which attitudes stand, such as belief in God, or belief in democracy as a political ideology. Values are attitudes or beliefs that contain a 'should' or 'ought' aspect, such as moral or ethical values.

Four significant features of attitudes are : Valence (positivity or negativity), Extremeness, Simplicity or Complexity (multiplexity), and Centrality

Valence (positivity or negativity) : The valence of an attitude tells us whether an attitude is positive or negative towards the attitude object.

Extremeness : The extremeness of an attitude indicates how positive or negative an attitude is.

Simplicity or Complexity (multiplexity) : This feature refers to how many attitudes there are within a broader attitude. An attitude system is said to be 'simple' if it contains only one or a few attitudes, and 'complex' if it is made up of many attitudes.

Centrality : This refers to the role of a particular attitude in the attitude system. For example, in the attitude towards world peace, a negative attitude towards high military expenditure may be present as a core or central attitude that influences all other attitudes in the multiple attitude system.

Multiple Choice Questions [1 Mark]

Q.1. When we meet people, we make inferences about their personal qualities is called___________.

(a) Impression formation

(b) Cognition

(c) Schema

(d) Pro – social behavior

Ans. (a)

Q.2. We assign causes to the behavior shown in specific social situations this process is called _______________.

(a) Impression

(b) Cognition

(c) Attribution

(d) Social facilitation

Ans. (c)

Q.3. The _____________ of an attitude indicates how positive or negative an attitude is.

(a) Simplicity

(b) Extremeness

(c) Centrality

(d) Complexity

Ans. (b)

Very Short Answer Type [1 Mark]

Q.1. Define Impression formation.

Ans. When we meet people, we make inferences about their personal qualities. This is called impression formation.

Q.2. What is centrality?

Ans. This refers to the role of a particular attitude in the attitude system. An attitude with greater centrality would influence the other attitudes in the system much more than non-central (or peripheral) attitudes would. For example, in the attitude towards world peace, a negative attitude towards high military expenditure may be present as a core or central attitude that influences all other attitudes in the multiple attitude system.

Short Answer Type - I [2 Marks]

Q.1. Mention two examples of Cognitive processes cannot be directly seen; they have to be inferred on the basis of externally shown behavior ?

Ans. Two such examples are social facilitation/ inhibition, i.e. the improvement/decline in performance in the presence of others, and helping, or pro-social behaviour, i.e. responding to others who are in need or distress.

Q.2. Discuss the difference between beliefs and value?

Ans. Beliefs refer to the cognitive component of attitudes, and form the ground on which attitudes stand, such as belief in God, or belief in democracy as a political ideology.

Values are attitudes or beliefs that contain a 'should' or 'ought' aspect, such as moral or ethical values. One example of a value is the idea that one should work hard, or that one should always be honest, because honesty is the best policy.

Short Answer Type - II [3 Marks]

Q.1. Mention any three significant features of attitude?

Ans. Three significant features of attitudes are : Valence (positivity or negativity), Extremeness, Simplicity:

i. **Valence (positivity or negativity) :** The valence of an attitude tells us whether an attitude is positive or negative towards the attitude object.

ii. **Extremeness :** The extremeness of an attitude indicates how positive or negative an attitude is. Taking the nuclear research example given above, a rating of 1 is as extreme as a rating of 5 : they are only in the opposite directions (valence). Ratings of 2 and 4 are less extreme. A neutral attitude, of course, is lowest on extremeness.

iii. **Simplicity or Complexity (multiplexity):** This feature refers to how many attitudes there are within a broader attitude. Think of an attitude as a family containing several 'member' attitudes. In case of various topics, such as health and world peace, people hold many attitudes instead of single attitude.

TOPIC 2

Summary

Attitude Formation and Change

In general, attitudes are learned through one's own experiences, and through interaction with others.

Process of Attitude Formation

- **Learning attitudes by association :** You might have seen that students often develop a liking for a particular subject because of the teacher.

- **Learning attitudes by being rewarded or punished :** If an individual is praised for showing a particular attitude, chances are high that s/he will develop that attitude further.

- **Learning attitudes through modelling (observing others) :** Often it is not through association, or through reward and punishment, that we learn attitudes.

- **Learning attitudes through group or cultural norms :** Very often, we learn attitudes through the norms of our group or culture. Norms are unwritten rules about behaviour that everyone is supposed to show under specific circumstances.

- **Learning through exposure to information** : Many attitudes are learned in a social context, but not necessarily in the physical presence of others. Today, with the huge amount of information that is being provided through various media, both positive and negative attitudes are being formed.

Factors that Influence Attitude Formation

- **Family and School Environment:** Particularly in the early years of life, parents and other family members play a significant role in shaping attitude formation. Learning of attitudes within the family and school usually takes place by association, through rewards and punishments, and through modelling.

- **Reference Groups :** Reference groups indicate to an individual the norms regarding acceptable behaviour and ways of thinking. Attitudes towards various topics, such as political, religious and social groups, occupations, national and other issues are often developed through reference groups.

Their influence is noticeable especially during the beginning of adolescence, at which time it is important for the individual to feel that s/he belongs to a group.

- **Personal Experiences :** Many attitudes are formed, not in the family environment or through reference groups, but through direct personal experiences which bring about a drastic change in our attitude towards people and our own life. A driver in the army went through a personal experience that transformed his life.

- **Media-related Influences :** Technological advances in recent times have made audio-visual media and the Internet very powerful sources of information that lead to attitude formation and change. The media can exert both good and bad influences on attitudes. On one hand, the media and Internet make people better informed than other modes of communication. The media can exert both good and bad influences on attitudes. On one hand, the media and Internet make people better informed than other modes of communication.

Attitude Change

- During the process of attitude formation, and also after this process, attitudes may be changed and modified through various influences. From a practical point of view, bringing about a change in people's attitudes is of interest to community leaders, politicians, producers of consumer goods, advertisers, and others.

Process of Attitude change

Three major concepts that draw attention to some important processes in attitude change are described below :

(a) The concept of balance, proposed by Fritz Heider is sometimes described in the form of the 'P-O-X' triangle, which represents the relationships between three aspects or components of the attitude. P is the person whose attitude is being studied, O is another person, and X is the topic towards which the attitude is being studied (attitude object). It is also possible that all three are persons.

(b) The concept of cognitive dissonance was proposed by Leon Festinger. It emphasises the cognitive component. Here the basic idea is that the cognitive components of an attitude must be 'consonant' (opposite of 'dissonant'), i.e., they should be logically in line with each other. If an individual finds that two cognitions in an attitude are dissonant, then one of them will be changed in the direction of consonance.

(c) The two-step concept was proposed by S.M. Mohsin, an Indian psychologist. According to him, attitude change takes place in the form of two steps. In the first step, the target of change identifies with the source. The 'target' is the person whose attitude is to be changed. The 'source' is the person through whose influence the change is to take place. Identification means that the target has liking and regard for the source. S/he puts herself/himself in the place of the target, and tries to feel like her/him.

Factors that Influence Attitude Change

Characteristics of the existing attitude : All four properties of attitudes mentioned earlier, namely, valence (positivity or negativity), extremeness, simplicity or complexity (multiplexity), and centrality or significance of the attitude, determine attitude change.

In addition, one must also consider the direction and extent of attitude change. An attitude change may be congruent — it may change in the same direction as the existing attitude (for example, a positive attitude may become more positive, or a negative attitude may become more negative).

On the other hand, an attitude change may be incongruent — it may change in a direction opposite to the existing attitude (for example, a positive attitude becomes less positive, or negative, or a negative attitude becomes less negative, or positive).

Source characteristics : Source credibility and attractiveness are two features that affect attitude change. Attitudes are more likely to change when the message comes from a highly credible source rather than from a low-credible source. For example, adults who are planning to buy a laptop are more convinced by a computer engineer who points out the special features of a particular brand of laptop, than they would be by a schoolchild who might give the same information.

The motives activated by the message also determine attitude change. For example, drinking milk may be said to make a person healthy and good-looking, or more energetic and more successful at one's job.

Target characteristics : Qualities of the target, such as persuasibility, strong prejudices, self-esteem, and intelligence influence the likelihood and extent of attitude change. People, who have a more open and flexible personality, change more easily. Advertisers benefit most from such people. People with strong prejudices are less prone to any attitude change than those who do not hold strong prejudices.

Attitude-Behaviour Relationship

Psychologists have found that there would be consistency between attitudes and behaviour when :

- the attitude is strong, and occupies a central place in the attitude system,

- the person is aware of her/his attitude,

- there is very little or no external pressure for the person to behave in a particular way. For example, when there is no group pressure to follow a particular norm,

- the person's behaviour is not being watched or evaluated by others, and

- the person thinks that the behaviour would have a positive consequence, and therefore, intends to engage in that behaviour.

Prejudice and Discrimination

Prejudices are examples of attitudes towards a particular group. They are usually negative, and in many cases, may be based on stereotypes (the cognitive component) about the specific group.

All members belonging to this group are assumed to possess these characteristics. Often, stereotypes consist of undesirable characteristics about the target group, and they lead to negative attitudes or prejudices towards members of specific groups. The cognitive component of prejudice is frequently accompanied by dislike or hatred, the affective component.

The genocide committed by the Nazis in Germany against Jewish people is an extreme example of how prejudice can lead to hatred, discrimination and mass killing of innocent people. Prejudices can exist without being shown in the form of discrimination. Similarly, discrimination can be shown without prejudice.

Social psychologists have shown that prejudice has one or more of the following sources :

- **Learning :** Like other attitudes, prejudices can also be learned through association, reward and punishment, observing others, group or cultural norms and exposure to information that encourages prejudice.

- **A strong social identity and ingroup bias :** Individuals who have a strong sense of social identity and have a very positive attitude towards their own group boost this attitude by holding negative attitudes towards other groups. These are shown as prejudices.

- **Scapegoating :** This is a phenomenon by which the majority group places the blame on a minority outgroup for its own social, economic or political problems.

- **Kernel of truth concept :** Sometimes people may continue to hold stereotypes because they think that, after all, there must be some truth, or 'kernel of truth' in what everyone says about the other group.

- **Self-fulfilling prophecy :** In some cases, the group that is the target of prejudice is itself responsible for continuing the prejudice. The target group may behave in ways that justify the prejudice, that is, confirm the negative expectations.

Strategies for Handling Prejudice

i. Education and information dissemination, for correcting stereotypes related to specific target groups, and tackling the problem of a strong ingroup bias.

ii. Increasing intergroup contact allows for direct communication, removal of mistrust between the groups, and even discovery of positive qualities in the outgroup.

iii. Highlighting individual identity rather than group identity, thus weakening the importance of group (both ingroup and outgroup) as a basis of evaluating the other person.

Social Cognition

'Cognition' refers to all those mental processes that deal with obtaining and processing of information. Extending this idea to the social world, the term 'social cognition' refers to all those psychological processes that deal with the gathering and processing of information related to social objects.

The processing of information related to social objects (particularly individuals, groups, people, relationships, social issues, and the like) differs from the processing of information related to physical objects.

Schemas and Stereotypes

A schema is defined as a mental structure that provides a framework, set of rules or guidelines for processing information about any object.

Schemas (or 'schemata') are the basic units stored in our memory, and function as shorthand ways of processing information, thus reducing the time and mental effort required in cognition.

Most of the schemas are in the form of categories or classes. Schemas that function in the form of categories are called prototypes, which are the entire set of features or qualities that help us to define an object completely.

In social cognition, category-based schemas that are related to groups of people are called stereotypes.

Multiple Choice Questions   [1 Mark]

Q.1. If we are interested to know why people behave in the ways they do is known as ___________.

    (a) Attribution

    (b) Empathy

    (c) Schema

    (d) Impress formation

Ans. (a)

Q.2. The 'P-O-X' triangle concept is given by__________?

(a) Fritz Heider

(b) S.M. Mohsin

(c) Festinger

(d) Bernard Wiener

Ans. (a)

Q.3. The two-step concept was proposed by__________.

(a) Festinger

(b) Carlsmith

(c) S.M. Mohsin

(d) Richard LaPiere

Ans. (c)

Q.4. __________ refers to all those mental processes that deal with obtaining and processing of information.

(a) Cognition

(b) Empathy

(c) Value

(d) Attitude

Ans. (a)

Q.5. The person who forms the impression is called the __________.

(a) Perceiver

(b) Target

(c) Steroyotypes

(d) Schema

Ans. (a)

Very Short Answer Type   [1 Mark]

Q.1. Explain the concept of cognitive dissonance.

Ans. The concept of cognitive dissonance was proposed by Leon Festinger. It emphasises the cognitive component. Here the basic idea is that the cognitive components of an attitude must be 'consonant' (opposite of 'dissonant'), i.e., they should be logically in line with each other. If an individual finds that two cognitions in an attitude are dissonant, then one of them will be changed in the direction of consonance.

Q.2. What is Kernel of truth concept?

Ans. Sometimes people may continue to hold stereotypes because they think that, after all, there must be some truth, or 'kernel of truth' in what everyone says about the other group. Even a few examples are sufficient to support the 'kernel of truth' idea.

Short Answer Type - I   [2 Marks]

Q.1. Mention two strategies for handling Prejudice?

Ans. i. Education and information dissemination, for correcting stereotypes related to specific target groups, and tackling the problem of a strong in group bias.

ii. Increasing intergroup contact allows for direct communication, removal of mistrust between the groups, and even discovery of positive qualities in the out group.

Q.2. Difference between schema and stereotypes.

Ans. A schema is defined as a mental structure that provides a framework, set of rules or guidelines for processing information about any object. Schemas (or 'schemata') are the basic units stored in our memory, and function as shorthand ways of processing information, thus reducing the time and mental effort required in cognition.

In social cognition, category-based schemas that are related to groups of people are called stereotypes. These are category-based schemas that are overgeneralised, are not directly verified, and do not allow for exceptions. For example, suppose you have to define a group G.

Short Answer Type - II   [3 Marks]

Q.1. Mention three aspects of Impression Formation.

Ans. The process of impression formation consists of the following three subprocesses :

i. **Selection :** we take into account only some bits of information about the target person,

ii. **Organisation :** the selected information is combined in a systematic way, and

iii. **Inference :** we draw a conclusion about what kind of person the target is.

Q.1. What is Attitude formation? Discuss the processes of attitude formation.

Ans. In general, attitudes are learned through one's own experiences, and through interaction with others. There are a few research studies that show some sort of inborn aspect of attitudes, but such genetic factors influence attitudes only indirectly, along with learning. Therefore, most social psychologists have focused on the conditions which lead to the learning of attitudes.

TOPIC 3

Summary

Process of Attitude Formation

The processes and conditions of learning may be different, resulting in varying attitudes among people.

- **Learning attitudes by association:** You might have seen that students often develop a liking for a particular subject because of the teacher. This is because they see many positive qualities in that teacher; these positive qualities get linked to the subject that s/he teaches, and ultimately get expressed in the form of liking for the subject. In other words, a positive attitude towards the subject is learned through the positive association between a teacher and a student.

- **Learning attitudes by being rewarded or punished:** If an individual is praised for showing a particular attitude, chances are high that s/he will develop that attitude further. For example, if a teenager does yogasanas regularly, and gets the honour of being 'Miss Good Health' in her school, she may develop a positive attitude towards yoga and health in general. Similarly, if a child constantly falls ill because s/he eats junk food instead of proper meals, then the child is likely to develop a negative attitude towards junk food, and also a positive attitude towards eating healthy food.

- **Learning attitudes through modelling (observing others) :** Often it is not through association, or through reward and punishment, that we learn attitudes. Instead, we learn them by observing others being rewarded or punished for expressing thoughts, or showing behaviour of a particular kind towards the attitude object. For example, children may form a respectful attitude towards elders, by observing that their parents show respect for elders, and are appreciated for it.

- **Learning attitudes through group or cultural norms:** Very often, we learn attitudes through the norms of our group or culture. Norms are unwritten rules about behavior that everyone is supposed to show under specific circumstances. Over time, these norms may become part of our social cognition, in the form of attitudes.

- Learning attitudes through group or cultural norms may actually be an example of all three forms of learning described above — learning through association, reward or punishment, and modelling. For example, offering money, sweets, fruit and flowers in a place of worship is a normative behaviour in some religions.

- **Learning through exposure to information :** Many attitudes are learned in a social context, but not necessarily in the physical presence of others. Today, with the huge amount of information that is being provided through various media, both positive and negative attitudes are being formed. By reading the biographies of selfactualized persons, an individual may develop a positive attitude towards hard work and other aspects as the means of achieving success in life.

Behaviour in the Presence of Others

One of the first observations made about social behaviour was that performance on specific tasks is influenced by the mere presence of others. This is called social facilitation. For example, Reena is about to participate in a music contest. She is very talented, yet she is feeling very nervous about the event.

i. Better performance in the presence of others is because the person experiences arousal, which makes the person react in a more intense manner.

ii. The arousal is because the person feels she or he is being evaluated. Cottrell called this idea evaluation apprehension. The person will be praised if the performance is good (reward), or criticised if it is bad (punishment).

iii. The nature of the task to be performed also affects the performance in the presence of others. For example, in the case of a simple or familiar task, the person is more sure of performing well, and the eagerness to get praise or reward is stronger.

iv. If the others present are also performing the same task, this is called a situation of co-action.

Pro-Social Behaviour

Throughout the world, doing good to others and being helpful is described as a virtue. All religions teach us that we should help those who are in need. This behaviour is called helping or pro-social behaviour.

Prosocial behaviour is very similar to 'altruism', which means doing something for or thinking about the welfare of others without any self-interest (in Latin 'alter' means 'other', the opposite of 'ego' which means 'self'). Some common examples of pro-social behaviour are sharing things, cooperating with others, helping during natural calamities, showing sympathy, doing favours to others, and making charitable donations.

Factors Influencing Pro-social Behaviour

- Pro-social behaviour is based on an inborn, natural tendency in human beings to help other members of their own species. This inborn tendency facilitates survival of the species.

- Pro-social behaviour is influenced by learning. Individuals who are brought up in a family environment that sets examples of helping others, emphasises helping as a value, and praises helpfulness, and showing more prosocial behaviour than individuals who are brought up in a family environment devoid of these features.

- Cultural factors influence pro-social behaviour. Some cultures actively encourage people to help the needy and distressed. In cultures that encourage independence, individuals will show less pro-social behaviour, because people are expected to take care of themselves, and not to depend on help from others.

Individuals in cultures suffering from a shortage of resources may not show a high level of pro-social behaviour

Pro-social behaviour is more likely to be shown by individuals who have a high level of empathy, that is, the capacity to feel the distress of the person who is to be helped, such as Baba Saheb Amte and Mother Teresa.

Pro-social behaviour is expressed when the situation activates certain social norms that require helping others.

Three norms have been mentioned in the context of pro-social behaviour :

(a) **The norm of social responsibility :** We should help anyone who needs help, without considering any other factor.

(b) **The norm of reciprocity :** We should help those persons who have helped us in the past.

(c) **The norm of equity :** We should help others whenever we find that it is fair to do so. For example, many of us may feel that it is more fair to help a person who has lost all belongings in a flood, than to help a person who has lost everything through gambling.

Pro-social behaviour is more likely to be shown by individuals who have a high level of empathy, that is, the capacity to feel the distress of the person who is to be helped, such as Baba Saheb Amte and Mother Teresa. Pro-social behaviour is also more likely in situations that arouse empathy, such as the picture of starving children in a famine.

Multiple Choice Questions   [1 Mark]

Q.1. The individual about whom the impression is formed is called the__________.

(a) Perceiver   (b) Target

(c) Steroyotypes   (d) Schema

Ans. (b)

Q.2. Pro-social behaviour is more likely to be shown by individuals who have a high level of__________.

(a) Equity   (b) Empathy

(c) Reciprocity   (d) Social loafing

Ans. (b)

Q.3. We should help those persons who have helped us in the past. Which of the following is this social norm?

(a) Reciprocity   (b) Equity

(c) Family norm   (d) Both (a) and (b)

Ans. (a)

Q.4. We wish to get praise and avoid criticism, therefore we try to perform well and avoid mistakes. This explanation is given by____________

(a) Bernard Wiener   (b) Fritz Heider

(c) Cottrell   (d) John Dollard

Ans. (c)

Q.5. ___________________if the target group is described as 'dependent' and therefore unable to make progress.

(a) Beliefs

(b) Values

(c) Self-fulfilling prophecy

(d) Attractiveness

Ans. (c)

Q.6. ___________________if the target group is described as 'dependent' and therefore unable to make progress.

(a) Beliefs

(b) Values

(c) Self-fulfilling prophecy

(d) Attractiveness

Ans. (c)

Q.7. If a teenager does yogasanas regularly, and gets the honour of being 'Miss Good Health' in her school, she may develop a positive attitude towards yoga and health in general.Which attitude change is this example ?

(a) Learning attitudes by being rewarded or punished

(b) Learning attitudes by being modelling

(c) Learning attitudes by being cultural norms

(d) Learning attitudes by being association

Ans. (a)

Q.8. ___________ refers to all those psychological processes that deal with the gathering and processing of information related to social objects.

(a) Social interaction

(b) Social cognition

(c) Social facilitation

(d) None of the above

Ans. (b)

Q.9. ________ is a phenomenon by which the majority group places the blame on a minority outgroup for its own social, economic or political problems.

(a) Value   (b) Schema

(c) Scapegoating   (d) All the above

Ans. (c)

Q.10. Refers to how many attitudes there are within a broader attitude.________.

(a) Inference   (b) Selection

(c) Multiplaxity   (d) Planning

Ans. (c)

Q.11. ___________________Means that the target has liking and regard for the source.

(a) Arousal   (b) Co-action

(c) Identification   (d) Social loafing

Ans. (c)

Very Short Answer Type   [1 Mark]

Q.1. Define impression formation.

Ans. When we meet people in public we start making conclusions about their personal qualities.This is called as impression formation.

Q.2. Define Social facilitation.

Ans. One of the first observations made about social behaviour was that performance on specific tasks is influenced by the mere presence of others. This is called social facilitation. For example, Reena is about to participate in a music contest. She is very talented, yet she is feeling very nervous about the event.

Short Answer Type - I　　[2 Marks]

Q.1. Mention two characters of Pro-social behavior.

Ans. Pro-social behaviour has the following characteristics.

It must :

i. aim to benefit or do good to another person or other persons,

ii. be done without expecting anything in return,

Q.2. Highlight the importance of schemas in social cognition.

Ans.
- Social schemas (schemata) are mental structure.

- They function as a framework to process social information. These schemas lead to emergence of prototypes.

- Prototypes are concepts which have most of the defining features of a concept, class or family.

- These are best representatives of the population.

- Various stereotypes emerge from these schemas. In other words stereotypes are category-based schemas.

Short Answer Type - II　　[3 Marks]

Q.1. Mention 3 strategies for handling prejudice.

Ans. Knowing about the causes or sources would be the first step in handling prejudice.

i. Education and information dissemination, for correcting stereotypes related to specific target groups, and tackling the problem of a strong ingroup bias.

ii. Increasing intergroup contact allows for direct communication, removal of mistrust between the groups, and even discovery of positive qualities in the outgroup. However, these strategies are successful only if : - the two groups meet in a cooperative rather than competitive context, - close interactions between the groups helps them to know each other better, and - the two groups are not different in power or status.

iii. Highlighting individual identity rather than group identity, thus weakening the importance of group (both ingroup and outgroup) as a basis of evaluating the other person.

Q.2. Describe the important factors that influence impression formation.

Ans. **Impression formation** is a process by which impression about others is converting into more or less induring cognitions or thoughts about them.In short, **impression formation** is a process through which we draw quick conclusion/ inferences regarding others.

Factors facilitating Impression Formation:

- Nature of the phenomena (familiar or unfamiliar).

- Personality traits of the perceiver.

- Social schemas stored in the mind of perceiver.

- Situational factors.

The process of impression formation consists of the following three sub-processes:

- **Selection:** We take into account only some bits of information about the target person.

- **Organization:** the selected information is combined in a systematic way.

- **Inference:** We draw a conclusion about what kind of person the target is.

Some **specific qualities,** that influence impression formation, are:

- The information presented first has a stronger effect than the information presented at the end. This is called the **primacy effect.**

- We have a tendency to think that a target person who has one set of positive qualities must also be having other specific positives that are associated with first set. This is known as **halo effect,** e.g., if we think that a person is 'tidy' then we are likely to think that this person must also be hard/working.

- Whatever information comes at the end may have a stronger influence on impression formation. This is known as the **recency effect**

NCERT Questions

Q.1. Differentiate between prejudice and stereotype.

Ans. Prejudices are negative attitude.

- These are bias about others.
- Prejudices are baseless and false.
- It refers to biased attitude formed about an individual or a group of people.
- These are usually negative.
- It has three components, i.e., A-B-C-

(a) Affective (Emotional i.e dislike or hatred).

(b) Behavioural (i.e., discrimination).

(c) Cognitive (Believes, i.e., stereotypes).

Stereotypes are cognitive **component of prejudice.** It is strongly influenced by the processing of incoming social information.

- These are **over-generalized beliefs,** e.g., girls are talkative.
- Stereotypes are category based schemas.
- These may be positive or negative or neutral.
- Stereotype has no emotional blending.
- From stereotypes, prejudices may emerge very easily.
- Stereotypes are usually formed for the groups.
- Stereotypes are pre conceived notions.

Q.2. Explain the concept of pro-social behaviour.

Or

Describe the factors influencing Pro-social behaviour. **(CBSE 2013)**

Ans. Pro-social behaviour is any positively valued behaviour that does good to another person, is done without any pressure from outside and without any expectation of a reward or a return.

Humans are social beings. Most of their activities are organized with the help of others. We cannot live and grow unless there is support from others. We often engage in helping others. Such efforts are considered as pro-social behaviour. For any behaviour to be pro-social, it should fulfil the following conditions:

- There has to be an intention to benefit the other person. Any pro-social act, which one accomplishes by compulsion or as a requirement of a job, does not merit to be called 'pro-social'.

- The behaviour should be considered socially desirable by the other members of the society. Obviously, helping a thief in stealing is not a pro-social behaviour.

- If an act intended to benefit others is also expect to benefit the helper, it cannot be termed as 'pro-social'.

The intentions and the consequent positive behaviour are more important considerations of pro-social behaviour than the actual benefits.

The other term which are used interchangeably with pro-social behaviour is **altruism.** The literal meaning of **altruism** is "doing things or acting for the interest of others without any ulterior motive." It is a behaviour that reflects an unselfish concern for the welfare of others. All charitable, humanitarian, philanthropic activities, which people do without any self-interest, come under the category of altruism behaviour.

Determinants of Pro-social Behaviour: The pro-social behaviour depends on many factors.

(i) Pro-social behaviour is based on an **inborn,** natural tendency in human beings to help other members of their own species.

(ii) Pro-social behaviour is influenced by **learning** through modelling and positive reinforcement in the family.

(iii)Cultural factors influence pro-social behaviour. Some cultures actively encourage people to help the needy and distressed. Individuals in cultures suffering from a shortage of resources may not show a high level of pro-social behaviour.

(iv) Pro-social behaviour is expressed when the situation activates certain 'social norms' that require helping others. Three norms have been mentioned in context of pro-social behaviour:

(a) The norms of **social responsibility**. We should help anyone who needs help without considering any other factors.

(b) The norms of **reciprocity**. We should help persons who have helped us in the past.

(c) The norms of **equity**. We should help others whenever we find that it is fair to do so.

(v) Pro-social behaviour is affected by the expected reactions of the person who is being helped. For example, people might be unwilling to give money to a needy person because they feel that the person might feel insulted, or may become dependent.

(vi) Pro-social behaviour is more likely to be shown individuals who have a high level of **empathy**, that is, the capacity to feel the distress of the person who is to be helped, e.g., Mother Teresa.

Factors inhibiting Pro-social Behaviour:

(a) Diffusion of Responsibility: Pro-social behaviour may be reduced when the number of bystanders is more than one. On the other hand, if there is only one bystander, this person is more likely to take responsibility and actually help the victim. It happens because each person thinks that others will take the responsibility.

(b) Feeling State of the Individual: Person in a bad mood, being busy with one's own problems or feeling that the person to be helped is responsible for his/her problem, may not help others.

Q.3. Is behaviour always a reflection of one's attitude? Explain with a relevant example.

Ans. An individual's attitude may not always be exhibited through behaviour. Likewise one's actual behaviour may be contrary to one's attitude towards a particular topic. Psychologists have found that there would be consistency between attitude and behaviour when:

(i) The attitude is strong and occupies a central place in the attitude system.

(ii) The person is aware of his/her attitudes.

(iii) Person's behaviour is not being watched or evaluated by others.

(iv) Person thinks that the behaviour would have a positive consequences.

Richard La Piere, an American social psychologist, conducted the following study. He asked a Chinese couple to travel across the United States, and stay in different hotels. Only once during these occasions they were refused service by one of the hotels. La Piere sent out questionnaires to managers of hotels and tourist homes in the same areas where the Chinese couple had travelled asking them if they would give accommodation to Chinese guest. A very large percentage said that they would not do so. This response showed a negative attitude towards the Chinese, which was inconsistent with the positive behaviour that was actually shown towards the travelling Chinese couple. Attitudes may not always predict actual pattern of one's behaviour.

Q.4. What are the factors that influence the formation of an attitude?

Ans. The following factors provide the context for the learning of attitude through various processes:

i. **Family and School Environment:** parents and other family-members play a significant role in attitude formation. Learning of attitudes within the family and school usually takes place by association, through rewards and punishment and through modelling.

ii. **Reference Groups:** Attitudes towards political, religious and social groups, occupations, national and other issues are often developed through reference groups. Reference groups indicate to an individual the norms regarding acceptable behaviour and ways of thinking. Various institutions, religion, culture and communities are form of reference groups.

iii. **Personal Experiences:** Many attitudes are formed, not in the family environment or through reference groups, but through direct personal experiences which bring about a drastic change in our attitude towards people and our own life.

iv. **Media Related Influences:** Technological advances have made audio-visual media and internet as very powerful sources for attitude formation. School textbooks also influence attitude formation. The media can be used to create consumerist attitude. The media can exert both good and bad influences on attitudes.

Chapter Practice

Multiple Choice Questions [1 Mark]

Q.1. Which of the following are the factors that Influence Attitude Chang

1. Valence
2. Extremeness
3. Complexity
4. Centrality

Choose the correct answer from the codes given below

(a) 1 2 and 3 only

(b) 2 3 and 4 only

(c) 1 3 and 4 only

(d) 1 2 3 and 4

Q.2. What is 'A' in A-B-C components?

(a) Arousal

(b) Attention

(c) Affective

(d) Attraction

Q.3. Schemas that function in the form of categories are called __________.

(a) Stereotypes

(b) prototypes

(c) perceivers

(d) None of the above

Q.4. The ____________ of an attitude tells us whether an attitude is positive or negative towards the attitude object.

(a) Centrality

(b) valence

(c) extremeness

(d) simplicity

Very Short Answer Type [1 Mark]

Q.5. What is actor-observer effect?

Q.6. What do you mean by Self-fulfilling prophecy ?

Short Answer Type - I [2 Marks]

Q.7. Mention two strategies for handling prejudice.

Q.8. Discuss two-step concept given by S.M mohsin?

Short Answer Type - II [3 Marks]

Q.9. State any four factors influencing pro-social behaviour.

Q.10. Mention any three sources of prejudice ?

Long Answer Type [5 Marks]

Q.11. Explain how the attribution made by an 'actor' would be different from that of an 'observer'.

Q.12. Explain the causes of group conflict. Discuss any three strategies for resolving conflicts.

CHAPTER 7

Social Influence and Group Processes

Summary

What is a Group?

A group may be defined as an organized system of two or more individuals, who are interacting and interdependent, who have common motives, have a set of role relationships among its members, and have norms that regulate the behaviour of its members.

Groups have the following salient characteristics:

- A social unit consisting of two or more individuals who perceive themselves as belonging to the group. This characteristic of the group helps in distinguishing one group from the other and gives the group its unique identity.

- A collection of individuals who have common motives and goals. Groups function either working towards a given goal, or away from certain threats facing the group.

- A collection of individuals who are interdependent, i.e. what one is doing may have consequences for others. Suppose one of the fielders in a cricket team drops an important catch during a match — this will have consequence for the entire team.

- Individuals who are trying to satisfy a need through their joint association also influence each other.

- A gathering of individuals who interact with one another either directly or indirectly.

- A collection of individuals whose interactions are structured by a set of roles and norms. This means that the group members perform the same functions every time the group meets and the group members adhere to group norms. Norms tell us how we ought to behave in the group and specify the behaviours expected from group members.

Teams are special kinds of groups. Members of teams often have complementary skills and are committed to a common goal or purpose. Members are mutually accountable for their activities. In teams, there is a positive synergy attained through the coordinated efforts of the members.

The main differences between groups and teams are:

- In groups, performance is dependent on contributions of individual members. In teams, both individual contributions and teamwork matter.

- In groups, the leader or whoever is heading the group holds responsibility for the work. However in teams, although there is a leader, members hold themselves responsible.

Group Formation

Proximity: Common interests, attitudes, and background are important determinants of your liking for your group members.

Similarity : Being exposed to someone over a period of time makes us assess our similarities and paves the way for formation of groups.

Common motives and goals : When people have common motives or goals, they get together and form a group which may facilitate their goal attainment.

Four important elements of group structure are :

Roles are socially defined expectations that individuals in a given situation are expected to fulfil. Roles refer to the typical behaviour that depicts a person in a given social context. As a daughter or a son, you are expected to respect elders, listen to them, and be responsible towards your studies.

Norms are expected standards of behaviour and beliefs established, agreed upon, and enforced by group members. They may be considered as a group's 'unspoken rules'. In your family, there are norms that guide the behaviour of family members.

Status refers to the relative social position given to group members by others. This relative position or status may be either ascribed (given may be because of one's seniority) or achieved (the person has achieved status because of expertise or hard work).

Cohesiveness refers to togetherness, binding, or mutual attraction among group members. As the group becomes more cohesive, group members start to think, feel and act as a social unit, and less like isolated individuals. Members of a highly cohesive group have a greater desire to remain in the group in comparison to those who belong to low cohesive groups.

Type of Groups

Major types of groups are enumerated below :

- Primary and secondary groups
- Formal and informal groups
- Ingroup and outgroup.

Primary and Secondary Groups : A major difference between primary and secondary groups is that primary groups are pre-existing formations which are usually given to the individual whereas secondary groups are those which the individual joins by choice.

Formal and Informal Groups : These groups differ in the degree to which the functions of the group are stated explicitly and formally. The functions of a formal group

are explicitly stated as in the case of an office organisation. The formation of formal groups is based on some specific rules or laws and members have definite roles. There are a set of norms which help in establishing order.

Ingroup and Outgroup : Just as individuals compare themselves with others in terms of similarities and differences with respect to what they have and what others have, individuals also compare the group they belong to with groups of which they are not a member.

The term 'ingroup' refers to one's own group, and 'outgroup' refers to another group. For ingroup members, we use the word 'we' while for outgroup members, the word 'they' is used.

Multiple Choice Questions　　[1 Mark]

Q.1. Being with people gives a sense of comfort, and protection is a reason for ____________

(a) Roles　　　　　(b) Security

(c) Status　　　　(d) Cohesiveness

Ans. (b)

Q.2. Suppose your school wins in an inter - institutional debate competition, you feel proud and think that you are better than others is an example of ______________.

(a) Status　　　　(b) Groupthink

(c) Norms　　　　(d) Roles

Ans. (a)

Q.3. Being a member of prestigious groups enhances one's self-concept an example of ______________.

(a) Status　　　　(b) Groupthink

(c) Security　　　(d) Self Esteem

Ans. (d)

Q.4. Often, after this stage, there is a stage of intragroup conflict which is referred to as__________________

(a) Performing　　(b) Norming

(c) Storming　　　(d) Forming satge

Ans. (c)

Q.5. _______ are expected standards of behaviour and beliefs established, agreed upon, and enforced by group members.

(a) Status   (b) Cohesiveness

(c) Norms   (d) Roles

Ans. (c)

Q.6. _________________ refers to togetherness, binding, or mutual attraction among group members.

(a) Status   (b) Cohesiveness

(c) Norms   (d) Roles

Ans. (b)

Very Short Answer Type   [1 Mark]

Q.1. Define Group.

Ans. A group may be defined as an organized system of two or more individuals, who are interacting and interdependent, who have common motives, have a set of role relationships among its members, and have norms that regulate the behavior of its members.

Q.2. Define Cohesiveness.

Ans. Cohesiveness refers to togetherness, binding, or mutual attraction among group members. As the group becomes more cohesive, group members start to think, feel and act as a social unit, and less like isolated individuals. Members of a highly cohesive group have a greater desire to remain in the group in comparison to those who belong to low cohesive groups.

Short Answer Type - I   [2 Marks]

Q.1. Mention two reasons why people join groups?

Ans. In general, people join groups for the following reasons:

i. Security: When we are alone, we feel insecure. Groups reduce this insecurity. Being with people gives a sense of comfort, and protection. As a result, people feel stronger, and are less vulnerable to threats.

ii. Status: When we are members of a group that is perceived to be important by others, we feel recognized and experience a sense of power. Suppose your school wins in an inter - institutional debate competition, you feel proud and think that you are better than others.

Q.2. Differentiate between Primary and secondary Group?

Ans. A major difference between primary and secondary groups is that primary groups are pre-existing formations which are usually given to the individual whereas secondary groups are those which the individual joins by choice.

Primary groups are central to individual's functioning and have a very major role in developing values and ideals of the individual during the early stages of development. In contrast, secondary groups are those where relationships among members are more impersonal, indirect, and less frequent.

Q.3. How Proximity and similarity help in group formation?

Ans. Proximity : Repeated interactions with the same set of individuals give us a chance to know them, and their interests and attitudes. Common interests, attitudes, and background are important determinants of your liking for your group members.

Similarity : Being exposed to someone over a period of time makes us assess our similarities and paves the way for formation of groups. Why do we like people who are similar? Psychologists have given several explanations for this. One explanation is that people prefer consistency and like relationships that are consistent.

Short Answer Type - II   [3 Marks]

Q.1. Differentiate between Formal and Informal Groups?

Ans. These groups differ in the degree to which the functions of the group are stated explicitly and formally.

i. The functions of a formal group are explicitly stated as in the case of an office organisation. The roles to be performed by group members are stated in an explicit manner.

ii. The formal and informal groups differ on the basis of structure. The formation of formal groups is based on some specific rules or laws and members have definite roles.

iii. There are a set of norms which help in establishing order. A university is an example of a formal group. On the other hand, the formation of informal groups is not based on rules or laws and there is close relationship among members.

Q.2. Mention any three salient characteristics of groups.

Ans. i. A social unit consisting of two or more individuals who perceive themselves as belonging to the group. This characteristic of the group helps in distinguishing one group from the other and gives the group its unique identity.

ii. A collection of individuals who have common motives and goals. Groups function either working towards a given goal, or away from certain threats facing the group.

iii. A collection of individuals who are interdependent, i.e. what one is doing may have consequences for others. Suppose one of the fielders in a cricket team drops an important catch during a match — this will have consequence for the entire team.

Long Answer Type [5 Marks]

Q.1. What is Group structure? What are the four important elements of group structure ?

Ans. During the process of group formation, groups also develop a structure. We should remember that group structure develops as members interact. Over time this interaction shows regularities in distribution of task to be performed, responsibilities assigned to members, and the prestige or relative status of members.

Four important elements of group structure are:

- Roles are socially defined expectations that individuals in a given situation are expected to fulfil. Roles refer to the typical behaviour that depicts a person in a given social context. You have the role of a son or a daughter and with this role, there are certain role expectations, i.e. including the behaviour expected of someone in a particular role. As a daughter or a son, you are expected to respect elders, listen to them, and be responsible towards your studies.

- Norms are expected standards of behaviour and beliefs established, agreed upon, and enforced by group members. They may be considered as a group's 'unspoken rules'. In your family, there are norms that guide the behaviour of family members. These norms represent shared ways of viewing the world.

- Status refers to the relative social position given to group members by others. This relative position or status may be either ascribed (given may be because of one's seniority) or achieved (the person has achieved status because of expertise or hard work). By being members of the group, we enjoy the status associated with that group. All of us, therefore, strive to be members of such groups which are high in status or are viewed favourably by others. Even within a group, different members have different prestige and status. For example, the captain of a cricket team has a higher status compared to the other members, although all are equally important for the team's success.

- Cohesiveness refers to togetherness, binding, or mutual attraction among group members. As the group becomes more cohesive, group members start to think, feel and act as a social unit, and less like isolated individuals. Members of a highly cohesive group have a greater desire to remain in the group in comparison to those who belong to low cohesive groups. Cohesiveness refers to the team spirit or 'we feeling' or a sense of belongingness to the group. It is difficult to leave a cohesive group or to gain membership of a group which is highly cohesive. Extreme cohesiveness however, may sometimes not be in a group's interest.

TOPIC 2

Summary

Influence of Group on Individual Behaviour

Since social facilitation has been briefly discussed in Chapter 6, we would try to understand the phenomenon of social loafing in this section.

Social Loafing

Social facilitation research suggests that presence of others leads to arousal and can motivate individuals to enhance their performance if they are already good at solving something. This enhancement occurs when a person's efforts are individually evaluated. It has been found that individuals work less hard in a group than they do when performing alone.

This points to a phenomenon referred to as 'social loafing'. Social loafing is a reduction in individual effort when working on a collective task, i.e. one in which outputs are pooled with those of other group members. An example of such a task is the game of tug-of-war.

It is not possible for you to identify how much force each member of the team has been exerting.

Group Polarisation

Groups show another tendency referred to as 'group polarisation'. It has been found that groups are more likely to take extreme decisions than individuals alone. Suppose there is an employee who has been caught taking bribe or engaging in some other unethical act.

After this interaction, your views may become stronger. This firm conviction is because of the following three reasons:

- In the company of like-minded people, you are likely to hear newer arguments favouring your viewpoints. This will make you more favourable towards capital punishment.

- When you find others also favouring capital punishment, you feel that this view is validated by the public. This is a sort of bandwagon effect.

- When you find people having similar views, you are likely to perceive them as ingroup. You start identifying with the group, begin showing conformity, and as a consequence your views become strengthened.

Conformity, Compliance, and Obedience

The term 'social influence' refers to those processes whereby our attitudes and behaviours are influenced by the real or imagined presence of other people. Throughout the day you may encounter a number of situations where others have tried to influence you and make you think in ways they want.

Kelman distinguished three forms of social influence, viz. compliance, identification, and internalisation.

In compliance, there are external conditions that force the individual to accept the influence of the significant other. Compliance also refers to behaving in a particular way in response to a request made by someone. For example, a member of a community group for 'clean environment' requests you to put a sticker on your bike that reads, 'Say No to Plastic Bags'. You agree to do so, not because of a group norm, or even because you personally believe in banning plastic bags .

Yet another form of behaviour is 'obedience'. A distinguishing feature of obedience is that such behaviour is a response to a person in authority. In the example given above, you may sign the letter more readily if a senior teacher or a student leader asks you to do so. In such a situation, you are not necessarily following a group norm but rather carrying out an instruction or an order.

Conformity

It seems that the tendency to follow a norm is natural, and does not need any special explanation. Yet, we need to understand why such a tendency appears to be natural or spontaneous. First, norms represent a set of unwritten and informal 'rules' of behaviour that provide information to members of a group about what is expected of them in specific situations.

The pioneering experiments on conformity were carried out by Sherif and Asch. They illustrate some of the conditions that determine the extent of conformity, and also methods that may be adopted for the study of conformity in groups. These experiments demonstrate what Sherif called the 'autokinetic effect'.

Determinants of Conformity

(i) Size of the group : Conformity is greater when the group is small than when the group is large. Why does it happen? It is easier for a deviant member (one who does not conform) to be noticed in a small group. However, in a large group, if there is strong agreement among most of the members, this makes the majority stronger, and therefore, the norm is also stronger. In such a case, the minority member(s) would be more likely to conform because the group pressure would be stronger.

(ii) Size of the minority : Take the case of the Asch experiment When the dissenting or deviating minority size increases, the likelihood of conformity decreases. In fact, it may increase the number of dissenters or non-conformists in the group.

(iii) Nature of the task : In Asch's experiment, the task required an answer that could be verified, and could be correct or incorrect. Suppose the task involves giving an opinion about some topic.

(iv) Public or private expression of behaviour : In the Asch technique, the group members are asked to give their answers publicly, i.e. all members know who has given which response.

(v) Personality : The conditions described above show how the features of the situation are important in determining the degree of conformity shown. We also find that some individuals have a conforming personality.

Compliance

It was stated earlier that compliance refers simply to behaving in response to a request from another person or group even in the absence of a norm. A good example of compliance is the kind of behaviour shown when a salesperson comes to our door.

In many situations, this happens because it is an easy way out of the situation. It is more polite and the other party is pleased. In other situations, there could be other factors at work. The following techniques have been found to work when someone wants another person to comply.

The foot-in-the-door technique : The person begins by making a small request that the other person is not likely to refuse. Once the other person carries out the request, a bigger request is made. Simply because the other person has already complied with the smaller request, he or she may feel uncomfortable refusing the second request. For example, someone may come to us on behalf of a group and give us a gift (something free), saying that it is for promotion.

The deadline technique : In this technique, a 'last date' is announced until which a particular product or 'an offer' will be available. The aim is to make people 'hurry' and make the purchase before they miss the rare opportunity.

The door-in-the-face technique : In this technique, you begin with a large request and when this is refused a later request for something smaller, the one that was actually desired, is made, which is usually granted by the person.

Obedience

When compliance is shown to an instruction or order from a person in authority, such as parents, teachers, leaders, or policemen, that behaviour is called obedience. Sometimes, it is because we believe that persons in authority must be obeyed. People in authority have effective means for enforcing their orders.

One person in each pair was the "learner", whose work was to memorise pairs of words. The other participant was the "teacher", who would read these words aloud and punish the learner when s/he made errors by giving her/him shock.

The instructions were so arranged that the teacher was faced with a dilemma — should s/he continue shocks even when they were increasingly painful? The experimenter kept on motivating the teacher to continue. In all, 65 per cent showed total obedience.

Cooperation and Competition

Behaviours in most social situations are characterised by either 'cooperation' or 'competition'. The rewards in cooperative situations are group rewards and not individual rewards. However, when members try to maximise their own benefits and work for the realisation of self-interest, competition is likely to result.

Deutsch investigated cooperation and competition within groups. College students were assigned to groups of five persons and were required to solve puzzles and problems. One set of groups, referred to as the 'cooperative group', were told that they would be rewarded collectively for their performance.

Although competition between individuals within a group may result in conflict and disharmony, competition between groups may increase within group cohesion and solidarity.

Prisoner's Dilemma Game, which is a two person game in which both parties are faced with cooperation or competition, and depending upon their choices both can win or lose, is often used to study cooperation or competition.

Conflict Resolution Strategies

Introduction of superordinate goals : Sherif's study, already mentioned in the section on cooperation and competition, showed that by introducing superordinate goals, intergroup conflict can be reduced. A superordinate goal is mutually beneficial to both parties, hence both groups work cooperatively.

Altering perceptions : Conflicts can also be reduced by altering perceptions and reactions through persuasion, educational and media appeals, and portrayal of groups differently in society. Promoting empathy for others should be taught to everyone right from the beginning.

Increasing intergroup contacts : Conflict can also be reduced by increasing contacts between the groups. This can be done by involving groups in conflict on neutral grounds through community projects and events.

Redrawing group boundaries : Another technique that has been suggested by some psychologists is redrawing the group boundaries. This can be done by creating conditions where groups boundaries are redefined and groups come to perceive themselves as belonging to a common group.

Structural solutions : Conflict can also be reduced by redistributing the societal resources according to principles based on justice. Research on justice has identified several principles of justice.

Negotiations : Conflict can also be resolved through negotiations and third party interventions. Warring groups can resolve conflict by trying to find mutually acceptable solutions.

Structural solutions : Conflict can also be reduced by redistributing the societal resources according to principles based on justice.

Respect for other group's norms : In a pluralist society like India, it is necessary to respect and be sensitive to the strong norms of various social and ethnic groups. It has been noticed that a number of communal riots between different groups have taken place because of such insensitivity.

Multiple Choice Questions   [1 Mark]

Q.1. _______________ have complementary skills and are committed to a common goal or purpose.

(a) Goal   (b) Team

(c) Crowd   (d) Audience

Ans. (b)

Q.2. Which of the following is not related to group formation?

(a) Proximity   (b) Similarity

(c) Storming   (d) Norming

Ans. (a)

Q.3. _______________ refers to togetherness, binding, or mutual attraction among group members.

(a) Cohesiveness   (b) Status

(c) Roles   (d) Norms

Ans. (a)

Q.4. 'Auto kinetic effect' was suggested by_____________.

(a) Kelman   (b) Sherif

(c) Milgram   (d) Freud

Ans. (b)

Q.5. Who wrote the book 'In the Minds of Men'?

    (a) Gardner Murphy (b) Deutsch

    (c) Milgram   (d) Henry stew

Ans. (a)

Q.6. Which of the following are not the important forms of social influence?

    (a) Conformity   (b) Compliance

    (c) Obedience   (d) Empathy

Ans. (d)

Q.7. Which of the following are not facilitate group formation?

    (a) Proximity   (b) Similarity

    (c) Goal   (d) Self esteem

Ans. (d)

Q.8. Who among the following distinguish three forms of social influence?

    (a) Kelman   (b) Sherif

    (c) Milgram   (d) Freud

Ans. (a)

Q.9. Which of the following are not the types of groups?

    (a) Primary   (b) Secondary

    (c) Formal   (d) Tertiary

Ans. (d)

Very Short Answer Type   [1 Mark]

Q.1. What is Social loafing?

Ans. Social facilitation research suggests that presence of others leads to arousal and can motivate individuals to enhance their performance if they are already good at solving something. It has been found that individuals work less hard in a group than they do when performing alone. This points to a phenomenon referred to as 'social loafing'.

Q.2. What is Bandwagon effect ?

Ans. When you find others also favouring capital punishment, you feel that this view is validated by the public. This is a sort of bandwagon effect.

When you find people having similar views, you are likely to perceive them as ingroup. You start identifying with the group, begin showing conformity, and as a consequence your views become strengthened.

Q.3. What is Autokinetic effect?

Ans. The pioneering experiments on conformity were carried out by Sherif and Asch. They illustrate some of the conditions that determine the extent of conformity, and also methods that may be adopted for the study of conformity in groups. These experiments demonstrate what Sherif called the 'autokinetic effect'

Short Answer Type - I   [2 Marks]

Q.1. Mention any two Determinants of Conformity.

Ans. i. Size of the group : Conformity is greater when the group is small than when the group is large. Why does it happen? It is easier for a deviant member (one who does not conform) to be noticed in a small group.

    ii. Size of the minority : Take the case of the Asch experiment Suppose the subject finds that after some rounds of judgment of the lines, there is another participant who starts agreeing with the subject's answer. When the dissenting or deviating minority size increases, the likelihood of conformity decreases. In fact, it may increase the number of dissenters or non-conformists in the group.

Q.2. Mention any two factors determine whether people will cooperate or compete.

Ans. Some of the important ones are given below:

    (i) Reward structure : Psychologists believe that whether people will cooperate or compete will depend on the reward structure. Cooperative reward structure is one in which there is promotive interdependence. Each is beneficiary of the reward and reward is possible only if all contribute. A competitive reward structure is one in which one can get a reward only if others do not get it.

(ii) Interpersonal communication : When there is good interpersonal communication, then cooperation is the likely consequence. Communication facilitates interaction, and discussion. As a result, group members can convince each other and learn about each other.

Q.3. How is one's identify formed?

Ans. • **Identity** refers to the aspect of one's self-concept that is based on group-membership.

• Our identity tells us what we are in a larger context.

• After one develops an identity, he/she internalises the norms emphasized in a group and adopts them.

• Identity provides a member of a group with a shared set of values, beliefs and goals about the social world.

• Identity helps to co-ordinate attitude and behaviour.

• The development of identity leads to the devaluation of the out group.

Q.4. What are the benefits of co-operation?

Ans. Groups may be co-operative or competitive. Technically, the behaviour that yields maximal joint profit for all the parties involved is called co-operation. The behaviour that yields maximal relative gain is labelled competition.

• Co-operative goals are those, which are defined in such a way that each individual can attain the goal if other members are also attaining their goals. There is interdependence in goal attainment.

Effects of co-operation:

• Goal achievement becomes easy.

• Interpersonal relations get strengthened.

• Cohesiveness rises in the group.

• Group-members become ready to work for others.

• Willingness to accept other's divergent view-point.

Q.1. Compare and contrast formal and informal groups, and in groups and out groups.

Ans. Formal Groups:

(i) The functions of a formal group are explicitly stated, as in an office organization, or social work club.

(ii) They have rigidly stated functions and the roles of the members are well-defined or imposed.

(iii) Formal groups have a chain of command for decision-making, e.g., military or bureaucracy. .

Informal Groups:

(i) Informal decision-making process may exist as parallel mechanisms.

(ii) Members of informal groups usually feel more comfortable to take decision in informal settings, e.g., tea time group or lunch group.

(iii) There are no elicit rules and regulations for informal group.

In-group:

(i) It is generally considered as 'me, my, we, or our' group.

(ii) People in in-group are viewed as having desirable behaviour and admirable traits,

(iii) It is always good, strong, cohesive, kind-hearted, open, relaxing and cool.

Out-group:

(i) It is considered as 'they' group.

(ii) Members are often perceived negatively.

(iii) It is always bad, dirty, damaging, dangerous and has people with negative emotions.

Q.2. Are you a member of a certain group? Discuss what motivated are you to join that groups.

Ans. Definitely I am member of various groups. In other words, I will say that there is no dimension of life where I am not related to a group because we all are social beings and for everything, we are dependent on this or that group. There are various reasons which motivate me and everybody to join a group. Some of them are as follows:

(i) **Security:** Groups reduce the feeling of insecurity. Being with people gives a sense of comfort and protection.

(ii) **Status:** When the group is perceived as important high profile and well known, then the members also feel recognized and 'experience a sense of power', e.g., being a student of high profile school.

(iii) **Self-esteem:** Being a member of a prestigious group enhances the individual's self-concept.

(iv) **Satisfaction of one's Psychological and Social Needs:** Groups satisfy one's social and psychological needs such as sense of belongingness, giving and receiving attention, love and power.

(v) **Group Achievement:** Groups help in achieving the goals which cannot be attained individually.

(vi) **Provide Knowledge and Information:** Group membership provides us knowledge and information and broadens our views.

Q.3. How does Tuck man's stage model help you to understand the formation of groups?

Ans. According to **Tuck man**, group formation takes place in following stages:

(i) **Forming Stage:** When group-members first meet, there is a great deal of uncertainty about the group, the goal, and how it is to be achieved.

(ii) **Storming:** There is a stage of inter group conflict. There is conflict among members about how the target of the group is to be achieved, who is to control the group and its resources, and who is to perform what task.

(iii) **Norming:** Group-members by this time develop norms related to group behaviour. This leads to development of a positive group identity.

(iv) **Performing:** At this stage, the structure of the group has evolved and is accepted by group-members. The group moves towards achieving the group goal.

(v) **Adjourning Stage:** In this stage, once the function is over or goal is achieved, the group may be disbanded.

These stages help in group formation. Which occurs on the basis of following factors:

(i) **Proximity:** Individuals with similar background, living in the same complex (e.g., going to the same school) may form groups on the basis of proximity.

(ii) **Similarity:** It has been observed that more the similarity in the attitudes, interest, beliefs and value system of two persons, greater the likelihood that they would form a group.

(iii) **Common Motives and Goals:** When a number of people have common objectives or goals, they tend to get together and form a group.

Q.4. How do groups influence our behaviour?

(CBSE 2008, 2014)

Ans. Group influence our behaviour in following three forms:

- 'Social facilitation' is a form of group influence.

- 'Social facilitation' refers to a concept that performance on specific task is influenced by the mere presence of others.

- Norman Triplett observed that individuals show better performance in presence of others, than when they are performing the same task alone.

Better performance in presence of others is because the person experiences According to arousal, which makes the person react in a more intense manner.

The arousal is because the person feels he or she is being evaluated. Cottrell called this idea **evaluation apprehension.** The person will be praised if performance is good (reward), he/she will be criticised if it is bad (punishment). We wish to get praise and avoid criticism, therefore we try to perform well and avoid criticism.

As in case of complex task, the person may be afraid of making mistakes. And the fear of criticism or punishment is stronger.

If the others present are also performing same task, this is called a **situation of co action.** When task is simple or a familiar one, performance is better under co-action than when the person is alone.

Task performing can be facilitated and improved or inhibited and worsened by the presence of others. If we are working together in a larger group, the less effort each member puts in. This phenomena is called **social loafing**, based on diffusion of responsibility.

Diffusion of responsibility can also be frequently seen in situations where people are expected to help.

II. 'Social loafing refers to reduction in motivation when people are functioning collectively.

* It is a form of group influence.

(i) Group members feel less responsible for the overall tasks being performed and therefore exert less effort.

(ii) Motivation of members may decrease because they realize that their contributions cannot be evaluated on the individual basis, so to why to work hard.

(iii)The performance of the group is not to be compared with that of the other groups.

(iv)There is improper co-ordination (or no co-ordination) among members.

III. Group polarization is a group influence which refers to the strengthening of groups initial position as a result interaction and discussion.

As a result of group discussion opinion shifts towards more extreme positions than those whicfi they initially held.

In group polarization, it has been found that groups are more likely to take extreme decisions than individuals alone. Group polarization occurs due to the following factors:

(i) In the company of like-minded people, people are likely to hear newer arguments favouring their view-points.

(ii) When people find others also favouring their view-point, they feel that their view is validated by the public. This is a sort of bandwagon effect.

(iii)When people find others having similar views, they are likely to perceive them as in-group.

Q.1. What are some of the causes of intergroup conflict? Think of any international conflict. Reflect on the human price of this conflict.

Ans. Conflict is a process in which either an individual or a group perceives that the others have opposite interest, and both try to contradict each other.

* In such conflicts intense feeling of 'We' and 'They' dominate.

* Both the groups believe that only their group (in group) will protect their interest. Individual group conflict occurs when the individuals, needs are different from the group's needs, goals or norms. **Inter group conflict** refers to the situation of conflict between groups. It often occurs to maintain the identity of the group different and stronger than the other groups.

Some Major Reasons for Group Conflicts:

1. One major reason is **lack of communication** and faulty communication between both parties. This kind of communication leads to suspicion, i.e., there is a lack of trust, and hence, conflict results.

2. Another reason for inter group conflict is **relative deprivation.** It arises when members of a group compare themselves with the members of another group, and L perceive that they do not have what they desire to have, which the other group has.

   In other words, they feel that they are not doing well in comparison to other groups. This may lead to feelings of deprivation and discontentment, which may trigger conflict.

3. Another cause of conflict arises when one party believes that it is **better than the other**, and what it is saying should be done. When this does not happen, both parties start accusing each other.

4. A feeling that the other group **does not respect the norms** of my group, and actually violates those norms, can cause conflict

5. Desire for **retaliation** for some harm done in the past could be another reason for conflict.

6. **Biased perceptions** are at the root of most conflicts.

7. Research has shown that when acting in groups, people are more competitive as well as more aggressive than when they are on their own. Groups compete over scarce resource, both material resources (e.g., territory) and money as well as social resources (e.g., respect and esteem).

8. **Perceived inequality** is another reason for conflict.

9. According to **Gardener Murphy** most conflicts begin in the minds of men and then go to the field.

Gardener Murphy, in his book '**In the Minds of Men**', explains intergroup conflicts at three levels:

(a) **Structural Level:** It includes high rates of poverty, economic and sound stratification, inequality, limited political and social opportunity, e.g., Tribal areas of Jharkhand and West Bengal becoming fertile ground for Naxal movement.

(b) **Group Level:** Social identity, realistic conflict between groups over resources and unequal power relations between groups lead to conflicts, e.g., Dalits in India or Women Empowerment Movement.

(c) **Individual Level:** It includes beliefs, biased attitudes and personality characteristics. These are important determinants.

Chapter Practice

Multiple Choice Questions [1 Mark]

Q.1. Socially defined expectations that individuals in a given situation are expected to fulfill known as______________

(a) Roles

(b) Norming

(c) Storming

(d) Cohesiveness

Q.2. Psychologists have identified the phenomenon of________________.

(a) Status

(b) Groupthink

(c) Norms

(d) Roles

Q.3. Common interests, attitudes, and background are important determinants of your liking for your group member's example which condition of group formation?

(a) Proximity

(b) Security

(c) Status

(d) Similarity

Q.4. Being with people gives a sense of comfort, and protection is a reason for ______________

(a) Roles

(b) Security

(c) Status

(d) Cohesiveness

Very Short Answer Type [1 Mark]

Q.5. What is group polarisation?

Q.6. What are norms?

Short Answer Type - I [2 Marks]

Q.7. Extreme cohesiveness within a group becomes harmful for functioning. Explain.

Q.8. What is the foot-in-the-door technique ?

Short Answer Type - II [3 Marks]

Q.9. Describe any two elements of group structure.

Long Answer Type [5 Marks]

Q.10. State three conditions which facilitate group formation.

Q.11. Discuss the Asch technique in brief?

CHAPTER 8

Psychology and Life

Summary

A branch of psychology called environmental psychology deals with various psychological issues pertaining to the human-environment interaction in a very broad sense of the term.

The minimalist perspective assumes that the physical environment has minimal or negligible influence on human behaviour, health and well being.

The instrumental perspective suggests that the physical environment exists mainly for use by human beings for their comfort and well-being.

The spiritual perspective refers to the view of the environment as something to be respected and valued rather than exploited.

Different Views of the Human-Environment Relationship

There is more than one way of looking at the human-environment relationship, depending largely on how this relationship is perceived by human beings.

A psychologist named Stokols (1990) describes three approaches that may be adopted to describe the human-environment relationship.

(a) The minimalist perspective assumes that the physical environment has minimal or negligible influence on human behaviour, health and wellbeing. The physical environment and human beings exist as parallel components.

(b) The instrumental perspective suggests that the physical environment exists mainly for use by human beings for their comfort and well-being. Most of the human influences on the environment reflect the instrumental perspective.

(c) The spiritual perspective refers to the view of the environment as something to be respected and valued rather than exploited. It implies that human beings recognise the interdependent relationship between themselves and the environment, i.e. human beings will exist and will be happy only as long as the environment is kept healthy and natural.

Multiple Choice Questions [1 Mark]

Q.1. Who describes three approaches that may be adopted to describe the human-environment relationship?

(a) Gorge stew   (b) Stokols

(c) Andrew freud   (d) Muller

Ans. (b)

Q.2. In Intimate distance how much distance is maintained?

(a) 18 inches

(b) 4 feet

(c) 10 feet

(d) Infinity

Ans. (a)

Q.3. Which of the following is not the features of Post-traumatic stress disorder (PTSD)?

(a) Immediate reaction

(b) Physical reaction

(c) Cognitive disorder

(d) Social reactions

Ans. (c)

Very Short Answer Type   [1 Mark]

Q.1. Define environmental psychology.

Ans. A branch of psychology called environmental psychology deals with various psychological issues pertaining to the human-environment interaction in a very broad sense of the term.

Short Answer Type - I   [2 Marks]

Q.1. Differentiate between Environment and ecology

Ans. i.   The word 'environment' refers to all that is around us, literally everything that surrounds us, including the physical, social, work, and cultural environment.

ii.   'Ecology' is the study of the relationships between living beings and their environment.

Short Answer Type - II   [3 Marks]

Q.1. Explain the different perspectives to understand the human-environment relationship.

Ans. A psycnologist named Stokols proposed three approaches to describe human-environment relationship:

(i) **The Minimalist Perspective:** This view assumes that physical environment has negligible influence on human behaviour. Both run parallel to each other.

(ii) **The Instrumental Perspective:** According to this approach, environment is simply provider. It is for the comfort of us. Human beings can use the environment as per their needs.

(iii) **The Spiritual Perspective:** It refers to the view of the environment as something to be respected and valued rather than exploited. Physical environment and human relationship are interdependent. The traditional Indian view about the environment supports spiritual perspective, worshipping Pipal, respect for rivers and mountains. Chipko Aandolan and movement by Bisnoi Community are examples of Indian perspective.

TOPIC 2

Summary

Environmental Effects on Human Behaviour

The human-environment relationship can be appreciated fully by understanding that the two influence each other, and depend on each other for their survival and maintenance.

- **Environmental influences on perception :** Some aspects of the environment influence human perception.

- **Environmental influences on emotions :** The environment affects our emotional reactions as well. Watching nature in any form, whether it is a quietly flowing river, a smiling flower, or a tranquil mountain top, provides a kind of joy that cannot be matched by any other experience.

- **Ecological influences on occupation,: living style and attitudes :** The natural environment of a particular region determines whether people living in that region rely on agriculture (as in the plains), or on other occupations such as hunting and gathering (as in forest, mountainous or desert regions), or on industries (as in areas that are not fertile enough for agriculture).

- **Human Influence on the Environment :** Human beings also exert their influence on the natural environment for fulfilling their physical needs and other purposes. All the examples of the built environment express human influence over the environment. For example, the human being started building something called 'houses' by changing the natural environment in order to provide shelter for herself/himself.

Noise, pollution, crowding, and natural disasters are some examples of environmental stressors, which are stimuli or conditions in the environment that create a stress for human beings.

Noise

Any sound that is annoying or irritating, and felt to be unpleasant is said to be noise. From common experience it is known that noise, especially for long periods of time, is uncomfortable, and puts people in an unpleasant mood.

Three characteristics of noise have been found to determine its effect on task performance, namely, intensity, predictability, and controllability of noise.

Pollution

Environmental pollution may be in the form of air, water, and soil pollution. Waste or garbage that comes from households or from industries are a big source of air, water, and soil pollution. Scientists know it very well that any of these forms of pollution is hazardous to physical health.

Specific psychological effects of air pollution have been reported by some researchers. For example, in one part of Kolkata, the psychological reactions to air pollution were compared between a group living in an industrial area, and a group living in a non-industrial residential area.

Pollution caused by leaks of dangerous chemical substances can cause other kinds of harm. The infamous Bhopal gas tragedy of December 1984 that claimed many lives also left behind psychological effects because of the gas. Many of those who had inhaled the poisonous gas, methylisocyanate (MIC) along with other substances, showed disturbances in memory, attention and alertness.

The presence of polluting substances in water and soil are hazardous for physical health. Some of these chemicals can also have damaging psychological effects. The presence of specific chemicals such as lead can cause mental retardation by affecting brain development.

Crowding

Most of us are familiar with crowds, which are large informal groups of persons coming together temporarily without any particular goal. For example, when a famous person suddenly appears on the road, people who are present in the situation at the time often collect around the scene, just to watch this person.

The experience of crowding has the following features :

- Feeling of discomfort,
- Loss or decrease in privacy,
- Negative view of the space around the person, and
- Feeling of loss of control over social interaction.

  Edward Hall, an anthropologist, mentioned four kinds of interpersonal physical distance, depending on the situation:
- Intimate distance (upto 18 inches) : The distance you maintain when you are talking privately to someone, or interacting with a very close friend or relative.
- Personal distance (18 inches to 4 feet) : The distance you maintain when you are interacting one-to-one with a close friend, relative, or even with someone not very close to you in a work setting or other social situation.
- Social distance (4 to 10 feet) : The distance you maintain when the interaction is formal, and not close. •Public distance (10 feet to infinity): The distance you maintain in a formal setting, where there is a large number of persons. For example, the distance of an audience from a public speaker, or a teacher in a classroom.

Multiple Choice Questions [1 Mark]

Q.1. Which of the following are not the causes of aggression?

   (a) Inborn tendency

   (b) Frustration

   (c) Child rearing

   (d) Schema

Ans. (d)

Q.2. Frustration-aggression theory was given by______.

   (a) John dollard   (b) Stokols

   (c) Andrew freud   (d) Muller

Ans. (a)

Q.3. Which of the following are not affected by Noise?

   (a) Thinking   (b) Memory

   (c) Learning   (d) Intelligence

Ans. (d)

Very Short Answer Type   [1 Mark]

Q.1. Give some examples of environmental stressor.

Ans. Noise, pollution, crowding, and natural disasters are some examples of environmental stressors, which are stimuli or conditions in the environment that create a stress for human beings.

Q.2. What is post-traumatic stress disorder (PTSD)?

Ans. Natural Disaster influence on human emotions is a traumatic experience that changes people's lives forever, and can last for a very long time after the actual event in the form of post-traumatic stress disorder (PTSD).

Q.3. What is personal space?

Ans. Personal space, or the comfortable physical space one generally likes to maintain around oneself, is affected by a high density environment.

Short Answer Type - I   [2 Marks]

Q.1. Mention any two psychological effect of Pollution.

Ans. i.   Greater tension and anxiety

    ii. Increase the aggression level of individuals.

Q.2. How crowding tolerance is different from competition tolerance?

Ans. i.   Crowding tolerance refers to the ability to mentally deal with a high density or crowded environment, such as a crowded residence (a large number of persons within a small room).

    ii. Competition tolerance is the ability to put up with a situation in which individuals would have to compete with many others for even basic resources, including physical space.

Short Answer Type - II   [3 Marks]

Q.1. Mention any three kinds of kinds of interpersonal physical distance.

Ans. i.   **Intimate distance (upto 18 inches) :** The distance you maintain when you are talking privately to someone, or interacting with a very close friend or relative.

    ii. **Personal distance (18 inches to 4 feet) :** The distance you maintain when you are interacting one-to-one with a close friend, relative, or even with someone not very close to you in a work setting or other social situation.

    iii. **Social distance (4 to 10 feet) :** The distance you maintain when the interaction is formal, and not close.

Q.2. Why personal space is important? Give three reasons for it.

Ans. The concept of personal space is important for the following reasons.

    i.   First, it explains many of the negative effects of crowding as an environmental stressor.

    ii. Second, it tells us about social relationships. For example, two persons sitting or standing close together are seen to be friends or related to each other. When you visit your school library, and if your friend is sitting at a table and the place next to her/him is empty, you like to sit next to her/him. But if a person you do not know is sitting at the table, even if the place next to her/him is empty, it is unlikely that you will sit next to this person.

    iii. Third, it gives us some idea about how physical space can be modified in order to reduce stress or discomfort in social situations, or to make social interaction more enjoyable and fruitful.

Long Answer Type [5 Marks]

Q.1. What is noise? Discuss the effects of noise on human behaviour.

Ans. Noise is defined as an unwanted sound or sounds that create an effective response. Some may not be disturbed by even a loud-speaker sound, on the other hand, some might even find whistle, tinkling of wind as noise. Thus, any sound "which an individual finds unwanted is **noise.**"

Noise (sound pollution) leads to adverse psychological effects. How the noise affect the individual depends on:

(a) its intensity (loudness), loud sound is often unpleasant and irritating.

(b) predictability, we can adapt more easily to a regular, predictable sound such as ' chirping of birds in the morning.

(c) Perceived Control: The negative effects of noise are reduced when individuals perceive that they have control over it.

Effects of noise (sound-pollution) on task performance:

(i) When the task being performed is a simple mental task, such as addition of numbers, noise does not affect overall performance whether it is loud or soft.

(ii) If the task being performed is very interesting, then, too, the presence of noise does not affect performance.

(iii) When the noise comes at intervals and in an unpredictable way, it is experienced as more disturbing than the noise being continuously present.

(iv) Difficult task performance requires full concentration, then intense, unpredictable and uncontrollable noise reduces the level of task performance. '

(v) When switching off the noise is within the control of the person, the numbers of ' errors in task performance decrease.

Q.2. What are the salient features of crowding? Explain the major psychological consequences of crowding.

Ans. Crowding: It is psychological crampedness. It manifests following features:

(a) Feeling of discomfort because of too many people or things around us the experience of physical restriction and sometimes the lack of privacy.

(b) Crowding is the person's reaction to the presence of a large number of persons within a particular area or space.

Features of Crowding; Crowding has the following features:

— Crowding gives feeling of discomfort.

— It gives a feeling that individual privacy is being threatened.

— It gives feeling that individual's personal space is being invaded.

— It gives negative view of a space around the person.

— Crowding develops feelings of loss of control over social interaction.

Crowding is studied by various psychologists in India and abroad.

Crowding is not always experienced in high density setting nor all people experience its negative effects. For example, Mela has high density but still people enjoy it.

Effects of Crowding and High Density:

(a) Crowding and High density may lead to abnormal behaviour and aggression. e.g., an increase in population has sometimes been found to be accompanied by an increase in violent crime.

(b) Crowding leads to **lowered performance on difficult tasks** that involve cognitive processes and has adverse effects on memory and the emotional state.

(c) Children growing up in very crowded households show **lower academic performance.** They also show a weaker tendency to continue working on a task if they are unsuccessful at it, compared to children growing up in non-crowded households. They experience greater conflicts with parents and get less support from their family members.

(d) The **nature of social interaction** determines the degree to which an individual will react to crowding. For example, in parties, large number of persons may not cause stress rather it may lead to positive emotional reactions.

(e) **Individuals** differ in the degree to which they show negative effects of crowding and also in the nature of these reactions.

Two kinds of tolerance can be mentioned that may explain these individual differences: (i) Crowding Tolerance (ii) Competition Tolerance

(i) **Crowding Tolerance;** It refers to the ability of a person to mentally deal with the high density or crowding environment, e.g., crowded residence.

- It is developed because people can use to manage people around them.

- It is modifying ones perception one holds regarding high density/crowded situations.

- Indians in general have more crowding tolerance.

(ii) **Competition Tolerance:** It is the ability to put up with a situation in which individuals would have to compete with many others for even basic resources including physical space.

Since there is a greater possibility of competition for resources in a crowded setting, the reaction to that setting would be influenced by the extent of tolerance for competition for resources.

(iii) Cultural Characteristics: It may determine the extent to which a particular environment is judged to be subjectively more crowded or less crowded.

TOPIC 3

Summary

Natural Disasters

Environmental stressors such as noise, various forms of pollution and crowding are the result of human behaviour.

Common examples of natural disasters are earthquakes, tsunamis, floods, cyclones, and volcanic eruptions. One finds examples of other disasters also, such as wars, industrial accidents such as the leaking of poisonous or radioactive elements in industrial plants, or epidemics (e.g., the plague that affected some parts of our country in 1994).

Promoting Pro-Environmental Behaviour

Pro-environmental behaviour includes both actions that are meant to protect the environment from problems, and to promote a healthy environment.

An American psychologist, John Dollard along with his collaborators, conducted research specifically to examine the frustration-aggression theory. This theory proposes that it is frustration that leads to aggression.

Multiple Choice Questions [1 Mark]

Q.1. ______ is the psychological feeling of not having enough space available.

(a) Group

(b) Team

(c) Crowding

(d) Conjust

Ans. (c)

Q.2. ________ and violence are among the major problems in today's society.

(a) Poverty   (b) Crowding

(c) Aggression   (d) Accident

Ans. (c)

Q.3. The distance you maintain in a formal setting is called______________.

(a) Social distance (b) Public distance

(c) Personal distance (d) Intimate disatence

Ans. (b)

Q.4. Which of the following is not environmental stressor?

(a) Noise (b) Pollution

(c) Crowding (d) Chronic Disease

Ans. (d)

Long Answer Type [5 Marks]

Q.1. Why is the concept of 'personal space' important for human beings? Justify your answer with the help of an example.

Ans. The concept of **personal space** refers to the personal physical distance that we maintain in our social interaction.

It is important for following reasons:

(i) It explains many of the negative effect of crowding as an environment stressor.

(ii) It tells us about social relations. For examples, two people sitting or standing close tighter are seen to be friends.

It gives us idea about how physical space can be modified in order to reduce stress or discomfort in real life situations.

Everyone has desire of personal space. Males generally have a larger personal space than females. Degree of personal space differ from culture to culture.

Personal space can vary between people, between situations and settings and between cultures.

Edward Hall, an anthropologist, mentioned four kinds of interpersonal physical distance—intimate distance, personal distance, social distance and public distance.

Q.2. What is pro-environmental behaviour? How can the environment be protected from pollution? Suggest some strategies.

Ans. **Pro-environmental behaviour** is the friendly and caring attitude of people who help to prevent environmental degradation and conserve natural resources.

For instance, change in life-style and attitude of the people like conserving energy resources, planting trees, reduction in noise (sound-pollution) and air-pollution.

Some Strategies to Protect Environment are:

(i) Reducing air-pollution by keeping vehicle in good condition or changing to non-fuel driven vehicle, stopping the practice of smoking.

(ii) Reducing noise (sound pollution) by ensuring that noise levels are low. e.g., discouraging needless honking on the road, or making rule regarding noisy music at certain hours.

(iii) Planting trees and ensuring their care.

(iv) Reducing the non-biodegradable packing of consumer goods.

(v) Laws related to construction (especially in urban areas) that violate optimal environment design.

(vi) Saying 'no' to plastic use in any form, thus reducing toxic wastes that pollute water, air and the soil.

Chapter Practice

Multiple Choice Questions   [1 Mark]

Q.1. The distance between houses in a colony feature is reflected which environmental design ?

    (a) Social interaction   (b) Human control

    (c) Creativity   (d) Social effect disroder

Q.2. Town planners and civil engineers are example of which environment design?

    (a) Social interaction   (b) Human control

    (c) Creativity   (d) None

Q.3. Which of the following is Public distance ?

    (a) 18 inches to 4 feet   (b) 4 feet to 10 feet

    (c) 10 feet to infinity   (d) Upto 18 inches

Q.4. Burning buses or other public property during a riot is called__________ and ________?

    (a) Deprivation   (b) Violence

    (c) Aggression   (d) Both (b) and (c)

Very Short Answer Type   [1 Mark]

Q.5. What is spiritual perspective in environment design?

Q.6. What is Poverty cycle?

Short Answer Type - I   [2 Marks]

Q.7. What are the major causes of Poverty ?

Q.8. Mention any two features of Post traumatic stress disorder (PTSD) ?

Short Answer Type - II   [3 Marks]

Q.9. Write down any three reactions that people with different intensities to natural disasters?

Q.10. What is interpersonal physical distance? Why there is negative reaction for crowding?

Long Answer Type   [5 Marks]

Q.11. Discuss the psychological impact of television viewing on human behaviour. How can its adverse consequences be reduced? Explain.

Q.12. Distinguish between 'instrumental aggression' and 'hostile aggression'. Suggest some strategies to reduce aggression and violence.

CHAPTER 9

Developing Psychological Skills

Summary

The term 'skill' may be defined as proficiency, facility or dexterity that is acquired or developed through training and experience. The Webster dictionary defines it as "possession of the qualities required to do something or get something done".

American Psychological Association (1973) in their task force constituted with the objective to identify skills essential for professional psychologists recommended at least three sets of skills. These are: assessment of individual differences, behaviour modification skills, and counselling and guidance skills.

Developing As An Effective Psychologis

Generally people pick up such terms from popular writings and media. There are a lot of common sense notions about human behaviour that one develops in the course of their lives.

The basic skills or competencies which psychologists have identified for becoming an effective psychologist fall into three broad sections, namely,

(a) General Skills,

(b) Observational Skills, and

(c) Specific Skills.

General Skills

These skills are generic in nature and are needed by all psychologists irrespective of their field of specialisation. These skills include personal as well as intellectual skills. It is expected that it will not be proper to provide any form of professional training (in clinical or organisational fields) to students who do not possess these skills.

Observational Skills

A psychologist engages in observing various facets of surroundings including people and varying events.

Naturalistic Observation is one of the primary ways of learning about the way people behave in a given setting.

Participant Observation is the variation of the method of naturalistic observation.

Advantages and Disadvantages of Observation

- Its major advantage is that it allows behaviour to be seen and studied in its natural setting.

- People from outside, or those already working in a setting, can be trained to use it.

- One disadvantage of it is that events being observed are subject to bias due to the feelings of the people involved as well as of the observers.

- Generally day-to-day activities in a given setting are fairly routine, which can go unnoticed by the observer.

- Another potential pitfall is that the actual behaviour and responses of others may get influenced by the presence of the observer, thus, defeating the very purpose of observation.

Specific Skills

(a) Communication Skills

- Speaking
- Active listening
- Body language or non-verbal skills

(b) Psychological Testing Skills

(c) Interviewing Skills

(d) Counselling Skills

- Empathy
- Positive regard
- Authenticity

Multiple Choice Questions [1 Mark]

Q.1. _______________ is one of the primary ways of learning about the way people behave in a given setting.

(a) Naturalistic Observation

(b) Participant Observation

(c) Empathy

(d) Authenticity

Ans. (a)

Q.2. Which of the following are not the characteristics of communication?

(a) Dynamic

(b) Continuous

(c) Irreversible

(d) Unpredictable

Ans. (d)

Q.3. The consistency between current and past patterns of behaviour, as well as harmony between verbal and non-verbal communication, is termed as____________;

(a) Cluster

(b) Congruency

(c) Interpretation

(d) Attitude

Ans. (b)

Very Short Answer Type [1 Mark]

Q.1. Define skill

Ans. term 'skill' may be defined as proficiency, facility or dexterity that is acquired or developed through training and experience.

Q.2. What do you understand by general skill?

Ans. These skills are generic in nature and are needed by all psychologists irrespective of their field of specialisation.

Short Answer Type - I [2 Marks]

Q.1. Mention two advantage of observation?

Ans. i.   Its major advantage is that it allows behaviour to be seen and studied in its natural setting.

ii. People from outside, or those already working in a setting, can be trained to use it.

Q.2. Define Naturalistic observation?

Ans. Naturalistic Observation is one of the primary ways of learning about the way people behave in a given setting. Suppose, you want to learn how people behave in response to a heavy discount provided by a company while visiting a shopping mall.

For this, you could visit the shopping mall where the discounted items are showcased and systematically observe what people do and say before and after the purchases have been made.

Q.3. What is Specific skill? Explain with example.

Ans. These skills are core/basic to the field of psychological service.

For example, psychologists working in clinical settings need to be trained in various techniques of therapeutic interventions, psychological assessment, and counselling. Similarly, organisational psychologists working in the organisational context need to have skills in assessment, facilitation and consultation, behavioural skills to bring about individual, group, team and organisational development besides research skills, etc.

TOPIC 2

▉ Summary

Characteristics of Communication

Communication is dynamic because the process is constantly in a state of change. As the expectations, attitudes, feelings, and emotions of the persons who are communicating change, the nature of their communication also changes.

Communication is continuous because it never stops, whether we are asleep or awake we are always processing ideas or thoughts. Our brain remains active.

Communication is irreversible because once we send a message we cannot take it back. Once we have made a slip of tongue, given a meaningful glance, or engaged in an emotional outburst, we cannot erase it. Our apologies or denials can make it light but cannot stamp out what was communicated.

Communication is interactive because we are constantly in contact with other people and with ourselves. Others react to our speech and actions, and we react to our own speech and actions, and then react to those reactions. Thus, a cycle of action and reaction is the basis of our communication.

Intrapersonal communication involves communicating with yourself. It encompasses such activities as thought processes, personal decision making, and focusing on self.

Interpersonal communication refers to the communication that takes place between two or more persons who establish a communicative relationship.

Public communication is characterised by a speaker sending a message to an audience.

Components of Human Communication

When we communicate, we encode (i.e., take ideas, give them meaning and put them into message forms), and send the idea through a channel. It is composed of our primary signal system based on our senses (i.e., seeing, hearing, tasting, smelling, and touching). The message is sent to someone who receives it using her or his primary signal system. S/he decodes (i.e., translates message into understandable forms).

Speaking

One important component of communication is speaking with the use of language. Language involves use of symbols which package meaning within them. To be effective, a communicator must know how to use language appropriately.

Communication takes place within a context. So one needs to consider the other's frame of reference, that is, the context used by the sender to say something

Listening

Listening is an important skill that we use daily. Your academic success, employment achievement, and personal happiness, to a large extent, depend upon your ability to listen effectively. Hearing and listening are not the same. Hearing is a biological activity that involves reception of a message through sensory channels. It is only a part of listening, a process that involves reception, attention, assignment of meaning, and listener's response to the message presented.

Reception

The initial step in the listening process is the reception of a stimulus or message. A message could be auditory and/or visual. The hearing process is based on a complex set of physical interactions that take place involving the ear and the brain.

Attention

Once the stimulus, i.e. the word or visual, or both, is received, it reaches the attention stage of the human processing system.

In this phase, the other stimuli recede so that we can concentrate on specific words or visual symbols. Normally your attention is divided between what you are attempting to listen to, and what is happening around you, and what is going on in your mind.

Paraphrasing

The person in doing this does not repeat your exact words. S/he makes a summary of the ideas just received and provides you with a restatement of what s/he understands. This is called 'paraphrasing'.

Assignment of Meaning

The process of putting the stimulus we have received into some predetermined category develops as we acquire language.

Role of Culture in Listening

Some cultures focus on controlling attention. Buddhism, for instance, has a notion called 'mindfulness'. This means devoting your complete attention to whatever you are doing. Training in 'mindfulness' which starts in childhood can help to develop longer attention spans and therefore, lead not only to better listening but also to sympathetic listening.

Body Language

We all know that it is possible to communicate a great deal even without using verbal language. We are aware that non-verbal acts are symbolic and closely connected to any talk in progress. Such non-verbal acts are part of what is called 'body language'.

Multiple Choice Questions [1 Mark]

Q.1. Which of the following is not an communication?

(a) Interactive (b) Irreversible

(c) Continous (d) Stastical

Ans. (d)

Q.2. _____________ is characterised by a speaker sending a message to an audience.

(a) Communication

(b) Social Communication

(c) Personal communication

(d) Interpersonal

Ans. (c)

Q.3. Which of the following is a Components of Human Communication?

(a) Decode (b) Encode

(c) Barcode (d) Both (a) and (b)

Ans. (d)

Short Answer Type - I [2 Marks]

Q.1. How communication is dynamic?

Ans. Communication is dynamic because the process is constantly in a state of change. As the expectations, attitudes, feelings, and emotions of the persons who are communicating change, the nature of their communication also changes.

Q.2. Define paraphrasing with example.

Ans. When someone is listening to you and told to restate what you said, at that time the person is not able to repeat your exact words/he makes a summary of the ideas just received and provides you with a restatement of what s/he understands. This is called "paraphrasing". It allows you to understand how much s/he understood of what was communicated.

Short Answer Type - II [3 Marks]

Q.1. Mention three characteristics of communication?

Ans. i. Communication is dynamic because the process is constantly in a state of change. As the expectations, attitudes, feelings, and emotions of the persons who are communicating change, the nature of their communication also changes.

ii. Communication is continuous because it never stops, whether we are asleep or awake we are always processing ideas or thoughts. Our brain remains active.

iii. Communication is irreversible because once we send a message we cannot take it back. Once we have made a slip of tongue, given a meaningful glance, or engaged in an emotional outburst, we cannot erase it. Our apologies or denials can make it light but cannot stamp out what was communicated.

Q.2. What is communication? Differentiate between Intrapersonal communication and Interpersonal communication?

Ans. communication is a conscious or unconscious, intentional or unintentional process in which feelings and ideas are expressed as verbal and/or non-verbal messages that are sent, received, and comprehended.

Human communication occurs on the intrapersonal, interpersonal, and public levels.

Intrapersonal communication involves communicating with yourself. It encompasses such activities as thought processes, personal decision making, and focusing on self.

Interpersonal communication refers to the communication that takes place between two or more persons who establish a communicative relationship.

Q.2. Which component of the communication process is most important? Justify your answer with relevant examples.

Ans. The most important component of communication is **speaking** with the use of language.

- Language involves **use of vocabulary which includes words by symbols.**

- **Communicator must know how to use words appropriately in organized and understandable form.**

- **It is necessary to be clear and precise.**

- Communication takes place within a context and needs to consider the other's frame of reference.

- It is important for the speaker to adjust his vocabulary level and choice of words to fit the level of the listener.

- Slang expressions, words unique to a culture, euphemism can become obstacles in good communication.

- Listening may appear as a passive behaviour, as it involves silence. But this is far from true.

- Listening requires a person to be attentive, patient, non-judgmental and have the capacity to analyze and respond.

- It is an active process.

- Hearing and listening are not the same, hearing is biological mechanism. It involves reception of a message through sensory channels.

Q.3. Explain three skills of communication.

Ans: Communication skills is one of the most important skills you will need to succeed in life.

We are going to discuss the following three skills of communication.

1. Speaking

   One important component of communication is speaking with the use of language.

   - To be effective, a communicator must know how to use language appropriately.

   - The communicator has to be clear and precise when using the words.

   - The listener has to understand what the communicator is trying to convey, so it is necessary for the communicator to adjust the vocabulary level and choice of words to

   fit the level of the listener.

2. Active Listening

   Listening is an important skill that we use daily.

   - Your academic success, employment achievement, and personal happiness, to a large extent, depend upon your ability to listen effectively.

   - Listening requires a person to be attentive, patient, non-judgmental and yet have the capacity to analyse and respond.

3. Body Language or non verbal skills

   Body language is composed of all those messages that people exchange besides words.

   - In case of body language a single non-verbal signal does not carry complete meaning.But factors like gestures, postures, eye contact, clothing style, and body movement all together are required.

   - An example is :crossing arms over the chest may suggest that a person likes to keep aloof. But, crossed arms accompanied by an erect posture, tightened body muscles, a set clenched jaw, and narrowing of the eyes are likely to communicate anger.

TOPIC 2

■ Summary

Psychological Testing Skills

The next set of competencies which psychologists require is concerned with the knowledge base of the discipline of psychology. They involve psychological assessment, evaluation and problem solving with individuals and groups, organisation, and the community. Psychologists have always been interested in understanding individual differences from the time of Galton in the late 19th century.

While using psychological tests an attitude of objectivity, scientific orientation, and standardised interpretation must be kept in mind.

Interviewing Skills

An interview is a purposeful conversation between two or more people that follows a basic question and answer format. The employment interview is one which most of you are likely to face. Some other formats are information gathering interview, counselling interview, interrogatory interview, radio-television interview, and research interview.

Opening of the Interview

The opening of interview involves establishing rapport between two communicators. The purpose is to make the interviewee comfortable. Generally, the interviewer starts the conversation and does most of the talking at the outset.

Body of the Interview

The body of the interview is the heart of the process. In this stage, the interviewer asks questions in an attempt to generate information and data that are required for the purpose.

Sequence of Questions

To accomplish the purpose of an interview, the interviewer prepares a set of questions, also called a schedule, for different domains, or categories s/he wants to cover.

Closing the Interview

While closing the interview, the interviewer should summarise what s/he has been able to gather. One should end with a discussion of the next step to be taken. When the interview is ending, the interviewer should give a chance to the interviewee to ask questions or offer comments.

Counselling Skills

Another prerequisite for developing as a psychologist is the competence in the domain of counselling and guidance. In order to develop these competencies, psychologists must undergo proper training and education under guided supervision.

Meaning and Nature of Counselling

Counselling provides a system for planning the interview, analysing the counsellor's and client's behaviour, and determining the developmental impact on the client. A counsellor is most often interested in building an understanding of the clients problem by focusing on what understanding the client has of her/his problem and how s/he feels about it.

Developing Effective Relation-ships

For most people who seek help from a counsellor, effective or satisfying relationships are almost non-existent or infrequent. Since change in behaviour is often created and supported by a network of social support, it is essential for clients to start developing more positive relationships with other persons.

Characteristics of Effective Helper

Authenticity : Your image or perception of yourself makes up your "I". The selfperceived "I" is revealed through ideas, words, actions, clothing, and your life-style. For example, friends tell you what they like and dislike about you. Your teachers and parents praise and/ or criticise you.

Positive Regard for Others: In a counselling-counsellor relationship, a good relationship allows freedom of expression. It reflects acceptance of the idea that the feelings of both are important. We should remember that when we form a new relationship, we experience feelings of uncertainty and anxiety.

Empathy: This is one of the most critical competencies that a counsellor needs to have. It is like stepping into someone else's shoes and trying to understand the pain and troubled feelings of the other person.

Paraphrasing: This skill has already been discussed in the section on communication earlier. You will recall that this involves the ability of a counsellor to reflect on what the client says and feels using different words.

Multiple Choice Questions [1 Mark]

Q.1. Which of the following is not one types of interview questions?

(a) Direct Question

(b) Open ended Question

(c) Bipolar question

(d) Closed ended Question

Ans. (d)

Q.2. ______________ means that your behavioural expressions are consistent.

(a) Empathy   (b) Authenticity

(c) Paraphrasing   (d) Ability to empathise

Ans. (b)

Q.3. Which of the following are bot the characteristics of Effective helper?

(a) Authenticity

(b) Paraphrasing

(c) Positive regard for others

(d) Schema

Ans. (d)

Q.4. Ability to examine and consider one's own motives, attitudes, behaviours is called __________.

(a) Expressive skills   (b) Reflective skills

(c) Personal skills   (d) Affective skills

Ans. (b)

Q.5. Desire to help others, openness to new ideas, honesty is called__________.

(a) Affective skills   (b) Reflective skills

(c) Personal skills   (d) Expressive skills

Ans. (c)

Very Short Answer Type [1 Mark]

Q.1. Define counseling.

Ans. Counselling involves helping relationship, that includes someone seeking help, and someone willing to give help, who is capable of or trained to help in a setting that permits help to be given and received.

Q.2. What is Interview in Psychology?

Ans. An interview is a purposeful conversation between two or more people that follows a basic question and answer format. Interviewing is more formal than most other conversations because it has a preset purpose and uses a focused structure. There are many kinds of interviews. The employment interview is one which most of you are likely to face.

Q.3. Define empathy with an example.

Ans. It is like stepping into someone else's shoes and trying to understand the pain and troubled feelings of the other person.

For example, if your friend loses her iPad and you feel really sad along with her

Short Answer Type - I [2 Marks]

Q.1. Mention two approaches of counseling.

Ans. Two approaches of counseling are as follows:

i. Counselling involves responding to the feelings, thoughts, and actions of the clients.

ii. Counselling involves a basic acceptance of the client's perceptions and feelings, without using any evaluative standards.

Q.2. Mention any two myths of counseling.

Ans. i. Counselling is not selection and placement of individuals onto jobs or for courses.

ii. Counselling is not the same as interviewing though interviewing may be involved.

Short Answer Type - II   [3 Marks]

Q.1. Mention three stages of Interview.

Ans. There is a basic format which is followed, regardless of the interview's purpose; i.e., an interview has three stages:

— Opening — The body — The closing

(a) Opening of the Interview:

1. In involves establishing report between the two communicators, so that the interview becomes comfortable.

2. Generally, the interviewer starts the conversation and does most of the talking at the outset. This serves two functions:

   (a) It establishes the goal of the interview

   (b) It gives the interviewee time to become comfortable with the situation and the interviewer.

(b) Body of the Interview:

1. This is the heart of the process.

2. In this stage, the interviewer asks questions in an attempt to generate information and data that are required to fulfil/required for the purpose.

(c) Closing of the Interview:

While closing the interview, the interviewer should:

1. Summarise what she/he has been able to gather.

2. Give a chance to the interviewee to ask questions or offer comments. One ' should end witfc a discussion of the next step to be taken.

Long Answer Type   [5 Marks]

Q.1. Explain the characteristics of an effective helper.

Ans. The counsellor has the responsibility for ensuring that her/his client is benefited from counselling and its therapeutic effects are achieved. The success of a counselling process depends on the skill, knowledge, attitude, personal qualities and behaviour of a counsellor, any or all of which can enhance or diminish the helping process. There are four qualities associated with effective counsellors. These include: (i) Authenticity, (ii) Positive regard for others, (iii) Ability to empathise, and (iv) Paraphrasing.

Authenticity

Authenticity means that your behavioural expressions are consistent with what you value and the way you feel and relate to your inner self-image. Your image or perception of yourself makes up your "I". The self perceived "I" is revealed through ideas, words, actions, clothing, and your life-style. All of these communicate your "I" to others. Those who come into close contact with you also build their own image of you for themselves, and they also sometimes communicate this image to you. For example, friends tell you what they like and dislike about you. Your teachers and parents praise and/ or criticise you.

Positive Regard for Others

In a counselling-counsellor relationship, a good relationship allows freedom of expression. It reflects acceptance of the idea that the feelings of both are important. We should remember that when we form a new relationship, we experience feelings of uncertainty and anxiety. Such feelings get minimised when a counsellor extends a positive regard to the client by accepting that it is all right to feel the way the client is feeling.

Empathy

Empathy is the ability of a counsellor to understand the feelings of another person from her/his perspective. It is like stepping into someone else's shoes and trying to understand the pain and troubled feelings of the other person.

Paraphrasing

It involves the ability of a counsellor to reflect on what the client says and feels using different words.

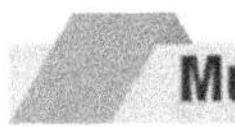

Chapter Practice

Multiple Choice Questions   [1 Mark]

Two statements are given in the question below as Assertion (A) and Reasoning (R). Read the statements and choose the appropriate option

Q.1. **Assertion(A) :** One important component of communication is speaking with the use of language.

Reasons(R) : To be effective, a communicator must know how to use language appropriately.

Options

(a) Both A and R are true, and R is the correct explanation of A.

(b) Both A and R are true, but R is not the correct explanation of A.

(c) A is true, R is false

(d) A is false, R is true

Q.2. Do you think knowledge of a product or communication skill is more important for a salesperson"? is an example of which interview question?

(a) Leading question

(b) Mirror question

(c) Close ended Question

(d) Direct Question

Q.3. ___________and ________________constitute essential ingredients in the counselling setting.

(a) Confidentiality

(b) privacy

(c) Mirror Question

(d) Both (a) and (b)

Q.4. It requires a yes or no response only in which type of interview question?

(a) Leading question   (b) Bipolar question

(c) Close ended Question   (d) Direct Question

Very Short Answer Type   [1 Mark]

Q.5. Define congruency .

Q.6. What is Bipolar Question ?

Short Answer Type - II   [3 Marks]

Q.7. Mention any three types of tips to Improve Your Listening Skills.

Q.8. Mention any three types of Interview Questions?

Long Answer Type   [5 Marks]

Q.9. What is the typical format of a counselling interview?

Q.10. What are the generic skills needed by all psychologists?

OR

What are the intellectual and personal skills required by the therapist to deal with the client.

ANSWERS & SOLUTIONS

Chapter-1

Variations in Psychological Attributes

1. (a) **2.** (b) **3.** (a) **4.** (c)

5. It refers to the measurement of psychological attributes of individuals and their evaluation, wherein multiple ways are involved in comparing the attributes.

6. Robert Sternberg

7. The characteristics of emotionally intelligent persons are :

- Perceive and be sensitive to your own's feelings and emotions.

- Perceive and be sensitive to others people's emotions by paying attention to their tone, body language and facial expressions.

8. As per Gardner , intelligence is not a single entity; rather distinct types of intelligences exist

Here are some important points as what Gardner feels on multiple intelligence.

(a) intelligences are independent of each other.

(b) Different types of intelligence interact and work together to find a solution to a problem.

9.

Psychometric Approach	Information-Processing Approach
This approach considers intelligence as an aggregate of abilities.	This approach deals on how an intelligent person acts.
It expresses the individual's performance in terms of a single index of cognitive abilities.	It mostly focuses mostly on emphasising studying cognitive functions underlying intelligent behaviour.

10. Here is a list that shows the relationship between creativity and intelligence.

- People with high IQ were not necessarily creative,creative ideas could come from persons who did not have a very high IQ.

- The same person, can be creative as well as intelligent but it is not necessary that intelligent ones must be creative.Intelligence, therefore, by itself does not ensure creativity.

- Relationship between creativity and intelligence is positive.

- All creative acts require some minimum ability to acquire knowledge and capacity to comprehend, retain, and retrieve. For example creative writers need facility in dealing with language. The artist must understand the effect that will be produced by a particular technique of painting, a scientist must be able to reason and so on.Hence, a certain level of intelligence is required for creativity but beyond that intelligence does not correlate well with creativity.

11. To know about the hereditary and environment influences on intelligence, the analysis is conducted mainly on twins and adopted children.

The observation are as follows:

- The intelligence of identical twins brought up together mostly shows 90% similarity.

- Twins separated in their childhood also shows similarity in terms of behaviour, personality and intellectual characteristics.

- The intelligence of identical twins brought up in different environments is almost 72%.

- Fraternal twins brought up together shows intelligence similarity of about 60%.

- Brothers and sisters brought up together shows intelligence similarity of about 50%.

- Siblings which are brought up separately shows intelligence similarity of about 25%.

- In case of adopted children intelligence is more close towards their biological parents rather than adoptive parents.As they grow , they slowly start picking up and get closer with intelligence of their adoptive parents.

- Children which are comes from deprived homes and later adopted in families having ,good food , good family background and quality schooling makes their intelligence improved.

So mostly all Psychologists come to a conclusion that intelligence is a product of complex interaction of heredity (nature) and environment (nurture).

12. As per Gardner , intelligence is not a single entity; rather distinct types of intelligences exist

Here are some important points as what Gardner feels on multiple intelligence.

(a)   intelligences are independent of each other.

(b)   Different types of intelligence interact and work together to find a solution to a problem.

Mr Gardner Identified 8 types of intelligence and here are the details:

Linguistic skill involved in using the language, how well he/she reads, speaks, writes and understand others.Poet and Writers are very strong in linguistic intelligence.

Logical-Mathematical skill mainly possess problem solving ability, very high on thinking logically,good at abstract reasoning and can solve mathematical problems with ease.Scientists and Nobel prize winners are good example with Logical-Mathematical Intelligence.

Spatial skill is more of understanding visual images and patterns. It refers to the abilities involved in forming, using, and transforming mental images. Pilots, sailors, sculptors, painters, architects, interior decorators, and surgeons are likely to have highly developed spatial intelligence.

Musical skill has more detail understanding of producing, creating and manipulating musical patterns. Persons high on this intelligence are very sensitive to sounds and vibrations, and in creating new patterns of sounds.

Bodily-Kinaesthetic is to make use of your whole body for problem solving or construction of products.Athletes, dancers, actors, sportspersons, gymnasts, and surgeons are likely to have such kind of intelligence

Interpersonal skill involves understanding behaviours , their motives , feelings and form a comfortable relationship with others. Psychologists, counsellors, politicians, social workers, and religious leaders are likely to possess high interpersonal intelligence

Intrapersonal skill deals with knowing one's internal strengths and limitations and using that knowledge to effectively relate to others. Philosophers and spiritual leaders present examples of this type of intelligence.

Naturalistics skill involves awareness of our relationship with natural world, i.e. analysing the beauty of species present, flora and fauna etc. Hunters, farmers, tourists, botanists, zoologists, and bird watchers possess more of naturalistic intelligence.

Chapter-2

Self and Personality

1. (c)   **2.** (b)   **3.** (a)   **4.** (b)

5. As an individual we always judge its value or worth, this judgment that we pass on ourselves is called self-esteem.

6. The Humanistic approach focuses on subjective experiences of individuals and their choices. Rogers emphasised the relationship between the 'real self' and the 'ideal self'. The congruence of these selves makes a person fully functioning. Maslow discussed personality in terms of the interplay of needs that motivated people. The needs could be arranged in a hierarchy from lower-order (survival related) needs to higher-order (development related) needs.

7. The psychoanalytic theory tells us that a large part of human behaviour is governed by unconscious motives. Direct methods of personality assessment cannot uncover the unconscious part of our behaviour.

   Projective techniques were developed to assess unconscious motives and feelings. These techniques are based on the assumption that a less structured or unstructured stimulus or situation will allow the individual to project her/his feelings, desires and needs on to that situation.

8. Psychodynamic theories face strong criticisms from many quarters. The major criticisms are as follows:

   (1) The theories are largely based on case studies; they lack a rigorous scientific basis.

   (2) They use small and atypical individuals as samples for advancing generalisations.

9. In case of interactional approach

   - Situation plays a very important role in determining our behaviour.

   - People will behave in a different way based on the reward / punishment on that particular situation.

   - The cross situational consistency of traits is found to be quite low.

   - The influence of situations can be noted by observing people's behaviour in places like a market, a courtroom, or a place of worship.

10. According to Freud's theory, the primary structural elements of personality are three, i.e. id, ego, and superego.

    i. Id : It is the source of a person's instinctual energy. It deals with immediate gratification of primitive needs, sexual desires and aggressive impulses. It works on the pleasure principle, which assumes that people seek pleasure and try to avoid pain.

    ii. Ego : It grows out of id, and seeks to satisfy an individual's instinctual needs in accordance with reality. It works by the reality principle, and often directs the id towards more appropriate ways of behaving.

    iii. Superego : The best way to characterise the superego is to think of it as the moral branch of mental functioning. The superego tells the id and the ego whether gratification in a particular instance is ethical.

11. • Observational method is a very powerful tool of psychological enquiry. It is an effective method of describing behaviour.

    • A scientific observation differs from day-to-day observation in many respects,

      (i) **Selection:** Psychologists do not observe all the behaviour that they encounter. Rather, they select a particular behaviour for observation.

      (ii) **Recording:** While observing, a researcher records the selected behaviour using different means, such as marking tallies for the already identified behaviour whenever they occur, taking notes describing each activity in greater detail using short hand or symbols, photographs, video recording, etc.

      (iii) After the observations have been made, psychologists analyse whatever they have recorded with a view to derive some meaning out of it.

      (iv) Observation is a skill. A good observation is a skill. A good observer knows what he/she is looking for, w'hom he/she wants to observe, when and where the observation needs to be made.

    • Observation can be of the following types :

    (a) Non-Participant vs. Participant Observation:

1. **Non-participant observation**

   (i) To observe the person or event from a distance.

   (ii) The observer may become part of the group being observed.

(iii) In the first case, the person being observed may not be aware that he/she is being observed. For example, you want to observe the pattern of interaction between teachers and students in a particular class..

(iv) Install a video camera to record the classroom activities, which you can see later and analyse. Alternatively, you may decide to sit in a corner of the class without interfering or participating in their everyday activities. This type of observation is called **non-participant observation.**

2. **Participant observation**

(i) In participant observation, the observer becomes a part of the school or the group of people being observed.

(ii) the observer takes some time to establish a rapport with the group so that they start accepting him/her as one of the group members.

(iii) the degree of involvement of the observer with the group being observed would vary depending upon the focus of the study.

The advantage of the observation method is that it enables the researcher to study people and their behaviour in a naturalistic situation, as it occurs. However, the observation method is labour-intensive, time-consuming, and is susceptible to the observer's bias. Our observation is influenced by our values and beliefs about the person or the event.

- **Acquiescence:** It is a tendency of the subject to agree with items/questions irrespective of contents.

- Testing and understanding personality require great skill and training.

- People become self-aware and conscious, hesitate to share thoughts and feelings and motivation. If they do it, it is done in a socially desirable manner. So, the real personality characteristics are not manifested.

12. Arihant wants to become a singer even though he belongs to a family of doctors. His family 'claims' to love him, but disapproves of his choice of career.

This fact warrants my attention towards an important terminology given by Carl **Rogers,** i.e., unconditional positive regard.

As the desire of Arihant to become a singer is contradicted by his family, it results in a situation of negative social conditions which will reduce his level of self-concept and self¬esteem.

His inability to fulfil his goal will prevent him from becoming a 'fully functioning person'. Moreover, his conception of an 'ideal self' involves him being a singer, while his 'real self' is not one due to familial pressure. This discrepancy between the real and ideal self results in dissatisfaction and unhappiness.

The provision of unconditional positive regard which includes empathy, love and warmth irrespective of other factors is necessary for Arihant.

According to **Rogers**, a person attains self-actualization only when people have reached their own fullest potential.

His inability to pursue singing will not allow self-actualization to occur which will prevent his psychological health and well-being.

Chapter-3

Meeting Life Challenges

1. (b)   2. (c)   3. (b)   4. (d)

5. 'Eustress' is the term used to describe the level of stress that is good for you and is one of a person's best assets for achieving peak performance and managing minor crisis.

6. Lazarus has distinguished between two types of appraisal, i.e. primary and secondary.

(i) Primary appraisal refers to the perception of a new or changing environment as positive, neutral or negative in its consequences.

(ii) When we perceive an event as stressful, we are likely to make a secondary appraisal, which is the assessment of one's coping abilities and resources and whether they will be sufficient to meet the harm, threat or challenge of the event.

7. **Some of these techniques are:**

Relaxation Techniques : It is an active skill that reduces symptoms of stress and decreases the incidence of illnesses such as high blood pressure and heart disease. Usually relaxation starts from the lower part of the body and progresses up to the facial muscles in such a way that the whole body is relaxed. Deep breathing is used along with muscle relaxation to calm the mind and relax the body.

Meditation Procedures : The yogic method of meditation consists of a sequence of learned techniques for refocusing of attention that brings about an altered state of consciousness. It involves such a thorough concentration that the meditator becomes unaware of any outside stimulation and reaches a different state of consciousness.

8. Some of the important sources of psychological stress are frustration, conflicts, internal and social pressures, etc.

(i) Frustration results from the blocking of needs and motives by something or someone that hinders us from achieving a desired goal.

(ii) Conflicts may occur between two or more incompatible needs or motives, e.g. whether to study dance or psychology.

(iii) Internal pressures stem from beliefs based upon expectations from inside us to ourselves such as, 'I must do everything perfectly'.

9. Life Events Changes, both big and small, sudden and gradual affect our life from the moment we are born. We learn to cope with small, everyday changes but major life events can be stressful, because they disturb our routine and cause upheaval.

Hassles These are the personal stresses we endure as individuals, due to the happenings in our daily life, such as noisy surroundings, commuting, quarrelsome neighbours, electricity and water shortage, traffic snarls, and so on.

Traumatic Events These include being involved in a variety of extreme events such as a fire, train or road accident, robbery, earthquake, tsunami, etc.

10. **Physiological Effects :** When the human body is placed under physical or psychological stress, it increases the production of certain hormones such as adrenaline and cortisol. It causes:

- Changes in heart-rate, blood-pressure levels, metabolism and physical activity.
- Slowing down of digestive system.
- Constriction of blood vessels.

Cognitive Effects : High levels of stress can lead to:

- Mental overload.
- Impairment in the ability to make sound decision.
- Poor concentration.
- Reduced short term memory.

Emotional Effects : Those who suffer from stress are more likely to experience:

- Mood swings.
- Erratic behaviour.
- Maladjustment with family and friends.
- Feeling of anxiety and depression.
- Increased physical and psychological tension.
- Intolerance.
- Impatience.

Behavioural Effects : Stress affects our behaviour in the form of:

- Eating less nutritional food.
- Increasing intake of stimulants such as caffeine or excessive consumption of cigarettes, alcohol and drugs.
- Disrupted sleep pattern.
- Reduced work performance.

11. Factors facilitating positive health and well-being are:

1. **Diet :** Diet can affect health independently or may enhance or modify the effects of stress in combination with other factors:

    (a) How much nutrition one needs depends on one's activity level, genetic structure,climate and health history. In fact, there is no one diet, which is ideal for everyone, in all situations.

    (b) Stress is supposed to affect diet and weight in many wrays. People, who are under stress or in a negative moods are often seen eating more. They seek 'comfort foods' or foods that make them feel better.

    (c) Stress may increase consumption of less healthy foods. Such people gain weight and loose stamina to fight stress.

    (d) Obesity and weight gain is a problem for a section of the society. A much larger section of the society, which is below the poverty line, suffer from malnutrition.

    (e) In the condition of poverty, women are the one who are most malnourished. Studies have shown that in India diets of female children and women are inadequate due to discriminatory practices.

2. **Exercise :**
    - Exercise is directly related to promoting positive health.
    - Two kinds of physical exercises essential for good health are 'stretching exercises' such as yogic asanas and 'aerobic exercises' such as jogging, swimming and cycling.
    - Stretching exercises have a calming effect.
    - Aerobic exercises increase the arousal level of the body.
    - Yogic asanas provide systematic stretching to all the muscles and joints of the body and massages the glands and other body organs.

    - Regular exercise reduces stress because it improves efficiency of vital body organs and improves immune system.
    - Positive health and well-being come through a positive attitude of the mind.
    - Positive health is the state of complete physical, mental, social and spiritual well¬being. It is not merely the absence of disease.
    - Positive health comprises high quality of personal relationships, a sense of purpose in life, self regard, mastery of life skills and resilience to stress, trauma and change.

3. **Positive Attitude :** Positive health and well-being can be realized by:
    - Perceiving the reality fairly accurately.
    - Tolerating and understanding different points of view.
    - Having a sense of purpose in life.
    - Having a sense of responsibility, accepting blame for failures and taking credit for success.
    - Being open to new ideas, activities, or ways of doing things.
    - Having a good sense of humour, to be able to laugh at oneself and absurdities of life helps to see things in their proper perspective.

4. **Positive Thinking :**
    - Positive thinking leads to a belief that adversity can be handled successfully whereas negative thinking and pessimism anticipate disaster.
    - Optimism, which is the inclination to expect favourable life outcomes is directly linked to psychological and physical well-being.
    - Optimists use more problem-focused coping and seek advice and help from others. This optimism function helps the individual to cope up stress effectively.

Chapter-4

Psychological Disorders

1. (c)   **2.** (a)   **3.** (b)   **4.** (d)

5. You might have met or heard of someone who was afraid to travel in a lift or climb to the tenth floor of a building, or refused to enter a room if s/he saw a lizard. You may have also felt it yourself or seen a friend unable to speak a word of a well-memorised and rehearsed speech before an audience. These kinds of fears are termed as phobias.

6. Another psychological model is the humanistic-existential model which focuses on broader aspects of human existence. Humanists believe that human beings are born with a natural tendency to be friendly, cooperative and constructive, and are driven to self-actualise, i.e. to fulfil this potential for goodness and growth.

7. Suicide can be prevented by being alert to some of the symptoms which include :

- changes in eating and sleeping habits
- withdrawal from friends, family and regular activities
- violent actions, rebellious behaviour, running away
- drug and alcohol abuse

8. Panic Disorder : frequent anxiety attacks characterised by feelings of intense terror and dread; unpredictable 'panic attacks' along with physiological symptoms like breathlessness, palpitations, trembling, dizziness, and a sense of losing control or even dying

9.
- Heroin intake significantly interferes with social and occupational functioning.
- Most abusers further develop a dependence on heroin, revolving their lives around the substance, building up a tolerance for it, and experiencing a withdrawal reaction when they stop taking it.
- The most direct and stopping it results in feelings of depression, fatigue, sleep problems, irritability and anxiety.
- Cocaine poses serious dangers. It has dangerous effects on psychological functioning and physical well-being.

10. Hypochondriasis

- Patients with hypochondriasis disorder has a persistent belief that s/he has a serious illness, despite medical reassurance, lack of physical findings, and failure to develop the disease.
- Hypochondriacs have an obsessive preoccupation and concern with the condition of their bodily organs, and they continually worry about their health.

Conversion disorder

- The symptoms of conversion disorders are the reported loss of part or all of some basic body functions.
- Paralysis, blindness, deafness and difficulty in walking are generally among the symptoms reported.

11. Dissociation can be viewed as a severe connections between ideas and emotions.

Dissociation involves feelings of unreality, estrangement, depersonalisation, and sometimes a loss or shift of identity.

Four conditions are included in this group:

- Dissociative amnesia: is characterised by extensive but selective memory loss that has no known organic cause (e.g., head injury).
- Dissociative fugue: has, as its essential feature, an unexpected travel away from home and workplace, the assumption of a new identity, and the inability to recall the previous identity.
- Dissociative identity disorder:often referred to as multiple personality, is the most dramatic of the dissociative disorders. It is often associated with traumatic experiences in childhood.
- Depersonalisation:involves a dreamlike state in which the person has a sense of being separated both from self and from reality.

12. • Negative symptoms of Schizophrenia are "pathological deficits" and include poverty of speech, blunted and flat affect, loss of volition, and social withdrawal.

• People with schizophrenia show alogia or poverty of speech, i.e. a reduction in speech and speech content.

• People with schizophrenia show less anger, sadness, joy, and other feelings than most people do. Thus they have blunted affect.

• Some show no emotions at all, a condition known as flat affect.

• Also patients with schizophrenia experience avolition, or apathy and an inability to start or complete a course of action.

• People with this disorder may withdraw socially and become totally focused on their own ideas and fantasies.

Chapter-5

Therapeutic Approaches

1. (d)   **2.** (a)   **3.** (b)   **4.** (d)

5. Logos is the Greek word for soul and Logotherapy means treatment for the soul. Victor Frankl, a psychiatrist and neurologist propounded the Logotherapy.

6. Non-specific factors attributable to the therapist are positive nature, absence of unresolved emotional conflicts, presence of good mental health, etc. These are called therapist variables.

7. Psychological disorders such as anxiety, depression, panic attacks, and borderline personality are treated with the help of Cognitive behaviour Therapy.

8. In occupational therapy, patients are taught skills such as

• candle making,

• paper bag making and

• weaving to help them to form a work discipline.

9. **(i)** there is systematic application of principles underlying the different theories of therapy,

(ii) persons who have received practical training under expert supervision can practice psychotherapy, and not everybody. An untrained person may unintentionally cause more harm than any good

(iii) the therapeutic situation involves a therapist and a client who seeks and receives help for her/his emotional problems (this person is the focus of attention in the therapeutic process)

10. Unconditional positive regard is the relation that the therapist shows towards the client during treatment. The therapist conveys by her/his words and behaviours that s/he is not judging the client and will continue to show the same positive feelings towards the client even if the client is rude or confides all the 'wrong' things that s/he may have done or thought about.

The therapist encourages this by being accepting, empathic, genuine and warm to the client.

11. • Systematic desensitisation is a technique introduced by Wolpe for treating phobias or irrational fears.

• The client is interviewed to elicit fear provoking situations and together with the client, the therapist prepares a hierarchy of anxiety-provoking stimuli with the least anxiety-provoking stimuli at the bottom of the hierarchy.

• The therapist relaxes the client and asks the client to think about the least anxiety-provoking situation.

• The client is asked to stop thinking of the fearful situation if the slightest tension is felt.

• Over sessions, the client is able to imagine more severe fear provoking situations while maintaining the relaxation.

• The client gets systematically desensitised to the fear.

12. • The treatment of psychological disorders has two components, i.e. reduction of symptoms, and improving the level of functioning or quality of life.

    • The patient with severe disorders like schizophrenia suffer from negative symptoms such as disinterest and lack of motivation to do work or to interact with people.Such patient needs rehabilitation to become self-sufficient.

    • The aim of rehabilitation is to empower the patient to become a productive member of society to the extent possible.

    • In rehabilitation, the patients are given occupational therapy, social skills training, and vocational therapy.

    • In occupational therapy, the patients are taught skills such as candle making, paper bag making and weaving to help them to form a work discipline.

    • Social skills training helps the patients to develop interpersonal skills through role play, imitation and instruction.

    • Cognitive retraining is given to improve the basic cognitive functions of attention, memory and executive functions.

    • Vocational training is given wherein the patient is helped to gain skills necessary to undertake productive employment.

Chapter-6

Attitude and Social Cognition

1. (d)   2. (c)   3. (b)   4. (b)

5. A distinction is also found between the attribution that a person makes for her/ his own positive and negative experiences (actor-role), and the attribution made for another person's positive and negative experiences (observer-role). This is called the actor-observer effect.

6. In some cases, the group that is the target of prejudice is itself responsible for continuing the prejudice. The target group may behave in ways that justify the prejudice, that is, confirm the negative expectations. For example, if the target group is described as 'dependent' and therefore unable to make progress, the members of this target group may actually behave in a way that proves this description to be true.

7. Thus, the strategies for handling prejudice would be effective if they aim at :

    (a) minimising opportunities for learning prejudices,

    (b) changing such attitudes

8. The two-step concept was proposed by S.M. Mohsin, an Indian psychologist. According to him, attitude change takes place in the form of two steps. In the first step, the target of change identifies with the source. The 'target' is the person whose attitude is to be changed. The 'source' is the person through whose influence the change is to take place.

9. • Pro-social behaviour is based on an inborn, natural tendency in human beings to help other members of their own species. This inborn tendency facilitates survival of the species.

    • Pro-social behaviour is influenced by learning. Individuals who are brought up in a family environment that sets examples of helping others, shows more prosocial behaviour than individuals who are brought up in a family environment devoid of these features.

    • Cultural factors influence pro-social behaviour. Some cultures actively encourage people to help the needy and distressed.In cultures that encourage independence, individuals will show less pro-social behaviour, because people are expected to take care of themselves, and not to depend on help from others.

    • Pro-social behaviour is affected by the expected reactions of the person who is being helped. For example, people might be unwilling to give money to a needy person because they feel that the person might feel insulted, or may become dependent.

10. Social psychologists have shown that prejudice has one or more of the following sources :

- **Learning :** Like other attitudes, prejudices can also be learned through association, reward and punishment, observing others, group or cultural norms and exposure to information that encourages prejudice.

- **A strong social identity and ingroup bias :** Individuals who have a strong sense of social identity and have a very positive attitude towards their own group boost this attitude by holding negative attitudes towards other groups.

- **Scapegoating :** This is a phenomenon by which the majority group places the blame on a minority outgroup for its own social, economic or political problems.

11. Actor observer phenomena refers to the tendency to attribute our own behaviour mainly to situational causes but the behaviour of others mainly to internal (dispositional) cause.

A distinction is found between the attribution that a person makes for actorrole and observer-role.

Person makes attribution for his/her own positive and negative experiences, it is actor role and the attribution made for another person's positive and negative experience is observer-role.

For example, if we get good marks, we will attribute it to our own ability and hard work (actor-role, internal attribution for a positive experience). If we get bad marks, we will say we were unlucky or test was difficult (actor-role, external attribution for negative experience).

On the other hand, if our classmate gets good marks, we will attribute his/her success to good luck or easy test (observer-role, external attribution for positive experience). If same classmate gets bad marks, we are likely to feel that his/her failure was because of low ability or due to lack of effort (observer-role, internal attribution for a negative experience).

The reason for the difference between the actor and observer roles is that people want to have a nice image of themselves, as compared to others.

12.
- "Social cognition" refers to all those psychological processes that deal with the gathering and processing of information related to social objects.

- These include all the processes that help in understanding, explaining and interpreting social behaviour.

- The processing of information related to social objects (particularly individuals, groups, people, relationships, social issues, and the like) differs from the processing of information related to physical objects.

- People as social objects may themselves change as the cognitive process takes place.

- For example a teacher who observes a student in school may draw conclusions differently than that of her mother at home. The student may show a difference in her/his behaviour, depending on who is watching her/him the teacher or the mother.

Schemas in Social Cognition

Social cognition is guided by mental units called schemas.

- A schema is defined as a mental structure that provides a framework, set of rules or guidelines for processing information about any object.

- Schemas (or 'schemata') are the basic units stored in our memory, and function as shorthand ways of processing information, thus reducing the time and mental effort required in cognition.

- Most of the schemas are in the form of categories or classes. Schemas that function in the form of categories are called prototypes which are the entire set of features or qualities that help us to define an object completely.

- In social cognition, category-based schemas that are related to groups of people are called stereotypes.

- An example is, suppose you have to define a group G. If you have never directly known or interacted with a member of this group, you will most likely use your 'general knowledge' about the typical member of group G. To that information you will add your likes and dislikes.If you have heard more positive things about group G, then your social schema about the whole group will be more positive and negative if you have heard negative information about that group i.e negative stereotype.

Chapter-7

Social Influence and Group Processes

1. (a) **2.** (b) **3.** (a) **4.** (b)

5. A group gets stronger as a result of discussions in the group. This strengthening of the group's initial position as a result of group interaction and discussion is referred to as group polarisation.

6. Norms are expected standards of behaviour and beliefs established, agreed upon, and enforced by group members.

In your family, there are norms that guide the behaviour of family members.

These norms represent shared ways of viewing the world.

7. • Groupthink is a consequence of Extreme cohesiveness.

- Groupthink is characterised by the appearance of consensus or unanimous agreement within a group.

- Groupthink is likely to occur in socially homogeneous, cohesive groups that are isolated from outsiders.

- Studies have shown that such a group has an exaggerated sense of its own power to control events, and tends to ignore or minimise cues from the real world that suggest danger to its plan.

8. The foot-in-the-door technique : The person begins by making a small request that the other person is not likely to refuse. Once the other person carries out the request, a bigger request is made. Simply because the other person has already complied with the smaller request, he or she may feel uncomfortable refusing the second request. For example, someone may come to us on behalf of a group and give us a gift (something free), saying that it is for promotion.

9. Roles

- Roles are socially defined expectations that individuals in a given situation are expected to fulfil.

- Roles refer to the typical behaviour that depicts a person in a given social context.

- In a role of a son or a daughter there are certain role expectations when in that role.

- An example is , as a daughter or a son, you are expected to respect elders, listen to them, and be responsible towards your studies.

Norms

- Norms are expected standards of behaviour and beliefs established, agreed upon, and enforced by group members.

- They may be considered as a group's "unspoken rules".

- In your family, there are norms that guide the behaviour of family members.

- These norms represent shared ways of viewing the world.

10. Basic to group formation is some contact and some form of interaction between people.

This interaction is facilitated by the following conditions:

Proximity

Repeated interactions with the same set of individuals give us a chance to know them, and their interests and attitudes. Common interests, attitudes, and background are important determinants of your liking for your group members.

Similarity

- Being exposed to someone over a period of time makes us assess our similarities and paves the way for formation of groups.

- The reason given by psychologist for group formation between similar people or liking between similar people is when two people are similar, there is consistency and they start liking each other.For example, you like playing football and another person in your class also loves playing football; there is a matching of your interests. There are higher chances that you may become friends.

- Another explanation given by psychologists is that when we meet similar people, they reinforce and validate our opinions and values, we feel we are right and thus we start liking them.

Common motives and goals

- When people have common motives or goals, they get together and form a group which may facilitate their goal attainment.

- Suppose you want to teach children in a slum area who are unable to go to school.You cannot do this alone because you have your own studies and homework. You, therefore, form a group of like-minded friends and start teaching these children. So you have been able to achieve what you could not have done alone.

11. Asch examined how much conformity there would be when one member of a group experiences pressure from the rest of the group to behave in a specific way, or to give a particular judgment. A group of seven persons participated in an experiment that was a 'vision test'. There was actually only one true subject. The other six participants were associates of the experimenter, or 'confederates' as they are called in social psychology. These confederates were given instructions to give specific responses. Of course, this was not known to the true subject. All participants were shown a vertical line (standard line) that had to be compared with three vertical lines of different lengths, A, B, and C (comparison lines). Participants had to state which of the comparison lines, A, B, or C, was equal to the standard line

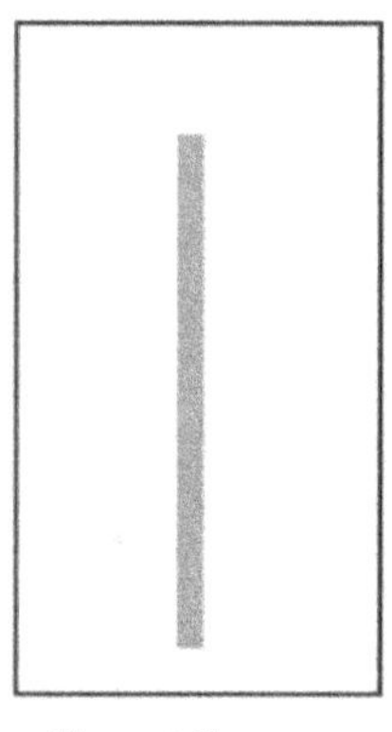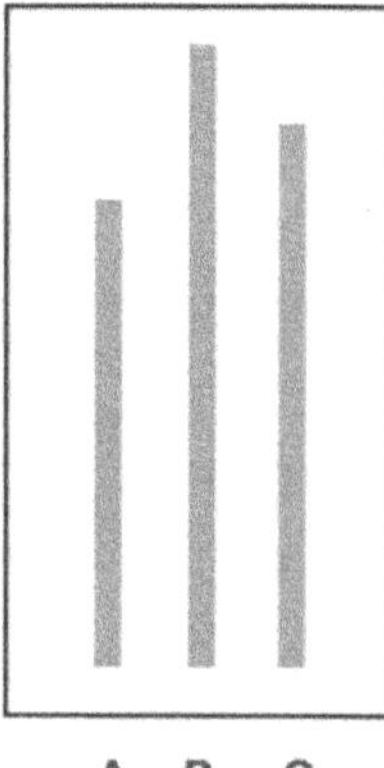

When the experiment began, each participant, by turn, announced her/his answer. The first five persons gave wrong answers (as they had been instructed to do so). The true subject's turn came last-but-one in each round. So the true subject had the experience of 5 persons giving incorrect answers before her/him. The last person (also a confederate) gave the same incorrect answer as the first five persons. Even if the true subject felt that these answers were incorrect, a norm had been presented to her/him. There were twelve trials.

It was observed that 67 per cent subjects showed conformity, and gave the same incorrect answer as the majority. Remember that this was a situation in which the answers were to be given publicly

Chapter-8

Psychology and Life

1. (a)   **2.** (c)   **3.** (c)   **4.** (d)

5. The spiritual perspective refers to the view of the environment as something to be respected and valued rather than exploited. It implies that human beings recognise the interdependent relationship between themselves and the environment, i.e. human beings will exist and will be happy only as long as the environment is kept healthy and natural.

6. The poverty cycle is another important cause of poverty that explains why poverty tends to continue among the same sections of society. Poverty begets poverty. Beginning with a low income and lack of resources, the poor go through low health and nutrition, lack of education, and lack of skills.

7. Major causes of Poverty are as follows :

   i.   Poverty is sometimes caused by natural disasters such as earthquakes, floods, and cyclones, or man-made disasters such as poisonous gas leaks.

   ii. When such events take place, people suddenly lose all their possessions and have to face poverty.

8. This disorder has the following features:

   i.   The immediate reaction to a disaster is commonly one of disorientation. People take some time to understand the full meaning of what the disaster has done to them.

   ii. Physical reactions, such as bodily exhaustion even without physical activity, difficulty in sleeping, change in the eating pattern, increased heartbeat and blood pressure, and getting startled easily can be found among the victims.

9. As in the case of the other environmental stressors, people react with different intensities to natural disasters.

In general, the intensity of reaction is affected by :

- The severity of the disaster, and the loss incurred (both in terms of property and life),

- The individual's general coping ability,

- Other stressful experiences before the disaster. For example, people who have experienced stress before may find it more difficult to deal with yet another difficult and stressful situation.

10. In social situations, human beings like to maintain a certain physical distance from the person with whom they are interacting. This is called interpersonal physical distance, and is a part of a broader concept called personal space, i.e. the physical space we like to have all around us.

One reason for the negative reactions to crowding, as described earlier, is the decrease in personal space. Personal space can vary between people, between situations and settings, and between cultures. Some average distances have been observed in certain cultures.

11. Television is one of the useful products of technological progress. It has both positive and negative effects. It has effects on cognitive processes and social behaviour.

   1. **T.V. provides large amount of information** in an attractive form and in visual mode, for which it became a powerful medium of instructions.

   2. Excellent programmes emphasise positive interpersonal attitudes and provide useful factual information, teaching children how to design and construct certain objects.

   3. T.V. watching may have an adverse effect on children's ability to concentrate on one target. Their creativity and ability to understand each other through social interaction is also significantly impaired.

4. Reduction in habit of reading and writing skills and also their outdoor activities such as playing is also reduced.

5. Watching violence on T.V. has been linked to greater aggressiveness in the viewers. As children are not mature enough to think of consequences, they simply imitate.

   - Some studies pointed out that merely watching violence on the television does not make children more aggressive. Other factors need to be present.

   - Other research findings show that watching violence may actually reduce the natural aggressive tendency of the viewers: what is 'bottled up' gets an outlet, thus cleans the system. This process is called **catharsis.**

6. Due to T.V. watching, consumerist attitude has developed. Numerous products are advertised and it is very natural for the viewer to get carried away.

12. **Aggression:** According to psychologists, **aggression** refers to any behaviour by a person that is intended to cause harm to another person or persons to take revenge. For example, aggression It can be demonstrated in actual action or through the use of harsh words or criticism or even hostile feelings against others.

    - **Violence:** Forceful destructive behavior towards another person or persons to attain some material gain is violence.

Instrumental Aggression:

The act of aggression is meant to obtain a certain goal or get others, possessions forcefully. For example, A bully slaps a new student in school so that he can snatch the new comer's chocolate. In violence, individual may or may not have the intention to harm others in terms of revenge. It is forceful destructive behaviour, e.g., hitting a person just to loot his money.

Hostile Aggression:

An expression of anger towards the target, with the intention of harming him/her even if the aggressor does not wish to obtain anything from the victim. For example, A criminal may beat up a person in the community for mentioning his name to the police. Aggression can be reduced by creating the appropriate attitude towards the general problem of growing aggression.

(a) **Parenting:**

   - Parents and teacher should be specially careful not to encourage aggression in any form. The use of punishment to bring about discipline also needs to be changed.

(b) **Modelling:**

   - Opportunities to observe and imitate the behaviour of aggressive models should be reduced drastically.

Portraying aggression as heroic behaviour should be particularly avoided because this may set the stage for learning through observation.

(c) **Implementing social justice and equality in society:**

   - It will help in reducing frustration levels and thereby curb aggressive tendencies at least to some extent.

(d) Inculcating **positive attitude** towards peace at the level of community or society. The father of our nation, Mahatma Gandhi, gave the world a new view to peace that was not simply the absence of aggression. This was non-violence. It should be taught to the younger generation.

Chapter-9

Developing Psychological Skills

1. (a)   2. (c)   3. (d)   4. (b)

5. A person's background and past patterns of behaviour are also considered when we analyse body language. The consistency between current

and past patterns of behaviour, as well as harmony between verbal and non-verbal communication, is termed as congruency.

6. It is a form of close-ended question. It requires a yes or no response. For example, "Would you like to work for the company?"

7. i. Recognise that both the sender as well as the receiver have equal responsibility in making effective communication.

   ii. Refrain from forming an early judgment about information that is being communicated. Be open to all ideas.

   iii. Be a patient listener. Do not be in a hurry to respond.

8. i. Direct Question: They are explicit and require specific information. For example, "Where did you last work?

   ii. " Open-ended Question: They are less direct and specify only the topic. For example, "How happy were you with your job on the whole?"

   iii. Close-ended Question: They provide response alternatives, narrowing the response variations. For example, "Do you think knowledge of a product or communication skill is more important for a salesperson?"

9. Interview refers to purposeful conversation through face-to-face interactions.

   - It follows a basic question-answer format.

   - First, the objectives of the interview are set.

   - The interviewer then prepares on interview format.

   - There is a basic format which is followed, regardless of the interview's purpose; i.e., an interview has three stages:

   — Opening — The body — The closing

A. Opening of the Interview:

1. In involves establishing report between the two communicators, so that the interview becomes comfortable.

2. Generally, the interviewer starts the conversation and does most of the talking at the outset. This serves two functions:

   (a) It establishes the goal of the interview

   (b) It gives the interviewee time to become comfortable with the situation and the interviewer.

B. Body of the Interview:

1. This is the heart of the process.

2. In this stage, the interviewer asks questions in an attempt to generate information and data that are required to fulfil/required for the purpose.

Sequence of Questions:

To accomplish the purpose of an interview, the interviewer prepares set of questions – called a schedule for different domains or categories he/she wants to cover.

1. To form the schedule, the interviewer must first decide on the domain/categories under which information is to be generated. For example for questions used in job interview (box 9.5), the interviewer selected various categories such as not use' of the organization last worked for, satisfaction with the past job, views on product etc.

2. These domains/categories and the questions within them are formed ranging from easy to answer to difficult to answer.

C. Closing of the Interview:

While closing the interview, the interviewer should:

1. Summarise what she/he has been able to gather.

2. Give a chance to the interviewee to ask questions or offer comments. One ' should end witfc a discussion of the next step to be taken.

10. Generic skills are important skills that are mandatory for all psychologists irrespective of their field of specialisation.

These skills include personal as well as intellectual skills.

- Interpersonal Skills: ability to listen and be empathic, to develop respect for/interest in other's cultures, experiences etc. These skills are expressed verbally and/or non-verbally.

- Cognitive Skills: ability to solve problems, engage in critical thinking and organised reasoning, and having intellectual curiosity and flexibility.

- Affective Skills: emotional control and balance, tolerance/understanding of interpersonal conflict, tolerance of ambiguity and uncertainty.

- Personality/Attitude: desire to help others, openness to new ideas, honesty/integrity/value ethical behaviour, personal courage

- Expressive Skills: ability to communicate one's ideas, feelings and information in verbal, non-verbal, and written forms.

- Reflective Skills: ability to examine and consider one's own motives, attitudes, behaviours and ability to be sensitive to one's own behaviour or others.

- Personal Skills: personal organisation, personal hygiene, time management, and appropriate dress.

CUET UG
Solved Paper 2022

PSYCHOLOGY
Class XII

1. Ravindra is 'Street Smart' as he is high on the ability to deal with environment demands encountered on a daily basis. He exhibits which type of intelligence according to Robert Sternberg ?

   A. Experiential
   B. Creativity
   C. Componential
   D. Contextual

2. The evidence for the genetic influence on intelligence comes from study of twins. Arrange the correlation dependent findings in descending order.

   A. Fraternal twins reared together
   B. Identical twins reared together
   C. Brothers. sisters reared together
   D. Siblings reared apart
   E. Identical twins reared in different environments

   Choose the correct answer form the options given below:

   A. B, C, A, D, E
   B. B, C, D, A, E
   C. B, E, A, C, D
   D. E, B, C, D, A

3. Highly talented people are sometimes called ______.

   A. Superior
   B. Gifted
   C. Prodigies
   D. Intellectually gifted

4. Raven's Progressive Matrices Test is an example of ______

   A. Group Test
   B. Verbal Test
   C. Non-verbal Test
   D. Performance Test

5. Which of the following statements are true about creativity ?

   A. Genetic factors play an important role

   B. Nurture affects creativity

   C. Creativity involves high emotional intelligence

   D. Creativity involves convergent thinking

   E. A minimum level of intelligence is required for creativity but beyond that intelligence doesn't matter.

   Choose the correct answer form the options given below:

   A. B, D and E only
   B. A, B and E only
   C. A, B and C only
   D. B, C and E only

6. Match the features of various people in List I with the type of intelligence in List II

List I (Features of People)	List II (Type of Intelligence)
A. Rahul is 'word-smart' as he can create linguistic images in his mind	I. Naturalistic Intelligence
B. Neha can think logically and critically as she can manipulate symbols to solve problems.	II. Interpersonal Intelligence
C. Mansi understands the feelings of other people. She has the ability to bond into a comfortable relationship.	III. Linguistic Intelligence
D. Anish recognizes the beauty of different species of flora and fauna	IV. Logical–Mathematical Intelligence

Choose the correct answer from the options given below:

A. A-I, B-II, C-III, D-IV

B. A-II, B-III, C-IV, D-I

C. A-IV, B-III, C-I, D-II

D. A-III, B-IV, C-II, D-I

7. Match the various theories of Intelligence in List I with the psychologists associated with the same in the List II

List I (Intelligence Theories)	List II (Psychologists)
A. Hierarchical Model of Intelligence	I. Louis Thurstone
B. Two–Factor Theory	II. Arther Jensen
C. Theory of Primary Mental Abilities	III. J.P. Guilford
D. Structure of Intellect Model	IV. Charles Spearman

Choose the correct answer from the options given below:

A. A-III, B-II, C-IV, D-I

B. A-IV, B-II, C-III, D-I

C. A-I, B-II, C-III, D-IV

D. A-II, B-IV, C-I, D-III

8. The notion of self-efficacy is related to__________.

A. Classical conditioning theory

B. Psychodynamic theory

C. Social learning theory

D. Analytical psychology

9. Match List I with List II

List I (Construct)	List II (Description)
A. Self-esteem	I. Ability to organize and monitor our own behaviour
B. Self-regulation	II. Ideas about our own attributes and ourself perception
C. Self-concept	III. Belief in our own ability to perform the task
D. Self-efficacy	IV. Judgement about our own value or worth

Choose the correct answer from the options given below:

A. A-IV, B-I, C-II, D-III

B. A-I, B-II, C-IV, D-III

C. A-II, B-III, C-IV, D-I

D. A-II, B-III, C-I, D-IV

10. Krish has unconscious aggressive feelings towards his father. He however refuses to accept this and instead feels that his father is very aggressive towards him. According to psychodynamic theory, which ego defence mechanism does it reflect?

A. Repression

B. Denial

C. Projection

D. Rationalization

11. 16 PF questionnaire is based upon:

A. Type Approach

B. Trait Approach

C. Behavioral Approach

D. Psychodynamic Approach

12. Which of the following is true about the relationship between culture and self with respect to Western and Asian/Indian cultures?

A. The western views seems to hold clear dichotomies between self and other.

B. In the Asian culture, the self and the group exist as two different entities with clearly defined boundaries.

C. In Indian culture, the self is generally separated from one's own group.

D. Western cultures are characterized as individualistic.

E. In the Indian culture, individual members of the group do not maintain their individuality.

Choose the correct answer from the options given below:

A. A, B, D only

B. B, C, E only

C. A, D, E only

D. B, C, D only

13. Identify the correct features related to the Projective Techniques.

A. The stimuli are relatively or fully unstructured and poorly defined.

B. Scoring and interpretation are easy so that they reveal a significant aspect of personality.

C. The respondent is informed that there are no correct or incorrect responses.

D. The respondent is usually not told about the purpose of assessment and method of scoring.

E. These are fairly structured measures that require respondents to give response in 'yes' or 'no'.

Choose the correct answer from the options given below:

A. A, C, D only

B. C, D, F only

C. E, A, B only

D. B, C, D only

14. The ______ is demanding, unrealistic and works according to the pleasure principle.

A. Id

B. Ego

C. Supergo

D. Hyperego

15. Arrange the following stages of psychosexual development in the right sequence.

A. Phallic Stage

B. Latency Stage

C. Oral stage

D. Anal Stage

E. Genital Stage

Choose the correct answer from the options given below:

A. E, A, B, C, D	B. C, D, A, B, E
C. A, C, D, B, E	D. D, A, E, B, C

16. Arrange following life events in terms of decreasing stress level (Holmes and Rahe)

    A. Change in eating habits   B. Illness of a family member

    C. Appearing for examinations   D. Unexpected accident

    E. Death of a close family member

    Choose the correct answer from the options given below:

    A. D, A, C, B, E   B. B, E, D, A, C

    C. E, D, B, C, A   D. C, A, E, D, B

17. Raman has very high expectations from himself related to his performance in competitive exams. Due to this, he is always under stress. Raman is facing which type of stress?

    A. Social stress   B. Psychic stress

    C. Psychological stress   D. Physical stress

18. 'Eustress' means:

    A. Response or reaction towards stressful situation   B. Bad or negative side of stress

    C. Good or positive side of stress   D. Strain

19. The assessment of damage that has already been done by a stressful event is called ______ according to Lazarus and his colleagues.

    A. Loss   B. Harm

    C. Threat   D. Physical Damage

20. ______is a subjective experience that uses imagery and imagination in order to effectively deal with stress.

    A. Creative Visualization   B. Biofeedback

    C. Relaxation   D. Free Association

21. Which of the following statements are TRUE for depression ?

    A. Men are at risk during young adulthood, while for women the risk is highest in early middle age.

    B. Genetic makeup plays no role in depression.

    C. Depression leads to a feeling of excessive guilt.

    D. Lack of social support can lead to depression.

    E. Women are more likely to report a depressive disorder.

    Choose the correct answer from the options given below:

    A. C, D, E only   B. A, B, E only

    C. A, D, B only   D. B, C, D only

22. The following disorders are under the category of neurodevelopmental disorders

    A. Autism Spectrum Disorder   B. Conduct Disorder

    C. Attention—Deficit/Hyperactivity Disorder   D. Specific Learning Disorder

    E. Somatic Symptom Disorder

Choose the correct answer from the options given below:

    A. B, C, A only   B. B, C, A only

    C. A, C, D only   D. E, A, B only

23. Seema is unable to control her preoccupation with specific ideas. She is unable to prevent herself from repeatedly thinking that her hands are dirty. This interferes"with her daily activities. Seema has :

    A. Anxiety Disorder   B. Depression

    C. Schizophrenia   D. Obsessive Compulsive Disorder

24. Match List I with List II

List I (Model)	List II (Cause of Abnormal Behaviour)
A. Psychodynamic	I. Irrational and illogical thinking
B. Humanistic-Existential	II. Maladaptive learning
C. Behavioural	III. Meaninglessness and inauthenticity
D. Cognitive	IV. Intrapsychic forces

Choose the correct answer from the options given below:

    A. A-I, B-II, C-III, D-IV   B. A-IV, B-III, C-II, D-I

    C. A-IV, B-III, C-I, D-II   D. A-II, B-III, C-IV, D-I

25. Match List I with List II

List I (Concept)	List II (Characteristics)
A. Verbal Aggression	I. Impairment in social interaction and communication skills, and stereotyped patterns of behaviours, interests and activities
B. Oppositional Defiant Disorder	II. Name calling, swearing
C. Specific Learning Disorder	III. Age inappropriate amount of stubbornness, defiance, disobedience, etc.
D. Autism Spectrum Disorder	IV. Difficulty in perceiving or processing information accurately manifested in problems with reading, writing and/or Maths

Choose the correct answer from the options given below:

    A. A-IV, B-III, C-I, D-II   B. A-II, B-III, C-IV, D-I

    C. A-I, B-III, C-II, D-IV   D. A-II, B-I, C-III, D-IV

26. Jung's personality theory describes which of the following constructs ?

    A. Psychosexual stages   B. Archetypes

    C. Personal goals   D. Social desirability

27. Exorcism i.e. removing the evil residing in the individual through counter magic and prayer is still commonly used. This can be explained by the _______ perspective.

    A. Biological   B. Supernatural

    C. Interactional   D. Psychological

28. Which of the following is not an eating disorder :

    A. Bulimia Nervosa   B. PTSD

    C. Anorexia Nervosa   D. Binge Eating

29. Which of the following does NOT help in strengthening students' self esteem ?

    A. Goals for the students should be general and unmeasurable.

    B. Providing opportunities for development of physical, social and vocational skills.

    C. Establishing a trustful communication.

    D. Accentuating positive life experiences.

30. Main features of ADHD are _______

    A. Low intelligence and inattention

    B. Lack of communication skills and low intelligence

    C. Inattention and lack of communication skills

    D. Inattention and Hyperactivity

31. Raju's deceitful behavior is non-aggressive but he violates the property rights of others by stealing. He is most likely to be diagnosed with _______ .

    A. Oppositional defiant disorder   B. Impulse control disorder

    C. Hyperactivity disorder   D. Conduct disorder

32. Sandeep and Harish are a part of the school football group. They are committed to the game and have developed a passion for it. Harish is the leader and he owns responsibility for their efforts. Thus, they both are a part of :

    A. Audience   B. Mob

    C. Team   D. Performers

33. Which of the following is NOT true about conformity ?

    A. When the group is large, it is easier to not conform as deviant cannot be easily noticed

    B. When a task requires an answer that can be verified, there will be greater conformity.

    C. When the group is small, there is greater conformity.

    D. Less conformity is found under private expression than under public expression.

34. Groups usually go through different stages of group formation as given by Tuckman.

    A. Group members develop norms related to group behavior.

    B. Group moves towards achieving the group goal.

    C. People meet and try to know each other and assess whether they will fit in.

    D. The group may be disbanded after goal is achieved.

    E. There is conflict between members about how to achieve the target of the group.

Choose the correct answer from the options given below:

    A. D, C, A, B, E   B. C, A, D, B, E

    C. D, A, C, B, E   D. C, E, A, B, D

35. Match the concepts in List I with their characteristics in List II

List I (Concept)		List II (Description)
A. Environment	I.	Refers to literally everything that surrounds us including the physical, social, cultural of work environment.
B. Ecology	II.	Deals with psychological issues pertaining to human-environment interaction.
C. Environmental Psychology	III.	Refers to the creativity of the human mind, as expressed in the work of architects and town planners
D. Environmental Design	IV.	Refers to the study of relationship between living beings and their environment

Choose the correct answer from the options given below:

    A. A-I, B-III, C-II, D-IV   B A-I, B-IV, C-II, D-III

    C. A-II, B-IV, C-III, D-I   D A-III, B-II, C-I, D-IV

36. _______ refers to the ability to understand the plight of another person and feel the same as the other person.

    A. Sympathy   B. Compassion

    C. Empathy   D. Insight

37. When the source of the message takes ideas, gives them meaning and puts them into message forms, it is referred as: _______

    A. Decoding   B. Noise

    C. Encoding   D. Paraphrasing

38. The consistency between current and past patterns of behavior, as well as harmony between verbal and non-verbal communication is termed as _______.

    A. Communication   B. Cluster

    C. Paraphrasing   D. Congruency

39. Pre-existing groups which an individual is born into, are called ______.

    A. Formal groups   B. Outgroup

    C. Primary group   D. Secondary group

40. When a person is brought up in a belief system that itself is the cause of poverty, then the belief system is known as ______.

    A. Poverty cycle   B. Culture of poverty

    C. Poverty pyramid   D. Social disadvantage

Passage:

Read the passage and answer the questions that follow :

Kavita has an irrational fear of going to the unfamiliar places. She avoids going to enjoyable picnics and excursions due to this fear. She wants to pursue psychology for which she has to move to a metropolitan city. She is worried about her fear of new places. Finally after thinking over the present situation and her goal of pursuing psychology, she decides to take help of a psychologist who uses behavioristic approach to treat her.

41. According to psychodynamic therapy, which factor is the cause of Kavita's disorder ?

    A. Faulty learning   B. Intrapsychic conflicts

    C. Faulty cognitions   D. Faulty living

42. Identify the disorder that Kavita is suffering from.

    A. Anxiety Disorder   B. Panic Disorder

    C. Separation Anxiety Disorder   D. Agoraphobia

43. Which of the following will be suitable therapeutic technique for Kavita to help her overcome the fear of unfamiliar places ?

    A. Transference   B. Systematic Desentization

    C. Logo therapy   D. Bio-medical therapy

44. Which principle is most likely followed in the therapy to treat Kavita ?

    A. Insight Principle   B. Emotional Intelligence

    C. Reciprocal Inhibition Principle   D. Life Instinct Principle

45. According to Behavior therapy, what is the main cause of Kavita's problem ?

    A. Genetic causes   B. Intrapsychic conflicts

    C. Existential anxiety   D. Faulty learning

Passage:

Read the passage and answer the questions that follow:

Pratap lost his young son due to a pothole accident some years ago. He decided to turn his pain into a purpose and now social media users are calling him a hero without a cape. For the last three years, Pratap has been filling up potholes in the city to ensure that no one else suffers the same fate. Pratap also starts planting trees in the city as he believes that environment is not simply for use by human beings but needs to be respected and valued. For this, he takes inspiration from a very famous movement in the Uttarakhand region which aimed to conserve forests. He also starts helping the poor in the community and observes that these poor people believe that they will continue to remain poor. Such beliefs have been passed on from one generation to another. He decides to change these beliefs by developing an advertisement in which he shows a pressure cooker that saves fuel and hence can help save money.

46. Pratap developed a negative attitude towards roads with potholes. Which of the following factor is responsible for this ?

    A. Family and school environment   B. Reference groups

    C. Personal experiences   D. Media related influences

47. Which view of human-environment relationship does Pratap believe in ?

    A. Minimalist perspective   B. Maximal perspective

    C. Instrumental perspective   D. Spiritual perspective

48. Pratap gets inspiration from which environment conservation movement of Uttarakhand that was aimed to conserve forests ?

    A. Rainbow movement   B. Red Vest movement

    C. Chipko movement   D. Bishnoi community movement"

49. The poor people in the community believe that they will always remain poor. This belief system is referred to as _______

    A. Poverty cycle   B. Culture of poverty

    C. Absolute poverty   D. Relative poverty

50. What kind of appeal does Pratap use in the advertisement ?

    A. Emotional appeal   B. Congruent appeal

    C. Rational appeal   D. Incongruent appeal

Answer Keys

1. (D)	**2.** (C)	**3.** (C)	**4.** (C)	**5.** (B)	**6.** (C)	**7.** (D)	**8.** (C)	**9.** (A)	**10.** (C)
11. (B)	**12.** (C)	**13.** (A)	**14.** (A)	**15.** (B)	**16.** (C)	**17.** (C)	**18.** (C)	**19.** (C)	**20.** (A)
21. (D)	**22.** (C)	**23.** (D)	**24.** (B)	**25.** (B)	**26.** (B)	**27.** (B)	**28.** (B)	**29.** (*)	**30.** (D)
31. (D)	**32.** (C)	**33.** (A)	**34.** (D)	**35.** (B)	**36.** (C)	**37.** (C)	**38.** (D)	**39.** (C)	**40.** (A)
41. (B)	**42.** (D)	**43.** (B)	**44.** (C)	**45.** (C)	**46.** (C)	**47.** (D)	**48.** (C)	**49.** (B)	**50.** (B)

Solution

1. (D) Contextual or practical intelligence involves the ability to deal with environmental demands encountered on a daily basis. It may be called 'street smartness' or 'business sense'.

2. (C) The intelligence of identical twins reared together correlate almost 0.90. Twins separated early in childhood also show considerable similarity in their intellectual, personality and behavioural characteristics. The intelligence of identical twins reared in different environments correlate 0.72, those of fraternal twins reared together correlate almost 0.60, and those of brothers and sisters reared together correlate about 0.50, while siblings reared apart correlate about 0.25.

3. (C) The highly talented are sometimes called 'prodigies'.

4. (C) Raven's Progressive Matrices (RPM) Test is an example of a non-verbal test. In this test, the subject examines an incomplete pattern and chooses a figure from the alternatives that will complete the pattern.

5. (B) There is no disagreement that creativity is determined by both heredity and environment. Limits of the creative potential are set by heredity, environmental factors stimulate the development of creativity.

6. (C) Naturalistic is useful in recognising the beauty of different species of flora and fauna, and making subtle discriminations in the natural world.

7. (D) In 1927, Charles Spearman proposed a two-factor theory of intelligence employing a statistical method called factor analysis. He showed that intelligence consisted of a general factor (g-factor) and some specific factors (s-factors).

8. (C) The notion of self-efficacy is based on Bandura's social learning theory. Bandura's initial studies showed that children and adults learned behaviour by observing and imitating others.

9. (A) Self-regulation refers to our ability to organise and monitor our own behaviour.

10. (C) In projection, people attribute their own traits to others. Thus, a person who has strong aggressive tendencies may see other people as acting in an excessively aggressive way towards her/him.

11. (B) Sixteen Personality Factor Questionnaire (16PF), for the assessment of personality. This test is widely used by psychologists.

12. (C) In the Western culture, the self and the group exist as two different entities with clearly defined boundaries.In the Indian culture, the self is generally not separated from one's own group; rather both remain in a state of harmonious co-existence.

13. (A) While the nature of stimuli and responses in these techniques vary enormously, all of them do share the following features:

    (1) The stimuli are relatively or fully unstructured and poorly defined.

    (2) The person being assessed is usually not told about the purpose of assessment and the method of scoring and interpretation.

    (3) The person is informed that there are no correct or incorrect responses.

    (4) Each response is considered to reveal a significant aspect of personality.

    (5) Scoring and interpretation are lengthy and sometimes subjective.

14. (A) Id : It is the source of a person's instinctual energy. It deals with immediate gratification of primitive needs, sexual desires and aggressive impulses. It works on the pleasure principle, which assumes that people seek pleasure and try to avoid pain.

15. (B) Freud claims that the core aspects of personality are established early, remain stable throughout life, and can be changed only with great difficulty. He proposed a five-stage theory of personality (also called psychosexual) development. Problems encountered at any stage may arrest development, and have long-term effect on a person's life.

16. (C)

Life Events	Mean Stress Score
Death of a close family member	66
Unexpected accident or trauma	53
Illness of a family member	52
Break-up with friend	47
Appearing for examinations	43
Change in eating habits	27

17. (C) These are stresses that we generate ourselves in our minds. These are personal and unique to the person experiencing them and are internal sources of stress. We worry about problems, feel anxiety, or become depressed. These are not only symptoms of stress, but they cause further stress for us.

18. (C) Eustress is the term used to describe the level of stress that is good for you and is one of a person's best assets for achieving peak performance and managing minor crisis.

19. (C) Harm is the assessment of the damage that has already been done by an event.

20. (A) Creative Visualisation : It is an effective technique for dealing with stress. Creative visualisation is a subjective experience that uses imagery and imagination.

21. (D) Psychological stress is accompanied by negative emotions and associated behaviours, including depression, hostility, anger and aggression. Negative emotion states are of particular concern to the study of effects of stress on health.

22. (C) A common feature of the neurodevelopmental disorders is that they manifest in the early stage of development. We will now discuss several disorders like Attention-Deficit/Hyperactivity Disorder (ADHD), Autism Spectrum Disorder, Intellectual Disability, and Specific Learning Disorder.

23. (D) People affected by obsessivecompulsive disorder are unable to control their preoccupation with specific ideas or are unable to prevent themselves from repeatedly carrying out a particular act or series of acts that affect their ability to carry out normal activities.

24. (B)Another psychological model is the humanistic-existential model which focuses on broader aspects of human existence. Humanists believe that human beings are born with a natural tendency to be friendly, cooperative and constructive, and are driven to self-actualise, i.e. to fulfil this potential for goodness and growth.

25. (B) Autism Spectrum Disorder is characterised by widespread impairments in social interaction and communication skills, and stereotyped patterns of behaviours, interests and activities.

26. (B) Jung claimed that there was a collective unconscious consisting of archetypes or primordial images. These are not individually acquired, but are inherited.

27. (B) Exorcism, i.e. removing the evil that resides in the individual through countermagic and prayer, is still commonly used. In many societies, the shaman, or medicine man (ojha) is a person who is believed to have contact with supernatural forces and is the medium through which spirits communicate with human beings.

28. (B) Another group of disorders which are of special interest to young people are eating disorders. These include anorexia nervosa, bulimia nervosa, and binge eating.

29.

30. (D) The two main features of ADHD are inattention and hyperactivityimpulsivity.

31. (D) The terms conduct disorder and antisocial behaviour refer to age-inappropriate actions and attitudes that violate family expectations, societal norms, and the personal or property rights of others.

32. (C) Teams are special kinds of groups. Members of teams often have complementary skills and are committed to a common goal or purpose. Members are mutually accountable for their activities. In teams, there is a positive synergy attained through the coordinated efforts of the members.

33. (A) Conformity is greater when the group is small than when the group is large. Why does it happen? It is easier for a deviant member (one who does not conform) to be noticed in a small group. In Asch's experiment, the task required an answer that could be verified, and could be correct or incorrect. Suppose the task involves giving an opinion about some topic.

34. (D) Tuckman suggested that groups pass through five developmental sequences. These are: forming, storming, norming, performing and adjourning.

When group members first meet, there is a great deal of uncertainty about the group, the goal, and how it is to be achieved. People try to know each other and assess whether they will fit in. There is excitement as well as apprehensions. This stage is called the forming stage.

Often, after this stage, there is a stage of intragroup conflict which is referred to as storming.

35. (B) The word 'environment' refers to all that is around us, literally everything that surrounds us, including the physical, social, work, and cultural environment. 'Ecology' is the study of the relationships between living beings and their environment. In psychology, the focus is on the interdependence between the environment and people, as the environment becomes meaningful with reference to the human beings who live in it.

36. (C) empathy is present when one is able to understand the plight of another person, and feel like the other person.

37. (C) we encode (i.e., take ideas, give them meaning and put them into message forms), and send the idea through a channel.

38. (D) A person's background and past patterns of behaviour are also considered when we analyse body language. The consistency between current and past patterns of behaviour, as well as harmony between verbal and non-verbal communication, is termed as congruency.

39. (C) A major difference between primary and secondary groups is that primary groups are pre-existing formations which are usually given to the individual whereas secondary groups are those which the individual joins by choice.

40. (A) It is not the individual, but a belief system, a way of life, and values, in which she/he is brought up, that is the cause of poverty. This belief system, called the 'culture of poverty', convinces the person that she/he will continue to remain poor, and the belief is carried over from one generation of the poor to the next.

41. (B) Psychodynamic therapy is of the view that intrapsychic conflicts, i.e. the conflicts that are present within the psyche of the person, are the source of psychological problems.

42. (D) Agoraphobia is the term used when people develop a fear of entering unfamiliar situations. Many people with agoraphobia are afraid of leaving their home.

43. (B) Systematic desensitisation is a technique introduced by Wolpe for treating phobias or irrational fears.

44. (C) The principle of reciprocal inhibition operates here. This principle states that the presence of two mutually opposing forces at the same time, inhibits the weaker force.

45. (C) Psychodynamic therapy is of the view that intrapsychic conflicts, i.e. the conflicts that are present within the psyche of the person, are the source of psychological problems.

46. (C) Pratap's personal experience developed negative attitudes towards road with potholes.

47. (D) The spiritual perspective refers to the view of the environment as something to be respected and valued rather than exploited.

48. (C) The Chipko movement's memorandum of demands included six principles: (a) only specific trees and vegetation suitable for a particular geographical region should be grown,

49. (B) It is not the individual, but a belief system, a way of life, and values, in which she/he is brought up, that is the cause of poverty. This belief system, called the 'culture of poverty', convinces the person that she/he will continue to remain poor, and the belief is carried over from one generation of the poor to the next.

50. (B) Congruent appeal.

CBSE

PSYCHOLOGY

Class XII

Time Allowed: 1½ hours   Maximum Marks: 40

General Instructions

Read the following instructions very carefully and strictly follow them :

1. This question paper contains three sections : **A**, **B** and **C**.
2. Section **A** has **24** questions. Attempt any **20** questions.
3. Section **B** has **24** questions. Attempt any **20** questions.
4. Section **C** has **12** questions. Attempt any **10** questions.
5. All questions carry **equal** marks.
6. There is no negative marking.

Section A

1. Intelligence Quotient (IQ) refers to

   (a) Chronological age divided by mental age and multiplied by 100

   (b) Chronological age multiplied by mental age and divided by 100

   (c) Mental age divided by chronological age and multiply by 100

   (d) Mental age multiplied by chronological age and divided by 100

2. _______ is an enduring belief about an ideal mode of behaviour.

   (a) Aptitude

   (b) Attitude

   (c) Value

   (d) Interest

3. Manifestation of _______ can be observed in a novel solution to a problem, an invention, composition of a poem, painting new chemical process an innovation in law, a breakthrough in preventing a disease and the like.

    (a) Creativity   (b) Attitudes

    (c) Education   (d) Intelligence

4. _______ is a set of skills that underlie accurate perception, appraisal, expression and regulation of emotions.

    (a) Emotional incompetenece   (b) Emotional intelligence

    (c) Perceptual skills   (d) Powerful emotions

5. Aptitude tests are available in ___

    (a) Three forms: independent, specialised and multiple aptitude test

    (b) Two forms: multidue and generalised aptitude tests

    (c) Two forms: independent and specialised tests

    (d) Two forms: independent and multiple aptitude tests

6. The _______ self emerges in relation with others and emphasizes such aspects of life as co-operation unity, affiliation, sacrifice, support, or sharing.

    (a) personal   (b) individual

    (c) social   (d) positive

7. _______ seeks to satisfy an individual's instinctual needs in accordance with reality.

    (a) Id   (b) ego

    (c) Superego   (d) Libido

8. For most behaviorists, the structural unit of personality is the ____.

    (a) Response   (b) Stimuli

    (c) Archetypes   (d) Emotions

9. Enhancement of people's self-concept possible by creating an atmosphere of ___

    (a) Conditional positive regard   (b) Unconditional positive regard

    (c) Unconditional and biased regard   (d) Identity crisis

10. _______ personality seem to process low motivation are patient and feel they have a lot of time and little work.

    (a) Type-A   (b) Type-B

    (c) Type-C   (d) Type-D

11. In _______ a person defends against anxiety by adopting behaviours opposite to her/his true feelings.

    (a) Reaction formation   (b) Rationalisation

    (c) Repression   (d) Regression

12. Archetypes can be found in___

(a) Consomus

(b) preconcious

(c) Myths, dreams arts and various traditions

(d) Sports-related activities and positive thinking

13. A _______ is considered as a relatively enduring attributes or quality on which one individual differs from another.

(a) Typology   (b) Personality

(c) Trait   (d) Persona

14. Social support may be in the form of ___ support when assistance is provided in the form of material aid such as money, goods, services etc.

(a) Emotional   (b) Tangible

(c) Informational   (d) Material

15. _______ is a stress management technique involving subjective experience using imagery and imagination

(a) Creative Visualisation   (b) Relaxation

(c) Mediation   (d) Biofeedback

16. Negative events are appraised for their possible____

(a) Harm, threat or commitment   (b) Harm, thought or controllability

(c) Hurt,threat, damage or challange   (d) Harm, threat or challange

17. _______ results from the blocking of needs and motives by something or someone that hinders from achieving the desired goal.

(a) Conflict   (b) Internal pressure

(c) Social presure   (d) Frustration

18. The state of physical, emotional and psychological exhaustion is known as

(a) burnout   (b) breakout

(c) resistance   (d) rustout

19. _______ refers to the measurement of psychological attributes of individuals and their evaluation, often using multiple methods in terms of certain standards of comparison

(a) actualisation   (b) assessment

(c) Attribute achievement   (d) Analysis

20. _______ is an exceptional general ability shown in superior performance in a wide variety of areas.

(a) Talent   (b) Intelligence

(c) Creativity   (d) Giftedness

21. It is the ____ that are attacked by the Human Immuno Deficiency Virus (IIIV), the virus causing Acquired Immuno Deficiency Syndrome (AIDS)

(a) B cells   (b) T-helper cells

(c) T cells   (d) Natural killer cells

22. In the _______ stage the parasympathetic nervous system calls for more cautious use of the body's resources.

(a) Alarm reaction   (b) Resistance

(c) Exhaustion   (d) Adaptation

23. _______ stresses are demands that change the state of our body. For example, we feel strained when we overexert ourselves, lack a nutritious diet or suffer an injury.

(a) Environmental   (b) Bodily

(c) Physical   (d) Health-related

24. _______ is a collective system of customs, beliefs, attitudes, and achievement in art and literature.

(a) Tradition   (b) Personality

(c) Culture   (d) Society

Section B

25. Vikas lags behind his peers in language and motor skills. He is trained in self-care as well as in simple social and communication skills. He also needs little supervision in everyday tasks. He is likely to be at the ____ level of intellectual disability.

(a) Mild (IQs 55 to approximately 70)

(b) Moderate (IQs 35-40 to approximately 50-55)

(c) Severe (IQs 20-25 to approximately 35-40)

(d) Profound (IQs below 20-25)

26. Latika is able to recall information accurately and derive general rules from the presented facts. According to Thurston the primary abilities she possesses most are ___

(a) Memory, and spatial relations

(b) Memory, spatial relations and anti-verbal comprehension

(c) Inductive resoning and spatial relations

(d) Inductive resoning and memory

27. Abdul realises that intelligence tests are of several types.

Which of the following is/are CORRECT explanation/explanations of the types of tests that he can use to assess intelligence?

i.   On the basis of their administration procedure, they can be categorised as either culture-fair or cultural-biased.

ii.   They can also be classified as either verbal or performance tests on the basis of the nature of items used.

iii.   Depending upon the extent to which an intelligence test favours one culture over another, it can be judged as either individual or group tests.

iv.   Abdul can choose a test depending on the purpose. This can be an individual group, verbal, non-verbal or performance test.

(a) i, ii and iii   (b) iii

(c) iii and iv   (d) ii and iv

28. Sheetal was provided feedback about her current physiological activity. This was also accompanied by relaxation training. This procedure to monitor and reduce the physiological aspects of stress is known as ___

(a) Meditation   (b) Relaxation

(c) Biofeedback   (d) Coping

29. Angel is high on the ability to think analytically and critically. Therefore, she performs well in academics. She is most likely to possess the following:

  i.   Contextual intelligence i.e. the analysis of information to solve problems.

  ii.   Componential intelligence which has three components, each serving a different function.

  iii. Experimental intelligence, which is the knowledge acquisition component.

  iv. Meta or a higher-order component, which involves planning about what to do and how to do it.

  v.   Performance component which involves actually doing things.

(a) iii, ii, iv and v   (b) i, iii, iv and v

(c) ii, iii and v   (d) ii, iv and v

30. Tanmay wants to assess how Geetika expresses in the face of a frustrating situation with the help of cartoon-like pictures. He presents a series of situations in which one person frustrates another, or calls attention to a frustrating condition. Tanmay is likely to be using the

(a) Thematic Apperception Test

(b) Rosenzweig's Picture-Frustration Study (P-F Study)

(c) Sixteen Personality Factor Test (16PF)

(d) Behavioural Analysis

31. Ivaan reaches the genital stage of psychosexual development. Which of the following is/ are NOT TRUE about this stage?

  i.   Ivaan has attained maturity in psychosexual development.

  ii.   This stage lasts from about seven years until puberty.

  iii. Physical growth continues and much of Ivaan's energy is channeled into social or achievement related activities.

  iv. Ivaan's sexuality, fears and repressed feelings of earlier stages are once again exhibited in this stage.

(a) i, ii,and iv   (b) ii

(c) ii and iii   (d) i and iii

32. Ankita scores high on the dimension of psychoticism this can be linked to psychopathology they represents ___

  i. A feeling of gratitude for others   ii. A tough manner of interacting with people.

  iii. A tendency to defy social conventions   iv. Socially conductive behaviour

  v. Hostility, egocentricity

(a) i, ii,iv and v   (b) i, iii, iv and v

(c) ii, iii, and v   (d) ii, iv and v

33. Christopher's personality is being assessed by a psychologist. Which of the following is/ are TRUE about assessment of personality?

    i.   It is an informal effort aimed at understanding his personality.

    ii. The goal of assessment is to understand and predict his behaviour with minimum error and maximum accuracy.

    iii. While assessing Christophers, the psychologist tries to study what he generally does or how he behaves in a given situation.

    iv. His assessment can also be useful for diagnosis training, placement counselling z and other purposes.

    (a) i, ii and iv   (b) ii

    (c) ii, iii, iv   (d) i, ii and iii

34. Assertion (A) : Pass model explains that state of arousal is basic to any behaviour as it helps in attending to stimuli. Arousal and attention enable a person to process information.

    Reason (R) : An optimal level of arousal focuses our attention to the relevant aspects of a problem. Too much or too little arousal would interfere with attention.

    (a) Both (A) and (R) are true (R) is the correct explanation of (A)

    (b) Both (A) and (R) are true and (R) is not the correct explanation of (A)

    (c) (A) is true, but (R) is false

    (d) (A) is false, but (R) is false

35. Assertion (A) : Alfred Binet was the first psychologist who tried to formalise the concept of intelligence in term of mental operations and has gave the concept of Intelligence Quotient (IQ)

    Reason (R) : Binet's one-factor theory of intelligence was rather simple as it arose from his interest in differentiating more intelligent from less intelligent individuals.

    (a) Both (A) and (R) are true (R) is the correct explanation of (A)

    (b) Both (A) and (R) are true and (R) is not the correct explanation of (A)

    (c) (A) is true, but (R) is false

    (d) (A) is false, but (R) is true

36. Assertion (A) : Behavioural ratings are frequently used for the assessment of personality in educational and industrial settings.

    Reason(R) : Naturalistic observation is free from observer bias.

    (a) Both (A) and (R) are true (R) is the correct explanation of (A)

    (b) Both (A) and (R) are true and (R) is not the correct explanation of (A)

    (c) (A) is true, but (R) is false

    (d) (A) is false, but (R) is true

37. Sunil avoids jealousy and sulking behaviour. He listens to what the other person says, And accepts the other person's opinions even if they are different from his own opinions. This will help him in ___

    (a) Being assertive   (b) Time management

    (c) Overcoming unhelpful habits   (d) Improving relationships

38. Assertion (A) : Roger emphasised the relationship between the 'real self' and the 'ideal self'.

Reason (R) : The congruence of these 'real' and 'ideal' selves makes a person fully functioning

(a) Both (A) and (R) are true (R) is the correct explanation of (A)

(b) Both (A) and (R) are true and (R) is not the correct explanation of (A)

(c) (A) is true, but (R) is false

(d) (A) is false, but (R) is true

39. Assertion (A) : Karen Horhey argued that psychological disorders were caused by disturbing interpersonal relationships during childhood.

Reason (R) : The goals that provide us with security and help us in overcoming the feeling of inadequacy are important in our personality development.

(a) Both (A) and (R) are true (R) is the correct explanation of (A)

(b) Both (A) and (R) are true and (R) is not the correct explanation of (A)

(c) (A) is true, but (R) is false

(d) (A) is false, but (R) is true

40. Assertion (A) : Psychodynamic theories face strong criticism from many quarters.

Reason (R) : The theories are largely based on the case studies. Thus they lack a rigorous scientific basis.

(a) Both (A) and (R) are true (R) is the correct explanation of (A)

(b) Both (A) and (R) are true and (R) is not the correct explanation of (A)

(c) (A) is true, but (R) is false

(d) (A) is false, but (R) is true

41. Assertion (A) : In psychological terms, personality refers to the physical or external appearance of an individual. For example, when we find someone 'good-looking' we often assume that the person also has a charming personality.

Reason (R) : Personality refers to out characteristic ways of responding to individuals and situations.

(a) Both (A) and (R) are true (R) is the correct explanation of (A)

(b) Both (A) and (R) are true and (R) is not the correct explanation of (A)

(c) (A) is true, but (R) is false

(d) (A) is false, but (R) is true

42. Reebika is experiencing stress due to noisy surroundings, commuting quarrelsome neighbours, electricity and water shortage. These resources of stress are ___

(a) Life events   (b) Hassles

(c) Traumatic events   (d) Environmental events

43. Randeep puts the work related issues under the carpet and refuses to accept or face them. This explains that he is ____ the task.

(a) Avoiding   (b) Procastinating

(c) Managing   (d) Approaching

44. Heena lost her husband in a car accident. this live event is traumatic. Which of the following is not true about the effects you can have all her?

    i.   stress can affect her behaviour in the form of eating less nutritional food disrupted sleep patterns and increased absenteeism and reduced work performance

    ii.   the cognitive effects of stress will be both and concentration and increased short term memory capacity

    iii. in her case this stress can start a vicious circle of decreasing confidence leading to more serious emotional problems

    iv. the effects of this stress will mostly be psychological in nature

(a) i and ii   (b) ii and iv

(c) ii and iii   (d) i, ii and iv

45. When Vikram was caught in a traffic jam he felt angry because he believed that the traffic should move faster to manage this thread he needs to _______

    i.   cope with stress on the basis of rigid deep-seated believes

    ii.   Reassess the way you think and learn coping strategies

    iii. allow himself to manage and regulate the emotional response that problem

    iv. handle the stressful situation pudding only covid activities in the coping strategies

(a) i, ii and iii   (b) i and iv

(c) ii and iii   (d) i, ii and iv

46. Assertion (A) : An individual's response to a stressful situation largely depends upon the perceived events and how they are interpreted.

Reason (R) : Lazarus has distinguished between two types of appraisal i.e primary and secondary.

(a) Both (A) and (R) are true (R) is the correct explanation of (A)

(b) Both (A) and (R) are true and (R) is not the correct explanation of (A)

(c) (A) is true, but (R) is false

(d) (A) is false, but (R) is true

47. Assertion (A) : High stress can produce unpleasant effect and cause our performance to deteriorate

Reason (R) : Eustress always turns into distress and also produces unpleasant effects

(a) Both (A) and (R) are true (R) is the correct explanation of (A)

(b) Both (A) and (R) are true and (R) is not the correct explanation of (A)

(c) (A) is true, but (R) is false

(d) (A) is false, but (R) is true

48. Assertion (A) : Life skills are abilities for adaptive and positive behaviour that enables effectively with the demands and challenges of everyday life

Reason (R) : to meet the challenges of life positive attitude positive thinking social support are some factors that can be of help

(a) Both (A) and (R) are true (R) is the correct explanation of (A)

(b) Both (A) and (R) are true and (R) is not the correct explanation of (A)

(c) (A) is true, but (R) is false

(d) (A) is false, but (R) is true

Section C

49. Narayanan Nair's intelligence can be primarily stated as ________ ability.

(a) Linguistic
(b) Logical-mathematical
(c) Naturalistic
(d) Bodily-kinesthetic

50. He honed finer sensibilities regarding his identity and meaning of his existence. Expression through dance also enhanced his self-awareness.

(a) Linguistic
(b) Bodily-kinesthetic
(c) Logical-mathematical
(d) Intrapersonal

51. Krishnappa was proud of Chowdiah's accomplishment at innovating the violin

The above statement reflects Chowdiah's ________

(a) Linguistic ability
(b) Musical ability
(c) Creative ability
(d) Logical-mathematical ability

52. Chwodiah's mother motivated him as she was convinced with the scholar's words. Thus Chowdiah was trained under Bidaram Krishnappa. Considering these factors, he became a successful violinist majorly because of the ____

(a) Hereditary influences
(b) Environmental processing
(c) Interaction of nature and nurture
(d) Environmental deprivation

53. In order to measure Narayanan Nair's and Chowdiah's intelligence, the tests should focus on measuring ____

(a) Componential intelligence
(b) Successive processing
(c) Multiple intelligence
(d) Uni or one factor of intelligence

54. Both Narayanan Nair and Chowdiah were successful in their fields as they were most likely to have ________

(a) The aptitude required for the career they pursued

(b) The interest required for the career they pursued

(c) Both the aptitude and interest required for the career they pursued

(d) The necessary passion for career they pursued

55. Which two approaches to personally can be explained by pictures 1A and 1B?

(a) Psychodynamic and cultural approaches
(b) Behavioral and humanistic approaches
(c) Cultural and humanistic approaches
(d) Cultural and behavioral approaches

56. Which of the following is TRUE about the Birhor community?

i.   Most of them live a nomadic life, which requires constant movement in small bands from one forest to another.

ii. In the Birhor society, children from an early age are allowed enormous freedom to move into forests and learn hunting and gathering skills.

iii. Their child socialisation practices are also aimed at making children dependent (do things with the help provided by elders).

iv. They are not achievement-oriented (they do not accept risks and challenges such as those involved in hunting)

(a) i, ii and iv
(b) i and ii
(c) ii and iv
(d) ii and iii

57. Which of the following is NOT TRUE about the approach to personality referred to in Picture IA?

(a) It expresses that people develop various personality qualities in an attempt to adapt to the ecological and cultural features of a group's life

(b) It promises that group's economic maintenance system plays a vital role in the origin of cultural and behavioral variations

(c) It promises that there is an inborn tendency among persons that directs them to actualise their inherited nature

(d) It states that rituals, ceremonies, religious practices, arts, games and play are the means through which people's personality gets projected in a culture

58. Biological and security needs are commonly found among human beings in all cultures. These needs are also known as _________ needs by Maslow.

(a) Survival   (b) Social

(c) Cross-cultural   (d) Growth

59. Why do people in hunting-gathering and agricultural societies develop and display different personality patterns?

(a) Because of reinforcement of a particular behaviour

(b) Because of different economic pursuits and cultural demands

(c) Because of rational thinking, learning and modelling

(d) Because of intrapsychic conflicts

60. Upon being assessed children belonging to the Birhor society are most likely to exhibit the following personality attributes :

i.   Independence(do many things without help from elders)

ii.   Autonomy(take several decisions for themselves)

iii.   Obedient to elders, nurturant to youngsters.

iv.   Achievement-oriented (accept risks and challenges such as those involved in hunting.)

(a) i, ii and iv   (b) i, ii and iii

(c) ii and iv   (d) ii and iii

Answer Keys

1. (c)	**2.** (c)	**3.** (a)	**4.** (b)	**5.** (d)	**6.** (c)	**7.** (b)	**8.** (a)	**9.** (b)	**10.** (b)
11. (a)	**12.** (c)	**13.** (c)	**14.** (b)	**15.** (a)	**16.** (d)	**17.** (d)	**18.** (a)	**19.** (b)	**20.** (d)
21. (c)	**22.** (b)	**23.** (c)	**24.** (c)	**25.** (a)	**26.** (d)	**27.** (a)	**28.** (c)	**29.** (d)	**30.** (b)
31. (c)	**32.** (c)	**33.** (c)	**34.** (a)	**35.** (d)	**36.** (c)	**37.** (d)	**38.** (a)	**39.** (b)	**40.** (a)
41. (d)	**42.** (b)	**43.** (a)	**44.** (b)	**45.** (c)	**46.** (a)	**47.** (c)	**48.** (b)	**49.** (d)	**50.** (d)
51. (c)	**52.** (b)	**53.** (c)	**54.** (c)	**55.** (b)	**56.** (b)	**57.** (c)	**58.** (a)	**59.** (b)	**60.** (a)

Solution

1. Mental age divided by chronological age and multiply by 100

2. Value is an enduring belief about an ideal mode of behaviour.

3. Creativity can be observed in a novel solution to a problem, an invention, composition of a poem, painting new chemical process an innovation in law, a breakthrough in preventing a disease and the like.

4. Emotional intelligence is a set of skills that underlie accurate perception, appraisal, expression and regulation of emotions.

5. Two forms : independent and multiple aptitude tests

6. The social self emerges in relation with others and emphasizes such aspects of life as co-operation unity, affiliation, sacrifice, support, or sharing.

7. Ego seeks to satisfy an individual's instinctual needs In accordance with reality.

8. For most behaviorists, the structural unit of personality is the response.

9. Enhancement of people's self-concept possible by creating an atmosphere of Unconditional positive regard.

10. Type B personality seem to process low motivation are patient and feel they have a lot of time and little work.

11. In reaction formation a person defends against anxiety by adopting behaviours opposite to her/his true feelings.

12. Archetypes can be found in Myths, dreams arts and various traditions

13. A trait is considered as a relatively enduring attributes or quality on which one individual differs from another.

14. Social support may be in the form of tangible support when assistance is provided in the form of material aid such as money, goods, services etc.

15. Creative visualization is a stress management technique involving subjective experience using imagery and imagination.

16. Negative events are appraised for their possible harm, threat or challange

17. Frustration results from the blocking of needs and motives by something or someone that hinders from achieving the desired goal.

18. The state of physical, emotional and psychological exhaustion is known as burnout.

19. Assessment refers to the measurement of psychological attributes of individuals and their evaluation, often using multiple methods in terms of certain standards of comparison

20. Giftedness is an exceptional general ability shown in superior performance in a wide variety of areas.

21. It is the T cells that are attacked by the Human Immuno Deficiency Virus (HIV), the virus causing Acquired Immuno Deficiency Syndrome(AIDS)

22. In the resistance stage the parasympathetic nervous system calls for more cautious use of the body's resources

23. Physical stresses are demands that change the state of our body. For example, we feel strained when we overexert ourselves, lack a nutritious diet or suffer an injury.

24. Culture is a collective system of customs, beliefs, attitudes, and achievement in are and literature.

25. Vikas lags behind his peers in language and motor skills. He is trained in self-care as well as in simple social and communication skills. He also needs little supervision in everyday tasks. He is likely to be at the mild level of intellectual disability.

26. Latika is able to recall information accurately and derive general rules from the presented facts. According to Thurston the primary abilities she possesses most are Inductive resoning and memory.

27. i. On the basis of their administration procedure, they can be categorised as either culture-fair or cultural-biased.

   ii. They can also be classified as either verbal or performance tests on the basis of the nature of items used.

   iii. Depending upon the extent to which an intelligence test favours one culture over another, it can be judged as either individual or group tests.

28. Sheetal was provided feedback about her current physiological activity. This was also accompanied by relaxation training. This procedure to monitor and reduce the physiological aspects of stress is known as Biofeedback.

29. Componential intelligence which has three components, each serving a different function. Meta or a higher-order component, which involves planning about what to do and how to do it. Performance component which involves actually doing things.

30. Tanmay wants to assess how Geetika expresses in the face of a frustrating situation with the help of cartoon-like pictures. He presents a series of situations in which one person frustrates another, or calls attention to a frustrating condition. Tanmay is likely to be using the Rosenzweig's Picture-Frustration Study (P-F Study).

31. This stage lasts from about seven years until puberty. Physical growth continues and much of Ivaan's energy is channeled into social or achievement- related activities.

32. A tough manner of interacting with people. A tendency to defy social conventions and Hostility, egocentricity.

33. The goal of assessment is to understand and predict his behaviour with minimum error and maximum accuracy .While assessing Christophers, the psychologist tries to study what he generally does or how he behaves in a given situation. His assessment can also be useful for diagnosis training, placement counselling z and other.

34. Pass model explains that state of arousal is basic to any behaviour as it helps in attending to stimuli. Arousal and attention enable a person to process information. An optimal level of arousal focuses our attention to the relevant aspects of a problem. Too much or too little arousal would interfere with attention.

35. Alfred Binet was the first psychologist who tried to formalise the concept of intelligence in term of mental operations and has gave the concept of Intelligence Quotient (IQ). Binet's one-factor theory of intelligence was rather simple as it arose from his interest in differentiating more intelligent from less intelligent individuals.

36. Behavioural ratings are frequently used for the assessment of personality in educational and industrial settings. Naturalistic observation is free from observer bias.

37. Sunil avoids jealousy and sulking behaviour. He listens to what the other person says, and accepts the other person's opinions even if they are different from his own opinions. This will help him in improving relationship.

38. Roger emphasised the relationship between the 'real self' and the 'ideal self'. The congruence of these 'real' and 'ideal' selves makes a person fully functioning.

39. Karen Horhey argued that psychological disorders were caused by disturbing interpersonal relationships during childhood. The goals that provide us with security and help us in overcoming the feeling of inadequacy are important in our personality development.

40. Psychodynamic theories face strong criticism from many quarters. The theories are largely based on the case studies. Thus they lack a rigorous scientific basis.

41. In psychological terms, personality refers to the physical or external appearance of an individual. For example, when we find someone 'good-looking' we often assume that the person also has a charming personality. Personality refers to out characteristic ways of responding to individuals and situations.

42. Reebika is experiencing stress due to noisy surroundings, commuting quarrelsome neighbours, electricity and water shortage. These resources of stress are hassles.

43. Randeep puts the work-related issues under the carpet and refuses to accept or face them. This explains that he is avoiding the task.

44. The cognitive effects of stress will be both and concentration and increased short term memory capacity and the effects of this stress will mostly be psychological in nature.

45. When Vikram was caught in a traffic jam he felt angry because he believed that the traffic should move faster to manage this thread he needs to Reassess the way you think and learn coping strategies and allow himself to manage and regulate the emotional response that problem.

46. An individual's response to a stressful situation largely depends upon the perceived events and how they are interpreted. Lazarus has distinguished between two types of appraisal i.e primary and secondary.

47. High stress can produce unpleasant effect and cause our performance to deteriorate. Eustress always turns into distress and also produces unpleasant effects.

48. Life skills are abilities for adaptive and positive behaviour that enables effectively with the demands and challenges of everyday life to meet the challenges of life positive attitude positive thinking social support are some factors that can be of help.

49. Bodily-kinesthetic is **a learning style often referred to as 'learning with the hands' or physical learning**. Basically, people with bodily-kinesthetic intelligence can learn more easily by doing, exploring, and discovering.

50. Individuals who are strong in intrapersonal intelligence are **good at being aware of their own emotional states, feelings, and motivations**. They tend to enjoy self-reflection and analysis, including daydreaming, exploring relationships with others, and assessing their personal strengths.

51. Creativity is **the ability to think about a task or a problem in a new or different way, or the ability to use the imagination to generate new ideas**. Creativity enables you to solve complex problems or find interesting ways to approach tasks. If you are creative, you look at things from a unique perspective.

52. Environmental processing that concen trates on the interaction between the physical world and human behaviour.

53. In order to capture the full range of abilities and talents that people possess, Gardner theorizes that **people do not have just an intellectual capacity, but have many kinds of intelligence, including musical, interpersonal, spatial-visual, and linguistic intelligences.**

54. **Aptitude refers to an individual's potential for acquiring some specific skills**. Aptitude tests are used to predict what an individual will be able to do if given proper environment and training. Interest is an individual's preference for engaging in one or more specific activities relative to others.

55. In brief, behaviorism is a psychological approach that emphasizes the importance of observable actions and scientific studies and suggests that the environment shapes behavior. Humanism approach, on the other hand, emphasizes the study of the whole person and inner feelings.

56. Most of them live a nomadic life, which requires constant movement in small bands from one forest to another.

57. It promises that there is an inborn tendency among persons that directs them to actualise their inherited nature

58. Biological and security needs are commonly found among human beings in all cultures. These needs are also known as **survival** needs by Maslow.

59. Because of different economic pursuits and cultural demands

60. Independence(do many things without help from elders). Autonomy(take several decisions for themselves). Achievement-oriented (accept risks and challenges such as those involved in hunting)

CBSE

PSYCHOLOGY

Class XII

Time Allowed : 2 Hours   *Maximum Marks : 35*

General Instructions

Please read the instructions carefully :

(i) There are **12** questions in this question paper.

(ii) This question paper is divided into **four** sections-**Section A, B, C** and **D**.

(iii) **Section A** has **three** questions, from Question Nos. **1** to **3**, carrying **2 marks** each. Answer to these questions should not exceed **40 words**.

(iv) **Section B** has three questions, from Question Nos. **4** to **6**, carrying **3 marks** each. Answer to these questions should not exceed **80 words**.

(v) **Section C** has four questions, from Question Nos. **7** to **10**, carrying **4 marks** each. Answer to these questions should not exceed **120 words**.

(vi) **Section D** has one case study. There are 2 questions based on this case study, Question Nos. **11** and **12**. Each question carries **2 marks**. Answer to these questions should not exceed **40 words**. Answer both questions.

SECTION A

1. (a) What is well-being ? (2)

OR

  (b) Differentiate between obsession and compulsion. (2)

2. Explain the characteristics of an attitude in terms of complexity and centrality. (2)

3. How does self-fulfilling prophecy help in strengthening prejudices ? Give an example to support your answer. (2)

SECTION B

4. (a) Imran is a forty-year-old male who complains of difficulty in breathing and other body-related symptoms. On being examined, the doctors were unable to find any medical explanation for his reported symptoms. Explain this disorder and discuss its various types. (3)

OR

(b) Richa is a young girl working as an officer in an organisation. One day she just disappeared from the city and after two years she was found on the banks of a river. Nobody there knew who she was and where she hand come form. But, one day she suddenly 'woke up' and wanted to know how she had reached the banks of the river. Explain this disorder and list the other disorders in the same category. (3)

5. Shyam believes that he should be loved by everybody, all the time. Most of his beliefs have a 'must' or 'should' component. When things don't go his way, he feels distressed. Suggest a suitable therapy that will make Shyam think deeper into his irrational belief system and help him to feel better. (3)

6. Mary found herself very lonely when she joined a new college, but soon felt at ease when she made friends and became a member of a 'hobby group' too. With the help of this example, discuss the conditions that lead to group formation. (3)

SECTION C

7. (a) Discuss the risk factors associated with suicides. What are the symptoms that help in identifying students in distress ? Examine some ways to foster positive self-esteem in students. (4)

OR

(b) What are the characteristics of neurodevelopmental disorders ? Describe any three neurodevelopmental disorders. (4)

8. (a) Describe the process of rehabilitation of the mentally ill in detail. (4)

OR

(b) Discuss the various techniques used in behaviour therapy to eliminate faulty behaviours. (4)

9. Quite often we see people getting themselves photographed while helping others or even when they are offering donations to the needy. Can we identify the attitudes of these people through their behaviour ? When would there be consistency between attitude and behaviour ? Explain. (4)

10. A teacher 'X' found that the project that she/he gave to a group of students, when submitted to her/him, lacked quality as compared to the ones submitted by individual students. What is the reason for this phenomenon and how can it be reduced ? Discuss. (4)

SECTION D

Read the following case study and answer the questions that follow :

Sundar, a college going 20-year-old male, has moved from his home town to live in a big city. He has continuous fear of insecurity and feels that the enemy soldiers are following him. He gets very tense when he spots anyone in a uniform and feels that they are coming to catch him. This intense anxiety is interfering with his work and relationship, and his friends are extremely concerned as it does not make any sense to them. Sundar occasionally laughs abruptly and inappropriately, and sometimes stops speaking mid-sentence, scanning off in the distance as though he sees or hears something. He expresses concern about television and radio in the room potentially being monitored by the enemies. His beliefs are fixed and if they are challenged, his tone becomes hostile.

11. Based on the symptoms being exhibited, identify the disorder. Explain the other symptoms that can be seen in this disorder.   (2)

12. Define delusion and inappropriate affect. Support it with the symptoms given in the above case study.   (2)

EXPLANATIONS

SECTION A

1. (a) The term 'well-being' includes many aspects such as, happiness, energy, leisure, peace with oneself, contentment and sensitivity to environment. Well-being involves not only happiness and pleasure but also experiencing/feeling satisfaction in life, presence of positive feeling or affect (e g. interest, love, surprise, pleasure) and the absence of negative feelings (e.g. anxiety, depression, stress).

OR

(b) *Obsessions* are intrusive thoughts that trigger intensely distressing feelings. At the same time, *Compulsions* are behaviours done to get rid of obsessions and decrease distress. This provides short-term relief but doesn't make the obsession disappear.

Obsessions and compulsions can become a cycle that's difficult to stop. The time you spend on compulsions might begin to take up so much of your day that you find it hard to get anything else done. This can affect your school, work, or personal life, leading to even more distress.

2. **Simplicity or Complexity (multiplexity) :** This feature refers to how many attitudes there are within a broader attitude. Think of an attitude as a family containing several 'member' attitudes. In case of various topics, such as health and world peace, people hold many attitudes instead of single attitude. An attitude system is said to be 'simple' if it contains only one or a few attitudes, and 'complex' if it is made up of many attitudes. Consider the example of attitude towards health and well-being. This attitude system is likely to consist of several 'member' attitudes, such as one's concept of physical and mental health, views about happiness and well-being, and beliefs about how one should achieve health and happiness. By contrast, the attitude towards a particular person is likely to consist of mainly one attitude.

Centrality : This refers to the role of a particular attitude in the attitude system. An attitude with greater centrality would influence the other attitudes in the system much more than non-central (or peripheral) attitudes would. For example, in the attitude towards world peace, a negative attitude towards high military expenditure may be present as a core or central attitude that influences all other attitudes in the multiple attitude system.

3. **Self-fulfilling prophecy :** In some cases, the group that is the target of prejudice is itself responsible for continuing the prejudice. The target group may behave in ways that justify the prejudice, that is, confirm the negative expectations. For example, if the target group is described as 'dependent' and therefore unable to make progress, the members of this target group may actually behave in a way that proves this description to be true. In this way, they strengthen the existing prejudice.

SECTION B

4. (a) Somatic symptom disorder involves a person having persistent body-related symptoms which may or may not be related to any serious medical condition. People with this disorder tend to be overly preoccupied with their symptoms and they continually worry about their health and make frequent visits to doctors. As a result, they experience significant distress and disturbances in their daily life.

Illness Anxiety Disorder : The person experiences worry about the possibility of developing a serious medical condition.

Conversion : The person suffers from a loss or impairment of motor or sensory function (e.g., paralysis, blindness, etc.) that has no physical cause but may be a response to stress and psychological problems.

OR

(b) **Dissociative amnesia :** The person is unable to recall important, personal information often related to a stressful and traumatic report. The extent of forgetting is beyond normal.

Depersonalisation/Derealisation Disorder : The person experiences a change in the person's sense of reality and perception of self.

Dissociative identity (multiple personality) Disorder : The person exhibits two or more separate and contrasting personalities, generally associated with a history of abuse.

5. Cognitive therapies locate the cause of psychological distress in irrational thoughts and beliefs. Albert Ellis formulated the Rational Emotive Therapy (RET). The central thesis of this therapy is that irrational beliefs mediate between the antecedent events and their consequences. The first step in RET is the antecedentbelief-consequence (ABC) analysis. Antecedent events, which caused the psychological distress, are noted. The client is also interviewed to find the irrational beliefs, which are distorting the present reality. Irrational beliefs may not be supported by empirical evidence in the environment. These beliefs are characterised by thoughts with 'musts' and 'shoulds', i.e. things 'must' and 'should' be in a particular manner. Examples of irrational beliefs are, "One should be loved by everybody all the time", "Human misery is caused by external events over which one does not have any control", etc.

6. Basic to group formation is some contact and some form of interaction between people. This interaction is facilitated by the following conditions:

- **Proximity :** Just think about your group of friends. Would you have been friends if you were not living in the same colony, or going to the same school, or may be playing in the same playground? Probably your answer would be 'No'. Repeated interactions with the same set of individuals give us a chance to know them, and their interests and attitudes. Common interests, attitudes, and background are important determinants of your liking for your group members.

- **Similarity :** Being exposed to someone over a period of time makes us assess our similarities and paves the way for formation of groups. Why do we like people who are similar? Psychologists have given several explanations for this. One explanation is that people prefer consistency and like relationships that are consistent.

- **Common motives and goals :** When people have common motives or goals, they get together and form a group which may facilitate their goal attainment. Suppose you want to teach children in a slum area who are unable to go to school. You cannot do this alone because you have your own studies and homework. You, therefore, form a group of like-minded friends and start teaching these children. So you have been able to achieve what you could not have done alone.

SECTION C

7. (a) Every suicide is a misfortune. Suicide takes place throughout the lifespan. Suicide is a result of complex interface of biological, genetic, psychological, sociological, cultural and environmental factors.

Some other risk factors are having mental disorders (especially depression and alcohol use disorders), going through natural disasters, experiencing violence, abuse or loss and isolation at any stage of life. Previous suicidal attempt is the strongest risk factor.

Any unexpected or striking change affecting the adolescent's performance, attendanceor behaviour should be taken seriously, such as:

- lack of interest in common activities
- declining grades
- decreasing effort
- misbehavior in the classroom
- mysterious or repeated absence
- smoking or drinking, or drug misuse

Strengthening students' self-esteem : Having a positive self-esteem is important in face of distress and helps in coping adequately. In order to foster positive selfesteem in children the following approaches can be useful:

- accentuating positive life experiences to develop positive identity. This increases confidence in self.
- providing opportunities for development of physical, social and vocational skills.
- establishing a trustful communication.
- goals for the students should be specific, measurable, achievable, relevant, to be completed within a relevant time frame.

OR

(b) A common feature of the neurodevelopmental disorders is that they manifest in the early stage of development. Often the symptoms appear before the child enters school or during the early stage of schooling. These disorders result in hampering personal, social, academic and occupational functioning. These get characterised as deficits or excesses in a particular behaviour or delays in achieving a particular age-appropriate behaviour.

Children who are impulsive seem unable to control their immediate reactions or to think before they act. They find it difficult to wait or take turns, have difficulty resisting immediate temptations or delaying gratification. Minor mishaps such as knocking things over are common whereas more serious accidents and injuries can also occur.

Hyperactivity also takes many forms. Children with ADHD are in constant motion. Sitting still through a lesson is impossible for them. The child may fidget, squirm, climb and run around the room aimlessly. Parents and teachers describe them as 'driven by a motor', always on the go, and talk incessantly.

8. (a) According to the socio-cultural model, abnormal behaviour is best understood in light of the social and cultural forces that influence an individual. As behaviour is shaped by societal forces, factors such as family structure and communication, social networks, societal conditions, and societal labels and roles become more important. Children from this kind of family may have difficulty in becoming independent in life. The broader social networks in which people operate include their social and professional relationships. Studies have shown that people who are isolated and lack social support, i.e. strong and fulfilling interpersonal relationships in their lives are likely to become more depressed and remain depressed longer than those who have good friendships. Socio-cultural theorists also believe that abnormal functioning is influenced by the societal labels and roles assigned to troubled people. When people break the norms of their society, they are called deviant and 'mentally ill'. Such labels tend to stick so that the person may be viewed as 'crazy' and encouraged to act sick. The person gradually learns to accept and play the sick role, and functions in a disturbed manner.

OR

(b) Behaviour therapies postulate that psychological distress arises because of faulty behaviour patterns or thought patterns. It is, therefore, focused on the behaviour and thoughts of the client in the present. The past is relevant only to the extent of understanding the origins of the faulty behaviour and thought patterns.

A range of techniques is available for changing behaviour.

Negative reinforcement and aversive conditioning are the two major techniques of behaviour modification. As you have already studied in Class XI, responses that lead organisms to get rid of painful stimuli or avoid and escape from them provide negative reinforcement. For example, one learns to put on woollen clothes, burn firewood or use electric heaters to avoid the unpleasant cold weather.

Aversive conditioning refers to repeated association of undesired response with an aversive consequence. For example, an alcoholic is given a mild electric shock and asked to smell the alcohol.

If an adaptive behaviour occurs rarely, positive reinforcement is given to increase the deficit. For example, if a child does not do homework regularly, positive reinforcement may be used by the child's mother by preparing the child's favourite dish whenever s/he does homework at the appointed time.

Systematic desensitisation is a technique introduced by Wolpe for treating phobias or irrational ears. The client is interviewed to elicit fearprovoking situations and together with the client, the therapist prepares a hierarchy of anxiety-provoking stimuli with the least anxiety-provoking stimuli at the bottom of the hierarchy.

The principle of reciprocal inhibition operates here. This principle states that the presence of two mutually opposing forces at the same time, inhibits the weaker force.

9. We usually expect behaviour to follow logically from attitudes. However, an individual's attitudes may not always be exhibited through behaviour. Likewise, one's actual behaviour may be contrary to one's attitude towards a particular topic.

Psychologists have found that there would be consistency between attitudes and behaviour when :

- the attitude is strong, and occupies a central place in the attitude system,
- the person is aware of her/his attitude,
- there is very little or no external pressure for the person to behave in a particular way. For example, when there is no group pressure to follow a particular norm the person's behaviour is not being watched or evaluated by others, and
- the person thinks that the behaviour would have a positive consequence, and therefore, intends to engage in that behavior.

That is, on the basis of their behaviour (telling others that the experiment was interesting, for only a small amount of money), they concluded that their attitude towards the experiment was positive ("I would not have told a lie for this small amount of money, which means that the experiment was actually interesting").

10. A number of strategies have been suggested by psychologists. Some of these are :

- **Introduction of superordinate goals :** Sherif's study, already mentioned in the section on cooperation and competition, showed that by introducing superordinate goals, intergroup conflict can be reduced.
- **Altering perceptions :** Conflicts can also be reduced by altering perceptions and reactions through persuasion, educational and media appeals, and portrayal of groups differently in society.
- **Increasing intergroup contacts :** Conflict can also be reduced by increasing contacts between the groups. This can be done by involving groups in conflict on neutral grounds through community projects and events.
- **Negotiations :** Conflict can also be resolved through negotiations and third party interventions. Warring groups can resolve conflict by trying to find mutually acceptable solutions.
- **Structural solutions :** Conflict can also be reduced by redistributing the societal resources according to principles based on justice.

- **Respect for other group's norms :** In a pluralist society like India, it is necessary to respect and be sensitive to the strong norms of various social and ethnic groups. It has been noticed that a number of communal riots between different groups have taken place because of such insensitivity.

SECTION D

11. Everyone has worries and fears. The term anxiety is usually defined as a diffuse, vague, very unpleasant feeling of fear and apprehension. The anxious individual also shows combinations of the following symptoms: rapid heart rate, shortness of breath, diarrhoea, loss of appetite, fainting, dizziness, sweating, sleeplessness, frequent urination and tremors.

    They include generalised anxiety disorder, which consists of prolonged, vague, unexplained and intense fears that are not attached to any particular object. The symptoms include worry and apprehensive feelings about the future; hypervigilance, which involves constantly scanning the environment for dangers. It is marked by motor tension, as a result of which the person is unable to relax, is restless, and visibly shaky and tense.

    Another type of anxiety disorder is panic disorder, which consists of recurrent anxiety attacks in which the person experiences intense terror. A panic attack denotes an abrupt surge of intense anxiety rising to a peak when thoughts of a particular stimuli are present. Such thoughts occur in an unpredictable manner.

12. People with schizophrenia may also experience delusions of reference in which they attach special and personal meaning to the actions of others or to objects and events. In delusions of grandeur, people believe themselves to be specially empowered persons and in delusions of control, they believe that their feelings, thoughts and actions are controlled by others.

    People with schizophrenia also show inappropriate affect, i.e. emotions that are unsuited to the situation. Negative symptoms are 'pathological deficits' and include poverty of speech, blunted and flat affect, loss of volition, and social withdrawal. People with schizophrenia show alogia or poverty of speech, i.e. a reduction in speech and speech content. Many people with schizophrenia show less anger, sadness, joy, and other feelings than most people do. Thus they have blunted affect. Some show no emotions at all, a condition known as flat affect. Also patients with schizophrenia experience avolition, or apathy and an inability to start or complete a course of action. People with this disorder may withdraw socially and become totally focused on their own ideas and fantasies.